RAISED UNDER STALIN

RAISED UNDER STALIN

Young Communists and
the Defense of Socialism

Seth Bernstein

CORNELL UNIVERSITY PRESS **ITHACA AND LONDON**

First published 2017 by Cornell University Press

Printed in the United States of America

Library of Congress Cataloging-in-Publication Data

Names: Bernstein, Seth, author.
Title: Raised under Stalin : young communists and the defense of socialism / Seth Bernstein.
Description: Ithaca : Cornell University Press, 2017. | Includes bibliographical references and index.
Identifiers: LCCN 2017004652 (print) | LCCN 2017005181 (ebook) | ISBN 9781501709883 (cloth : alk. paper) | ISBN 9781501712029 (epub/mobi) | ISBN 9781501709388 (pdf)
Subjects: LCSH: Socialism and youth—Soviet Union—History. | Vsesoiuznyĭ leninskiĭ kommunisticheskiĭ soiuz molodezhi—History. | Youth—Soviet Union—History. | Soviet Union—History—1925–1953.
Classification: LCC HQ799.R9 B385 2017 (print) | LCC HQ799.R9 (ebook) | DDC 305.2350947084—dc23
LC record available at https://lccn.loc.gov/2017004652

Cornell University Press strives to use environmentally responsible suppliers and materials to the fullest extent possible in the publishing of its books. Such materials include vegetable-based, low-VOC inks and acid-free papers that are recycled, totally chlorine-free, or partly composed of nonwood fibers. For further information, visit our website at www.cornellpress.cornell.edu.

Contents

Figures

Acknowledgments

I have put myself in a great deal of intellectual debt while writing this book. At the risk of forgetting some of my obligations, though, I will keep these acknowledgments short. Lynne Viola deserves a special place in this work. Her guidance was fundamental as I wrote and revised this book. My Higher School of Economics colleague Oleg Khlevniuk has my particular appreciation for reading the entire manuscript and providing detailed suggestions that improved it. In addition, the first ranks of recognition must include Doris Bergen, Michael David-Fox, Thomas Lahusen, David Shearer, and Alison Smith.

A number of colleagues provided me with invaluable assistance as readers, commentators, and supporters. These include Susan Grant, Anna Hajkova, Aaron Hale-Dorrell, Sam Hirst, Rob Hornsby, Matthew Lenoe, Vojin Majstorovic, Tracy McDonald, Brandon Miller, Lilia Topouzova, Jon Waterlow, and Zbigniew Wojnowski. In addition, Oleg Budnitskii and Liudmila Novikova not only provided me with important suggestions on my work but also with a home in Moscow where I could finish this manuscript.

Writing this book would have been impossible without the help of archivists in Kiev, Moscow, Petrozavodsk, and Riazan. I will single out the incomparable Galina Mikhailovna Tokareva, who never tired of seeing me after several years in the former Komsomol Archive (now a part of the Russian State Archive of Social-Political History). Elena Pozdniak of the State Archive of Riazan Province first introduced me to archival research as a young postgraduate student and welcomed me back in subsequent years. Maria Panova organized a formative research trip to the Security Service of Ukraine (SBU) Archive in Kiev.

It has been a pleasure working with Cornell University Press. In particular, Roger Haydon not only curated this publication but also provided insightful comments on the manuscript. This work also benefited significantly from the readings of the two anonymous reviewers. I am grateful for Karen Laun's excellent coordination of this book's production and Carolyn Pouncy's thorough editing.

This book has led me far from my friends and family in the United States. My parents, Jim Bernstein and Lynn Franklin, and sister Miranda Bernstein have been supportive no matter where my curiosity has taken me. My Moscow family, Tanya and Teo Glakhov, made the book worth writing.

I have not acquired financial debt while writing this book thanks to several organizations. I received generous funding from the Vanier Canada Graduate Scholarship. The International Research and Exchanges Board sponsored my archival research to Russia and Ukraine in 2010–11. A Petro Jacyk Graduate Scholarship allowed me to travel to Ukraine for research. The study has been funded by the Russian Academic Excellence Project "5–100." The Higher School of Economics and its International Center for the Study of World War II and Its Consequences provided me with a salary, excellent colleagues, and resources for archival research in Russia, Ukraine, and the United States.

An early version of chapter 3 appeared as "Class Dismissed? New Elites and Old Enemies among the 'Best' Socialist Youth in the Komsomol, 1934–41" in *Russian Review* 74, no. 1 (2015): 97–116. I appreciate the journal's permitting me to reproduce sections of the article in this book.

Note on Conventions

This work generally uses the Library of Congress transliteration system. In the case of well-known names and places such as Joseph Stalin or Moscow, it uses the conventional spelling. In general, the author has opted to translate Russian administrative territories into English rather than using the Russian. A *raion* is a district, a *krai* is a territory, and an *oblast'* is a province. Archival references are abbreviated from Russian archives as f. for *fond* (collection), op. for *opis'* (inventory), and l. for *list* (page), and correspondingly from Ukrainian archives as f. for *fond*, op. for *opys*, spr. for *sprava* and ark. for *arkush*.

RAISED UNDER STALIN

Introduction

THE FIRST SOCIALIST GENERATION

The day after Germany invaded the Soviet Union, Nina Kosterina wrote in her diary, "Do you remember, Nina Alekseevna, how you secretly dreamed of living through big, important events, through tumult and danger? Well here you go—war!" Born in 1921, Kosterina was a devoted activist in the Young Communist League (Komsomol) during the formative period of Soviet socialism. Her enthusiasm endured the Great Terror despite her father's arrest and her regrets over denouncing a friend whose parents were "enemies of the people." The Komsomol taught her how to be a "cultured" Soviet young person and rewarded her with higher education, access to recreation, even food. As war in Europe and Asia threatened, her role as an ideal Soviet citizen increasingly included training marches and firearms practice. She and other Soviet young people knew that war was coming. Soon after the invasion, Kosterina volunteered for a partisan battalion and, like so many of her peers, perished before the end of 1941.[1]

This book is a study of young communists like Nina Kosterina, who grew up in the wake of revolution and in the midst of war. They might have heard about prerevolutionary times but had never experienced life without Soviet rule. Only the oldest could recall a period when Joseph Stalin was not the absolute leader of the country. By the end of the 1930s, nearly a third of all young people joined

---

1. Kosterina, *Diaries*, June 23, 1941.

1

the Komsomol, the vanguard organization of politically engaged Soviet youth (see Table 1 in appendix). The decade was a turbulent period of mass violence but also a time when people believed in a brighter future. After years of upheaval, Stalin declared in 1934 that the country had become the most advanced political entity in the world—the first socialist state. It seemed possible that within their lifetime, the children of the revolution might build the communist state that Marx had predicted.

As preparation for the socialist present and the communist future, the country's leaders called for a new program of moral socialization, "communist upbringing." Party leaders and Komsomol activists believed they were building a new society, but there was no blueprint for raising the first socialist generation. Decisions about how to create the ideal youth were filled with tensions: How should the regime channel enthusiasm without unleashing radicalism? Was the Komsomol a political organization of activists or a mass organization for socialization? What divided irredeemable "enemies of the people" from wayward youth? Stalinist youth leaders resolved these questions based on the problems of the day. Above all, socialist youth culture and Stalinist socialism more broadly were shaped by war. As the USSR prepared for conflict and experienced World War II, youth leaders discovered that building a socialist society meant to discipline and militarize young people.

Examining Soviet youth culture across the 1941 divide highlights the continuities between the prewar and wartime periods. Undoubtedly, Germany's invasion of the USSR transformed the lives of Soviet citizens. The war was a life and death struggle that touched virtually every person in the USSR. Yet the entire period from 1929 to 1945 can be seen as an unbroken time of crisis that provided young people with opportunities even as it surrounded them with violence. Socialist practices of reward and terror evolved, growing into wartime practices of mass mobilization and coercion. When the war arrived, there was no shift from building socialism to defending it. The two goals were inseparable.

In virtually every country, young people represent hopes for the future. This was particularly so in the USSR, where youth was at the center of Soviet leaders' attempts to transform society. Soviet people born around the time of the Bolshevik Revolution felt epochal changes that that shaped their identities as a generation. The formation of the first Soviet generation was also inseparable from Bolshevik conceptions about how youth should develop. Soviet leaders believed they had created a regime unlike any the world had seen and anticipated that the postrevolutionary state would produce "new people" from the young. Under the control of a Marxist regime, these "new people" were supposed to become physically and morally stronger than the older generations as they built the communist future.[2] At the same time, party leaders, like their counterparts throughout the modern world, felt anxiety over the malleability of youth and its seeming vulnerability to harmful influences.[3] The Bolsheviks' perceived enemies—domestic capitalists, foreign agents, and hooligans, among others—threatened to corrupt the future of the Soviet Union. Youth's development into "new people" or their transformation into enemies became a measure of the Bolshevik regime's success in its mission to fulfill the aspirations of the October Revolution.

In addition to youth's figurative importance, young people played an important role as supporters of the new state. In the first years of Soviet rule, only a fraction of the population belonged to the Communist Party and the regime could count on just a small number of nonparty supporters as well. Among both groups, young people made up a large proportion. The Bolsheviks' desperate need for loyalists to govern an enormous country thrust politically active youth into posts whose significance was unprecedented for young people in the modern world.[4] The regime's reliance on the young throughout the interwar period and during World War II increased concerns over their reliability, lack of experience, and turbulent nature. Anxieties over the future and the present of youth motivated the regime to cultivate the children of the revolution through discipline, terror, and reward.

The Komsomol was the regime's main instrument in its efforts to shape and mobilize the young generation. Founded in the midst of the Russian civil war in 1918, it was a unique youth organization in several key respects. The league formed from the merger of various pro-Bolshevik young workers' unions and student organizations. Its mission was to aid the new Soviet regime by generating support among young men and women and organizing them to work on its behalf. Unlike nearly all other contemporary, adult-led organizations, young people were the driving force in the Komsomol. Although the Communist Party had substantial control over the league, at the local level youth cells often enjoyed autonomy.[5] Komsomol members were usually older than participants in similar youth organizations in other countries. During the 1930s, their average age

---

2. The classic treatment of generations is Karl Mannheim, "Problem of Generations." See 304, in particular, for the definition of a generation as a cohort of youth whose collective identity coalesced based on the experience of similar, novel problems. For a discussion of generational thinking in the USSR, see Fürst, *Stalin's Last Generation*, 14–16.

3. On youth broadly, see Gillis, *Youth and History*, 182–83. On the Soviet politics of generation during the 1920s, see Gorsuch, *Youth in Revolutionary Russia*, 12–15.

4. Tirado, *Young Guard!*, 89, 93.

5. Guillory, "'We Shall Refashion Life on Earth!,'" 5.

was around twenty, with members' ages spanning from fourteen well into their thirties.

The relative independence of pro-Soviet youth culture was a source of concern for the country's leaders. During the 1920s, party leaders loathed the political indifference of some Komsomol youth. Non-Soviet culture coexisted uneasily with the new regime under the semi-market economy of the New Economic Policy (NEP). Bolsheviks feared that young people would imbibe the anti-Soviet attitudes of "bourgeois" life.[6] At the same time, the opposite danger existed of young radicalism. A significant subculture of young activists became disillusioned with the relatively moderate NEP regime and advocated a renewal of class warfare on behalf of proletarians. Young civil war veterans, in particular, asked why they had fought for the Bolsheviks if the regime would not create a true workers' state.[7] The strong support Lev Trotsky and other oppositionists enjoyed among young people in the 1920s only made Stalin and his allies warier of the demographic.[8] Compounding this independence was a sense of moral superiority to the older cohorts. Youth's status as "new people" fostered a consciousness of their special generational destiny.[9]

As Stalin and his supporters rejected the relative moderation of NEP in the late 1920s, the regime's relationship to youth culture also altered. The threat of a war with neighboring states motivated Stalin to push for radical, state-led modernization. He declared 1929 the year of the Great Turn, when the country would begin its transformation through forced-pace industrialization and the collectivization of agriculture. Although many young people did not support these policies, a significant portion of radicals believed the Great Turn marked the continuation of the 1917 revolution that would create a workers' state. As Stalin's "revolution from above" unleashed young radicals, it destroyed the relatively independent political culture that had enabled their subculture to thrive. By the end of the 1920s, Komsomol cells transformed from semi-independent supporters of the Soviet state into a wholly dependent resource for the regime.[10] The revolution from above created a virtual civil war between the regime and the countryside.[11] The key cause of conflict was the broad coercive license that leaders gave to police and activists of all ages to repress those who resisted Stalin-

---

6. Gorsuch, *Youth in Revolutionary Russia*, 22–26.
7. Guillory, "We Shall Refashion Life on Earth!," 57–59.
8. Gorsuch, *Youth in Revolutionary Russia*, 80–95.
9. Krylova, "Soviet Modernity in Life and Fiction: The Generation of the 'New Soviet Person' in the 1930s," xiii.
10. See Neumann, *Communist Youth League*, 206–9.
11. Viola, *Peasant Rebels under Stalin*, 13–44.

ist policies. Nonetheless, Stalin's extraordinary dependence on youth activists intensified intergenerational conflict and exacerbated the explosion of violence in the country. By 1933, Stalin's regime had won its war in the countryside but at a tremendous cost of lives and turmoil.

A central story of the creation of Stalinist socialism in the 1930s was the regime's attempt to stabilize the country as war loomed. Japan threatened the Soviet Far East, while the rise of the Nazi Party in Germany appeared to make war in Europe inevitable. At the same time, Soviet officials obsessed over the potential "fifth column" of supposed domestic enemies among former oppositionists and "class aliens." The People's Commissariat of Internal Affairs (NKVD), Stalin's secret police, repressed these perceived enemies mercilessly. The connected problems of a looming war and domestic repression created dangers and opportunities for Soviet youth. Stalinist leaders remained wary of youth as an impressionable, volatile population that threatened social order. At the same time, the regime continued to rely on young people, who were better educated than the previous generation at a time when the country needed competent workers and soldiers.

Stalinist leaders turned to official youth culture in their attempts to create a stable, loyal generation. Through the Komsomol, they enacted a cultural revolution from above, an intervention in the social and political behavior of young citizens that was meant to accompany the economic transformation of socialism. Like an honors society or a church group, the Komsomol organized activities meant to create a sense of community through recreation and moral socialization. The development of "communist upbringing," though, was inextricable from the pragmatic search for social stability. By promoting conventional education, refined behavior, and a militarized discipline, the "cultured" behavior that the Komsomol promoted in the 1930s opposed the iconoclastic attitudes of young radicals of the 1920s.[12] Youth leaders supported traditional gender roles and hoped to incorporate young mothers and their families into the big family of Stalinist socialism.[13] Over the course of the decade, the league's membership more than tripled, exposing millions of new members to this program (see Table 1 in appendix).

---

12. On Stalinist promotion of *kul′turnost′* ("culturedness") see Fitzpatrick, "Becoming Cultured," in *Cultural Front*; and Kelly, *Refining Russia*, especially chapter 4.

13. On the Stalinist turn to traditional gender norms, see Goldman, *Women, the State, and Revolution*, 296–344. For the argument that women could find multiple gender roles in Stalinist socialism, see Shulman, *Stalinism on the Frontiers of Empire*, 12–24; and Krylova, *Soviet Women in Combat*, 60.

The flood of youth into the Komsomol highlighted the tension between the inclusionary and the exclusionary aspects of Stalinism. Until the mid-1930s, the league had favored the Bolsheviks' "class allies" and their children—workers and, to a lesser extent, peasants. As Komsomol and regime leaders envisioned the future of a classless communist society, though, membership criteria in the Komsomol increasingly focused on the meritocratic measures of education and professional achievements. Although these new membership policies reignited conflicts over the dilution of the Komsomol's proletarian identity, the central anxiety in youth culture lay in the regime's treatment of "enemies of the people."[14] The presence of millions of young people whose families had been marginalized in various campaigns of repression raised uncomfortable questions about the future of Soviet society. In a time when war loomed, was it safer to socialize the children of "enemies" in official youth culture or to deny them the opportunity to sabotage the regime from within the Komsomol? The answer to this question was always ambiguous and contested.

Anxieties about who could be a young communist provide an important window onto Stalinist concepts of redemption. As the Komsomol transformed into a mass youth organization, its leaders increasingly relied on corrective punishments for youth who transgressed the intertwined rules of political and polite society. It was never clear, though, when young people crossed the line from misbehavior to being an "enemy of the people." For acts of drunkenness, sexual misbehavior, and vulgar verses of poetry, thousands of youth would face punishments that blurred the boundary between discipline and repression. When police determined that young people had broken the law, youth became criminals whose unlikely return to society lay in hard labor in the Gulag.[15] Terror was not only a destructive force, however, but one that shaped Stalinist society. Most young communists were not arrested and instead experienced repression as a disciplinary process, amplified by the moral panic over hooliganism and "degeneracy" in the Soviet press.[16] The threat of corruption convinced Komsomol leaders that it was crucial to retain young people within the bounds of Soviet political culture, where they might be reformed into worthy defenders of the USSR.

---

14. For the argument that proletarian anxiety was still a key factor in the 1930s, see Krylova, "Identity, Agency, and the 'First Soviet Generation'" in *Generations in Twentieth Century Europe*, ed. Lovell, 104–11.

15. Barnes, *Death and Redemption*, 2.

16. This work draws on the sociologist Stanley Cohen's conception of moral panics, where the interaction of media, police, politicians, and society produce a cohesive narrative about a deviant subculture from incoherent or nonexistent groups. See Cohen, *Moral Panics and Folk Devils*, 1–12.

Repression was inextricable from young communists' experience of Stalinism as a time of opportunity. The Great Terror of 1937–38, in particular, created a large number of empty positions now open to young cadres.[17] The expansion of the industrial economy in the 1930s also generated a demand for educated workers. During wartime, these aspects of Stalinist social mobility merged. Mass violence on the Eastern Front created even more demand for young people as soldiers and ensured that those who survived would rise rapidly. Although social mobility was a result of upheaval, it was also the product of deliberate policies. Komsomol leaders advertised that devotion to the regime and efforts to perform well in school, on the job, or on the battlefield would provide tangible advantages. In turn, Komsomol members increasingly expected that their activism would result in rewards.

Material incentives were just one reason youth became young communists. Undoubtedly, a large number of young people joined the Komsomol to gain access to higher education or a better job. Others felt coerced into joining by superiors or their peers. Still others became what scholars have called "Stalinist subjects," internalizing the regime's goal to build socialism and their own place within this historical mission.[18] These motivations frequently coexisted and over-lapped. A young person could believe in the mission to transform the Soviet Union into a communist state and see their admission to university as proof of its righteousness. Gauging the relative importance of these factors is difficult because evidence about young people's motivations is necessarily anecdotal. It is clear, though, that youth leaders in the late 1930s primarily strove to forge reliable, pliant subjects rather than self-reflective historical actors. In a period of increasing tensions, youth leaders wanted to create an army—figuratively and literally—of young loyalists.

Soviet youth culture's origins in the revolution and civil war made it unique in the modern world, but the atmosphere of crisis in the 1930s created similarities with contemporary organizations in authoritarian states. Stalin's Soviet Union, like other authoritarian regimes, sought a total claim over the public socialization of youth. Germany's Hitler Youth and League of German Girls were especially successful at incorporating a large majority of age-eligible ethnic German youth and inculcating them with Nazi racial ideology.[19] Mussolini's National Boys Organization (Opera Nazionale Balilla) and its successor the Gioventù Italiana del Littorio similarly claimed to have included a majority of Italian youth in their

---

17. See Fitzpatrick, *Education and Social Mobility*, 242–43; and Hough, *Soviet Prefects*, 38–55.

18. Halfin, *From Darkness to Light*, 1–38; Krylova, "Soviet Modernity in Life and Fiction," 1–40; Hellbeck, *Revolution on My Mind*, 9–10.

19. Kater, *Hitler Youth*, 15.

ranks, although they exercised a lesser influence than the youth organizations of Germany.[20] The Komsomol would not include a majority of age-eligible youth until well after Stalin's death. Nonetheless, the authoritarian urge to raise youth for the regime transformed the Komsomol from a relatively small league dominated by activists into a mass organization for cultivating youth with a broad pan-Soviet identity.[21]

In the USSR and contemporary states, the threat of war shaped the basic assumption that youth organizations should militarize the young for the state. Soviet practices of militarization intensified over the interwar period, partially in concert with its would-be enemies. Of course, the Soviet state had always been militaristic, meaning that it glorified the military and the victories of the civil war.[22] In contrast to militarism, the historian Michael Geyer defines militarization as "the contradictory and tense social process in which civil society organizes itself for the production of violence."[23] In the USSR, groups like the Komsomol provided a regime-approved substitute for civil society organizations and a vehicle for militarizing programs. While the Komsomol engaged in militarism during celebrations of the Red Army, it also prepared youth in overt and subtle ways for the never-ending task of defending socialism. Practices of social discipline, mobilization, and paramilitary training evolved in the prewar years and continued after the German invasion.

The increasing importance of militarization in youth culture reveals the adaptability of Stalinism. Like the years of World War I and civil war, when wartime practices became ingrained in Bolshevik conceptions of how to rule a state, the early period of socialism was a formative period in the USSR.[24] There was no roadmap from socialism to communism, because there had been no other socialist country. By the 1930s, some aspects of socialism, like the planned economy and the dominant role of the Communist Party, were taken as a given. In other areas, though, socialism was an experiment with trial and error. The central crisis of socialism was one of impending war with the associated necessities of eliminating potential

---

20. Koon, *Believe, Obey, Fight*, 31–32, 234.

21. Even as Soviet leaders sought to create a pan-Soviet identity, national politics still existed in the USSR. As Yuri Slezkine, "USSR as a Communal Apartment," 415, argues, Soviet nationalities policy carved out a national identity and territory for each group that complemented the pan-Soviet identity that the Komsomol hoped to foster.

22. Gillis, "Introduction," in *Militarization of the Western World*, ed. Gillis, 1–2.

23. Geyer, "The Militarization of Europe, 1914–1945," in *Militarization of the Western World*, ed. Gillis, 79.

24. On Bolshevik adoption of civil war-era governing practices, see Holquist, *Making War, Forging Revolution*, 6–7.

enemies and preparing society in advance of conflict.[25] When Soviet leaders and people militarized socialism in the tense atmosphere of the prewar decade, they interpreted it as a natural development of Marxist historical progress.

Stalin was the central figure in defining what socialism would be after the revolution from above, but young activists played an important role in designating youth's role in socialism at the local level. The leading figures in the party could not and would not provide directives for every aspect of life under socialism. The ambiguities of socialism's direction forced organizers to read signals from various sources: from the pages of *Pravda*; from rumors they heard when the NKVD arrested local party officials; or from their own notions of what was right and necessary. Sometimes youth activists' interpretations inspired excesses of ideological fervor and so-called political hooliganism, while uncertainty led to passivity among others. Understandings of what a young communist should be shifted over time. Emblematic of this flexibility was Aleksandr Kosarev, the leader of the Komsomol from 1929 to 1938. In the 1920s, he was a firebrand proletarian who had fought in the civil war and mocked the bourgeois fashions of NEP-era capitalists. After the advent of socialism, though, he donned a suit and became an advocate of discipline and refinement. He explained, "Our party does not recognize eternal laws. . . . The Komsomol, too, must change its goals."[26]

During the crisis-filled early years of socialism, Soviet leaders transformed society. Commentators in the interwar period often called the USSR a "young state" referring to its recent founding but also to its reliance on the young. When the Soviet Union emerged from World War II, it was no longer a young state. The victory came at a terrible cost for the first Soviet generation. Fighting on the front lines decimated those born in the years after the revolution. According to Soviet leaders, though, the victory validated the way the country had raised its youth during the interwar period—above all during the formative years of socialism. The challenge of the postwar years would be to rebuild and expand Stalin's socialism on the model of the 1930s.

A Note on Sources

This book examines youth culture in various geographical and hierarchical contexts of the Soviet Union. The main actors are the young activists who shaped and implemented official youth culture. Their viewpoint is preserved in

---

25. For a similar argument about the impact of war on the development of Stalinist policing, see Shearer, "Elements Near and Alien," 841–42.

26. RGASPI, f. 1m, op. 2, d. 115, l. 14.

the archives of the Communist Party and Komsomol in Russia (RGASPI) and Ukraine (TsDAHO), the records of related administrations in Soviet sport and education at the State Archive of the Russian Federation (GARF), in the Soviet youth press, and in films of the time. Archival materials include stenographic records of meetings, bureaucratic correspondence, statistical records, summary reports, and letters from ground-level activists. These central records contain information not only from Moscow but from all regions of the country, providing an all-Soviet perspective on the spread of Stalinist youth culture. Materials from the archive of the Security Service of Ukraine (SBU) reveal the important viewpoint of Stalin's security services on the danger that youth supposedly posed and faced.

Although the primary focus of this book is organizers, it also explores the experiences of ordinary youth under Stalinism as far as source limitations allow. Because so many young people born after the revolution died in World War II, sources like memoirs and diaries are relatively scarce. Many memoirists survived the war because the regime had classified them as "anti-Soviet," and they were thus excluded from military service. They provide a significant part of the story of Soviet youth under Stalin, but one that reflects a particular experience. Similarly, the recollections of those who left the USSR during or after the war were influenced by the Cold War divide. Besides ego sources, this study uses archival records of local youth groups in and around Kiev, Moscow, Petrozavodsk, Riazan, and Smolensk. Studies that rely on individual accounts or regional sources often face the choice of creating case studies or weaving these materials into a broader narrative. This book opts for the latter, integrating the stories of individual, regional, and central actors in Soviet youth culture into a wider account of Stalinism.

YOUTH IN THE STALIN REVOLUTION

Revolutions overthrow not only political regimes but also generational hierarchies. They demand organizers, supporters, and soldiers, giving young people
opportunities beyond traditional age-based social orders. After the October Revolution, the enormous needs of the Soviet state meant that young activists gained
an unusual amount of authority as they were funneled into the army and administration of the new regime.[1] The Bolshevik Revolution not only invested youth
with influence, it inspired them with revolutionary ideals about the construction
of a socialist workers' state. The first decade and a half of Soviet power unleashed
young people's enthusiasm, and their empowerment brought them into conflict
with their elders inside and outside the regime.

In the 1920s, the spirit of the 1917 revolutions and the sense that the new
regime was not fulfilling its promises made many into radicals during a time of
relative moderation. In 1921, with the economy in shambles after seven years of
war, Lenin instituted the New Economic Policy, a period of "economic breathing
space" that allowed limited autonomy in the peasant economy and in industry
following the nationalization of many sectors and use of coercion during War
Communism.[2] Not all young people became radicals even in the Komsomol, but

---

1. Tirado, *Young Guard!*, 89, 93.
2. "Plan doklada V. I. Lenina o zamene razverstki nalogom," *Pravda*, March 21, 1931. Lenin used
the term "breathing space" only in his drafts, and it is unclear whether his characterization of NEP's

a fervent base of young organizers grew disillusioned with the relative moderation of NEP. They were mostly male, urban factory workers, the emblematic constituency of the youth league.[3] The Bolsheviks had promised a paradise for proletarians after the overthrow of prerevolutionary elites. Instead, young workers found themselves suffering from high levels of unemployment in the cities while cultural and educational institutions were still dominated by non-Bolshevik elites.[4] These factors and the relative autonomy local youth organizations enjoyed during NEP fostered an internal "cultural revolution"—a process of radicalization among activists that occurred throughout the 1920s.[5] As much as young radicals directed their anger against workers' supposed class enemies, they also targeted their elders broadly, claiming the mantle of revolution for youth.

When Stalin's regime abandoned NEP for a radical solution to lackluster industrial growth at the end of the decade, it encouraged young people to protest openly against voices of moderation.[6] Although they empowered young radicals, Stalin and his inner circle did not share their iconoclastic outlook. Instead, the country's leadership enabled young zealots to turn their cultural revolution outward as a cudgel against common enemies in various spheres of the country's political, cultural, and economic life.[7] Although some activists volunteered, the regime pressed millions of other young people into service through the Komsomol, mobilizing them toward the transformation of the country.

A core component of Stalin's revolution was the collectivization of agriculture and its exploitation to pay for industrialization. Stalin had become convinced that rich peasants (so-called kulaks) were impeding food supplies to the cities. He responded to grain crises by sending outside activists, including large numbers of youth organizers, to the countryside to extract grain by force. When Stalin initiated the collectivization of the entire countryside in late 1929, the violence of the campaign and the license the regime gave its agents led to inescapable

---

durability changed over time. The publication of his working notes in 1931, with the characterization of NEP as an implicitly temporary "breathing space," gave legitimacy to the ongoing collectivization campaign. On War Communism and the transition to NEP, see Carr, *Bolshevik Revolution*, 2:147–279.

3. In January 1927, for instance, this core group was primarily a subset of the 836,760 members who claimed to have a worker background, either from their own experiences or through their parents. Komsomol members who registered as being factory workers at the time were 583,403. The total membership was just under two million. RGASPI, f. 1m, op. 126, d. 336, ll. 18–23.

4. On workplace generational tensions, see Koenker, "Fathers against Sons/Sons against Fathers." On education in the 1920s, see David-Fox, *Revolution of the Mind*, 79; Fitzpatrick, *Education and Social Mobility*, 68–88.

5. David-Fox, "What Is Cultural Revolution?," 182, 186.

6. Fitzpatrick, "Cultural Revolution as Class War," in *Cultural Revolution in Russia*, 25.

7. For a sampling of literature on the cultural revolution, see Fitzpatrick, *Cultural Revolution in Russia*.

abuses of power—"excesses," in the language of Stalinism. The perpetrators of these excesses were not only young, just as opponents of collectivization were not always old. When young people spoke out, though, their actions often bore the signs of youthful maximalism and generational conflict.

Stalin's revolution succeeded in remaking the Soviet economy, but its effects were also devastating. By 1932, the large majority of households in grain-growing regions had joined collective farms.[8] In spite of agriculture's increased pliancy to grain extraction, though, there was a severe shortfall in requisitions in 1932–33. When state representatives fulfilled party leaders' demands to take supposed excess grain from the peasantry, the result was a famine that killed millions. In the midst of famine, Stalinist leaders assumed that many activists had been disloyal to the regime and had shown their true colors as kulak saboteurs. The Komsomol, like the party, undertook a membership purge following collectivization that expelled a large proportion of its membership for supposed opposition to collectivization. The purge punctuated the end of a tumultuous period for Soviet youth. The relative independence of youth culture in the 1920s had given young radicals the space to form as a group and gave license to generational conflict. During the turmoil of the revolution from above, though, pro-Soviet youth culture came entirely under the control of Stalin's regime.

From Radical Activists to State Radicalism

The tenth anniversary of the October Revolution in 1927 was a time for celebration, reflection, and dissent. Amid parades and films commemorating the Bolshevik victory, discord about the future path of the Soviet Union lurked.[9] Soon after the celebrations, the party's Central Committee expelled a number of Stalin's opponents, including prominent figures like Lev Trotsky, Lev Kamenev, and Grigorii Zinov'ev. Although Kamenev and Zinov'ev were one-time allies of Stalin, they had joined Trotsky in the so-called United Opposition, hoping to overturn the semicapitalist NEP economy and Stalin's creeping domination of the country. Beaten by Stalin, the leadership of the opposition went into exile or recanted. Even as the organized opposition dissolved, though, the radical challenge from below continued, often led by youth. High urban unemployment—20 percent in January 1925, and nearly 50 percent among

---

8. Davies and Wheatcroft, *Years of Hunger*, 1–2.

9. For a discussion of the anniversary of the October Revolution, see Corney, *Telling October*, 175–200.

young adults in 1928—contributed to popular dissatisfaction with the NEP system among young people.[10] It seemed to many that the new regime was failing to improve conditions for workers.

Although they lived in the supposed dictatorship of the proletariat, many youth felt that Soviet officials were helping everyone but young proletarians. At the end of the civil war, Lenin and other Soviet leaders had concluded that there were not enough party-loyal technical specialists to support the economy. The new state needed the nonparty technical intelligentsia to rebuild the country's industrial sector. For this reason, until the late 1920s regime leaders defended technical professionals from "specialist baiting" (*spetseedstvo*), verbal and even physical attacks by radicals.[11] Activists also targeted segments of the population that appeared to be prospering from the semicapitalist economy. At a factory Komsomol meeting in Sokolniki district (Moscow) organized to celebrate the tenth anniversary of the October Revolution, one young man said, "The pride of the party C[entral] C[ommittee] is that it has fostered kulaks in the country-side, and in the city it continues to help the Nepmen [private entrepreneurs] get rich."[12] Peasants' alleged wealth was another source of hostility for young workers, but so were rural migrants to the cities. Worker activists feared that peasant migrants would overwhelm their factories and youth cells.[13]

Activists also criticized the new regime for its failure to overturn hierarchies in higher education. Like specialists in industry, Soviet leaders gave the academy considerable autonomy, and much as they had before the revolution, universities admitted relatively few workers or peasants as students. In the 103 traditional institutions of higher education in Russia, students classified as proletarians made up only 21.8 percent of enrollment in 1925.[14] Responding to the persistence of the traditional academy, communist academics founded a parallel system of party-loyal higher education institutions that the Bolsheviks hoped would train a new generation of pro-Soviet intellectuals.

Despite the presence of this alternative academy, young radicals remained dissatisfied with workers' access to higher education. One clandestine group of young people from a village in Cheliabinsk territory, uncovered by United State Political Administration (OGPU) agents in November 1927, printed a wall

---

10. Chase, *Workers, Society, and the Soviet State*, 141–43, 150–51; Gorsuch, *Youth in Revolutionary Russia*, 36–40.

11. Fitzpatrick, "Cultural Revolution as Class War," 8–9; Bailes, *Technology and Society*, 44–68.

12. RGASPI, f. 1m, op. 23, d. 683, l. 58. On the Nepmen, see Ball, *Russia's Last Capitalists*.

13. Guillory, "We Shall Refashion Life on Earth!," 98–110. Tirado, "Komsomol and Young Peasants."

14. David-Fox, *Revolution of the Mind*, 79.

FIGURE 1.1. Young Communists at the Komsomol's Petrograd Political School in 1920. The future Komsomol leader Aleksandr Kosarev (age sixteen) is in the third row with his hand on the shoulder of a comrade. Rossiiskii Gosudarstvennyi Arkhiv Sotsial'no-Politicheskoi Istorii (RGASPI), f. 1m, op. 18, d. 2472, l. 26.

newspaper containing a characteristic critique, "Educational institutions are full of the brats of the bourgeois and former bureaucrats."[15]

In addition to class-based criticisms, generational differences sparked dissent among young activists in the 1920s. As the historian Diane Koenker has noted of the printing industry, Soviet protections for young workers like adolescents' six-hour maximum workday made employers reluctant to hire them. Moreover, the prerevolutionary system of apprenticeship persisted, causing dissatisfaction among apprentices who felt stifled by their masters.[16] Shock work—conducting extraordinarily difficult labor or finding ways to increase production (e.g., through minimizing absenteeism)—became a means for youth to subvert the power structure of the factories and gain experience and authority.[17] At the Krasnyi Proletariat machine tool factory on the outskirts of Moscow, the head of a Komsomol workshop cell named Anikiev initiated a shock brigade after reading

15. RGASPI, f. 1m, op. 23, d. 664, l. 13.

16. Koenker, "Fathers against Sons/Sons against Fathers."

17. Shearer, "Language and Politics of Socialist Rationalization," 597–98.

about a similar effort in a *Pravda* article in 1924. Around the same time and probably related to the brigade, league members began unsanctioned efforts to monitor the factory's administration. An activist later recalled that young people scrutinized "the condition of the factory, [if] the factory was making a profit, [and] the status of orders." Anikiev commented that some youth, particularly those from the countryside, opposed the cell's activities. Voluntary increases in labor norms and inspections of workshops were especially unpopular. Krasnyi Proletariat's administration, too, resisted youth activists' interference in the factory's management. As one organizer said, "The party cell didn't approve of Komsomol members' activities." Understandably, leaders at the factory probably viewed the youth cell's actions as meddling.[18]

Revolutionary iconoclasm also manifested itself in young communists' attacks on religion. In a large-scale campaign in the winter of 1922–23, the Komsomol Central Committee sanctioned an alternative to traditional religious festivals, Komsomol Christmas. Thousands of young people in hundreds of towns marched in demonstrations during the holiday. Although leaders hoped to promote the rationalism of the communist regime, the demonstrators often engaged in vicious ridicule of the old ways of religious belief. Indeed, young communists critiqued not only religion but also representatives of the perceived NEP counterrevolution—even Lenin.[19] The scornful, carnival-like atmosphere at these events drew the reproach of Komsomol and party leaders. Party leaders may have shared many of the protesters' beliefs but viewed mockery as counterproductive. Rather than mocking the religious, party leaders hoped to enlist the broader population's support for the NEP regime, while gradually making Soviet people understand the reactionary nature of religion through education. With this goal in mind, central leaders forbid the organization of Komsomol holidays until 1928.[20]

In part, the generational animosity that emerged at factories and during antireligious festivals occurred because a number of the representatives of the "young generation" were no longer so young. Although new members had joined the Komsomol during the 1920s, by the end of the decade those activists who became members during the civil war had grown older, exceeding its age limits. Many itched for the conflict and drama of their early years.[21] Others wanted political

---

18. GARF, f. 7952, op. 3, d. 98, ll. 9, 72; d. 94, l. 14.

19. Neumann, "Revolutionizing Mind and Soul?" 255–58; Husband, *"Godless Communists,"* 58–59.

20. On the broader history of religious coexistence and accommodation during NEP, see Husband, *"Godless Communists."* See 64–65 on Komsomol holidays.

21. On the trauma of the civil war and the desire for renewed revolution as a cure to boredom, see Guillory, "Shattered Self of Komsomol Civil War Memoirs."

or social advancement that was often unavailable to them. After the Lenin Levy, the party's recruiting campaign following Lenin's death, it became difficult for Komsomol members to join the party. At the Moscow Higher Technical School (MVTU), one in five Komsomol members were above the league's age limit. For overage members, it was "unthinkable not to join the party [and] simply leave the Komsomol," according to one organizer at MVTU.[22] Political authorities at the university said that older members were beginning to oppose the Komsomol from within, resentful of "the party for using Komsomol members during the civil war as a political and military force and then abandoning them."[23] Reacting to protest from aging youth activists, Komsomol General Secretary Nikolai Chaplin had announced the league's official policy in 1927: overage members would leave the league to join the "nonparty active," its nonmember supporters, but not receive automatic party membership.[24] Mocking this statement, a Komsomol activist from MVTU said that overage youth would not go to the "party active but to the party archive." Other organizers asserted that the discontent among older activists could lead to the formation of an oppositionist group or even another party.[25]

As political and generational tensions in youth culture continued into the late 1920s, the threat of war played a significant role in the development of the relationship between youth and the Soviet regime. During the civil war, the Bolsheviks had fought against a foreign intervention by the Entente and against Poland on the country's western borders.[26] Although the USSR made peace with its former opponents in the 1920s and even established commercial relations with some, Soviet leaders remained convinced that war would someday resume with the capitalist world. In March 1927, British authorities raided the London branch of the All Russian Cooperative Society (ARCOS), believing that the Soviet trade outfit was a cover for espionage. The raid set off a conflagration of rumors among political elites and ordinary citizens that the USSR would soon be at war with British-backed Poland or with the United Kingdom itself.[27]

Reactions toward a potential war were mixed, but many activists believed that such a conflict would reinvigorate the revolutionary struggle that the NEP regime had waylaid. Reports on young people's attitudes in the Komsomol

---

22. RGASPI, f. 1m, op. 23, d. 671, l. 28.
23. Ibid., 20.
24. Ibid., 32–33.
25. RGASPI, f. 1m, op. 23, d. 683, ll. 100, 101ob.
26. On the intervention, see Novikova, *Provincial "Counterrevolution,"* chapter 4.
27. For a longer discussion of popular reactions to the war scare, see Velikanova, *Popular Perceptions of Soviet Politics in the 1920s,* 85–117.

indicated that some organizers were eager to give up their membership to avoid the rapid conscription they expected the league to conduct. Others were eager to fight, tired of "babying the foreign bourgeois."[28] Foreign enemies were not the only targets of scorn. Young people railed against the perceived representatives of the NEP counterrevolution: capitalists and Jews. A twenty-four-year-old peasant from Sumy district in Ukraine said, "When the war starts we'll beat the commissars and Jews with their briefcases." A peer from the same town offered an alternative, "First we'll beat the Nepmen and then we'll see what needs to be done."[29] Perhaps the most pervasive enemies young people decried, though, were Soviet officials. Calls to "beat party bureaucrats" reflected activists' view that war would be an opportunity to overturn NEP by removing established officials. Moreover, the disproportionate prevalence of Jews in the party meant that many calls against the bureaucracy merged with popular antisemitism.[30] But embedded in this critique was also hostility toward the authority of party elders over young activists.

War did not materialize, yet the threat of conflict nonetheless had an impact on Soviet politics. There is reason to believe that Soviet leaders were skeptical about the possibility of war in 1927.[31] It is clear, however, that Stalin believed the war scare was evidence of intensifying tensions between capitalist states and the Soviet Union. The USSR would go to war with the bourgeois world someday, and pessimistic military reports about the country's readiness for such a conflict gave Stalin no relief.[32] The "capitalist encirclement" of a Soviet state whose industrial capacity had scarcely recovered to pre-World War I levels made the prospect of war even more threatening. Meanwhile, supposed enemies of the Soviet regime within the country seemed to pose a greater danger as the external threat grew. At a meeting of youth leaders in 1927, Nikolai Chaplin announced that "the period of breathing space is over." The time when the Soviet regime would accommodate "alien classes and social groups," he said, would necessarily end as international tensions increased.[33]

An important break from the conciliation of NEP toward these alien classes came in 1928 as Stalin spearheaded attacks against nonparty specialists who

---

28. RGASPI, f. 1m, op. 23, d. 792, ll. 41, 43.

29. RGASPI, f. 1m, op. 23, d. 743, ll. 2, 14.

30. Kostyrchenko, *Tainaia politika Stalina*, 59–60.

31. Stone, *Hammer and Rifle*, argues that Soviet leaders enacted few practical measures in reaction to the war scare in 1927 and initiated the militarization of the Soviet economy only in response to the Japanese threat in the early 1930s.

32. Harris, "Encircled by Enemies," 520–21.

33. RGASPI, f. 1m, op. 23, d. 792, l. 1v.

had supposedly sabotaged industrial development in the country. In the North Caucasian coal-mining town of Shakhty, OGPU officials raised charges of sabotage against fifty-three foreign and Soviet technical workers in March 1928, resulting in five executions and forty-four prison sentences.[34] Stalin seems to have believed the accusations against the engineers, but his denunciations also encouraged radicals in the country who were hostile toward nonparty experts. The campaign against "bourgeois specialists" was just one piece of the regime's more aggressive stance toward old elites and the supporters of moderation. The increasing repression toward these groups unleashed a cultural revolution in which radical activists in education, cultural life, and the economy overthrew gradualist party leaders and prerevolutionary figures whose careers had survived the rise of the Bolsheviks. Radicals' attacks on the cultural establishment were permitted and sometimes instigated by the Stalinist leadership. At the same time, these activists were semi-independent actors who found that, after years of resentment and radicalization, they finally had the opportunity to renew their revolutionary struggle on behalf of the working class.

The cultural revolution had perhaps its greatest impact on the arts and in education, as young organizers upturned existing hierarchies. In the world of the theater, activists from the influential Leningrad Theater of Working-Class Youth (TRAM) called for the "liquidation of MKhAT [Moscow Art Theater, an established institution] as a class," an appeal for the destruction of nonrevolutionary cultural forms that echoed contemporaneous calls for violence against kulaks and other class enemies.[35] In universities, students and young academics attacked supposed rightists among figures in the administration and faculty. University professors were subjected to a reelection campaign in 1929–30, where 219 of 1,062 were at least temporarily removed from their positions. As significant as this purge was for halting many academics' careers, the purge represented the destruction of the academy as an independent sphere in the USSR.[36] Young activists in education also pushed for the regime to dismantle the traditional school system. A radical working within the People's Commissariat of Enlightenment (Narkompros) named Vasilii Shul'gin characterized education as "the old dying order; the old type of relationship between adults and children, 'bosses' and 'subordinates,' the 'teacher' and the 'pupil.'" Emboldened by the Shakhty trial and the broader move away from NEP moderation, Shul'gin and young

---

34. See Bailes, *Technology and Society*, 69–94.
35. Quoted in Clark, *Petersburg*, 268. On TRAM, see Mally, *Revolutionary Acts*, 109–45.
36. David-Fox, *Revolution of the Mind*, 258; Fitzpatrick, *Education and Social Mobility*, 193–98.

activists from the Komsomol replaced ousted officials in Narkompros, forcing the resignation of its moderate leader Anatolii Lunacharskii in 1929.[37]

The cultural revolution also encouraged young people's radical rebellion against moderate managers and specialists in industry. At the Krasnyi Proletariat factory in Moscow, a young, Komsomol-affiliated engineer named Gorbunkov led the charge against older technical specialists, writing a critical letter to the factory's party secretary about their role in the plant's troubles. The technical director of the trust supervising his factory learned about these criticisms and summoned Gorbunkov to intimidate him into ceasing his attacks on specialists. Although he was chastised by a leading member of the technical intelligentsia, Gorbunkov received support from the factory's party chief and continued his attack.[38] Among those radicals who continued to oppose Stalin's rule, many supported his assault on nonparty specialists. A circle of young oppositionists calling itself the Group of Bolshevik Leninists wrote in a letter to party leaders that the discoveries of saboteur-specialists at Shakhty and elsewhere "signal a grave danger."[39]

Stalinist demands for forced industrialization became another cudgel in the hands of activists. In March 1927, the party Central Committee released a decree "On Rationalization," demanding that the industrial sector increase capital reinvestment and therefore economic growth by improving efficiency and accountability. At the same time, the decree prohibited factory managers from lowering costs by implementing policies that would worsen workers' conditions or compensation. These requirements were effectively impossible for enterprise directors to fulfill. When they failed to meet the Central Committee's demands, worker-activists could hammer industrial leadership on its shortcomings.[40] The push for forced-paced industrialization in the First Five-Year Plan of 1928–32 placed even more pressure on management. Eschewing the gradualist approach of the NEP period, Stalin demanded extraordinary growth in manufacturing and enlisted ordinary workers to support the plan against opponents in the factories.[41]

---

37. Fitzpatrick, *Education and Social Mobility*, 141–46; Holmes, *Kremlin and the Schoolhouse*, 120.

38. GARF, f. 7952, op. 3, d. 94, ll. 97–98. David Shearer argues based on the case of Gorbunkov and others that the rift in the factories was not only between specialists and nonspecialists but also between different generations of specialists. For more on the conflict at Krasnyi Proletariat and among other groups of technical intelligentsia, see Shearer, *Industry, State, and Society*, 134–63.

39. RGASPI, f. 1m, op. 23, d. 820, l. 69.

40. On the rationalization campaign, see Shearer, "Language and Politics of Socialist Rationalization," 592–95.

41. Davies, *Soviet Economy in Turmoil*, 62.

Komsomol cells often provided the organizational framework for this regime-approved protest. Young workers from the league had already been organizing shock brigades for years, and now their efforts gained official sanction.[42] The Komsomol's Central Committee called for the expansion of "socialist competitions" among shock workers, where brigades from rival factories competed to increase productivity, signing contracts with their opponents to set the goals for the contest.[43] No matter who won the competition, the real winners were Stalinist leaders, radical activists, and young specialists. Their attempts to increase efficiency at the local level undercut the standing of managers and specialists who might have opposed forced-pace industrialization.[44]

Even youth who did not work in factories caught shock work fever. Vadim Iasnyi, a teenager from Rostov-on-Don, was a pupil in school and not a factory worker. Nonetheless, he took on the mentality of shock labor. In 1930, Iasnyi and his classmates vowed to finish their standard seven-year schooling several months early as a tribute to Stalinist exhortations to complete the First Five-Year Plan a year ahead of schedule. To the dismay of his teachers, Iasnyi and his theater brigade gained permission to miss classes in order to perform motivational agit-prop plays at local factories. Iasnyi's group, like the broader agit-prop theater movement, had approval from the Soviet trade union organization. In 1930, the trade unions demanded that cultural activity among factory workers should increase their productivity as it entertained them. Agit-prop brigades like Iasnyi's consisted of amateurs who performed not only on the stage but in the factory itself, urging workers to contribute to the five-year plan.[45] The license Iasnyi received from his performances gave him a sense of worth beyond his years. He wrote about his teachers in his diary, "We almost felt ourselves equal to them."[46]

For some shock workers, material incentives played a key role in driving activism. Members of brigades received a shock worker card and occasional bonuses for their work. A common complaint in the Komsomol leadership was that the movement created "fake shock workers," who became brigade members only for the rewards.[47] A worker-activist from the Dinamo factory in Moscow named Mileshin complained to the Komsomol's Central Committee that once his

---

42. As Matthew Payne notes, the regime found in shock brigades a "moral community" of supporters that both challenged hierarchies and strove for increased efficiency. Payne, *Stalin's Railroad*, 211.

43. See GARF, f. 7952, op. 3, d. 569, l. 35.

44. Shearer, "Language and Politics of Socialist Rationalization," 595–601.

45. Mally, *Revolutionary Acts*, 150–51.

46. Iasnyi, *God rozhdeniia—deviat'sot semnadtsatyi*, 17.

47. RGASPI, f. 1m, op. 23, d. 964, l. 17ob.

factory began to set quotas for shock work, laborers tried to exploit the system: "He [a factory worker] demands—give me this many [quota units], because I have to earn this amount."[48] These shock workers' self-interest ran counter to the Komsomol leadership's hopes for selfless activism. Nonetheless, official backing of the campaign gave youth groups on the factory floor reason to accede to workers' demands both for authority in the factory and for compensation.

Groups of Light Cavalry (Legkaia kavaleriia)—a voluntary youth inspectorate—provided another outlet for youth empowerment. Nikolai Bukharin was said to have initiated the group, suggesting to a meeting of Komsomol leaders in 1928 that the league organize autonomous groups of youth that would monitor bureaucracy and corruption.[49] Ironically, the Komsomol leadership soon set the Light Cavalry to work in support of Stalinist programs of industrialization and grain requisitions, policies that Bukharin opposed.[50] These groups staged "raids" to test the efficiency and accountability of stores, factories, and collective farms. Effectively the role of the cavalry was as a young counterpart to the Workers' and Peasants' Inspectorate (Rabkrin), a powerful government agency that spearheaded the campaign for state-controlled industrialization.[51] In some cases, Light Cavalry brigades simply attached themselves to Rabkrin as unpaid workers. Moscow's Komsomol, for instance, sent 150 Light Cavalry members to work directly under the city's Rabkrin administration.[52]

Outside of the Light Cavalry's involvement with Rabkrin, its brigades conducted raids on their own, coming into conflict with enterprise managers and sometimes worrying even the Komsomol's leadership. In the Moscow-Narva district of Leningrad, Light Cavalry activists at a factory checked the work records of Komsomol members for tardiness and successfully lobbied for the factory to fire one worker for his twenty-eight instances of lateness. Another group inspecting a Leningrad canning workshop complained that its work was hampered because workers had grown wary of releasing information to the brigade: "Today I point out [shortcomings in the workshop to the Light Cavalry], and a week later I'll feel the anger of the administration."[53] Work in the Light Cavalry inflated some group members' sense of authority to levels that central Komsomol leaders considered dangerous. A youth league report on cavalry groups from 1929 asserted

48. RGASPI, f. 1m, op. 23, d. 925, l. 11.
49. RGASPI, f. 1m, op. 23, d. 866, ll. 1, 29.
50. Cohen, *Bukharin and the Bolshevik Revolution*, 270–336.
51. Shearer, *Industry, State, and Society*, 76–110.
52. RGASPI, f. 1m, op. 23, d. 866, l. 13.
53. RGASPI, f. 1m, op. 23, d. 927, l. 1.

that many had "taken on the functions of the OGPU." Rather than reporting findings to authorities for action, groups were taking matters into their own hands. At one enterprise in Arkhangelsk, the Light Cavalry confiscated all the materials the plant had failed to keep secure. A brigade in a Ukrainian town shut down stores for not having proper change.[54] Through shock brigades and Light Cavalry groups, the center's push for industrialization granted authority to youth who supported it.

Despite their fervor and symbolic importance, dedicated activists were only a prominent minority amid a majority of comparatively indifferent young people who faced increasing pressure from central authorities to mobilize. In the 1920s, central Komsomol leaders had supported a moderate program that focused on cultivating proletarian ideals among youth. Youth leaders advocated vocational education through factory apprenticeships, believing that they would generate working-class solidarity among a generation that would not face exploitation under capitalism. Local youth cells had a great deal of independence from central control, though. Radical activists found a milieu that nurtured their zeal for the class warfare of the revolution and civil war.[55] Other cells organized recreational activities like dances or films, denounced by radicals as frivolous. Some youth groups existed only on paper.[56]

The autonomous space these groups enjoyed began to close in the late 1920s. From 1927 onward, Stalin's regime increasingly viewed youth as a population to be mobilized through Komsomol cells on behalf of state projects. In that year, Stalin pushed forward rapid industrialization in the First Five-Year Plan. The plan established a schedule for economic growth with production norms that extended from entire industries to individual workers on the shop floor. In support of the plan, central Komsomol leaders increasingly associated youth activism with participation in norm fulfillment and overfulfillment. Despite some activists' warnings that the shock work movement would lose its vitality if prescribed from above, by the early 1930s a widely propagated slogan would demand 100 percent participation of league members in shock brigades.[57]

The mobilization of youth in the factories generated resistance. Saratov's Komsomol secretary claimed that many youth viewed socialist competitions as a form of pressure—"a cabal for workers." The secretary then made a common,

---

54. RGASPI, f. 1m, op. 23, d. 965, ll. 14–16.
55. Guillory, "We Shall Refashion Life on Earth!," 5; Gorsuch, *Youth in Revolutionary Russia*, 80–85.
56. Gorsuch, *Youth in Revolutionary Russia*, 71–75.
57. RGASPI, f. 1m, op. 23, d. 994, l. 10.

convenient assertion that peasant migrants in the factories were the main source of opposition.[58] But young workers from the cities also chafed as the regime demanded they work harder. When senior factory workers met with Komsomol leaders to discuss the problems of proletarian youth in 1928, a worker named Lobanov from the Krasnyi fakel factory claimed that youth outside the Komsomol "did not take [shock work] seriously." Non-Komsomol youth in the fitting brigade "nearly struck" when the youth league in the factory tried to force them into shock work.[59]

Management and older workers pushed back against shock work, too. At the Tbilisi train car factory, older workers and the party leadership considered "shock workers 'rivals' and almost enemies." When a Komsomol member had claimed his workshop head was "garbage" that needed to be thrown out, a master responded, "Don't mess in others' affairs." The Tbilisi Komsomol also claimed that the secretary of the party committee at the tram workshop threatened that the last person who had criticized the leadership too fervently had been accused of anti-Soviet nationalism.[60] An anonymous letter addressed from the Krasnyi Putilovets factory in Leningrad to Stalin and Kalinin in 1930 derided Komsomol-led shock work: "You like it that Komsomol members shout, but they are really dumbbells and sheep who don't understand anything."[61] At a mill in Ivanovo province, two female shock workers received a threatening letter for organizing their brigade. It said: "You're undermining our work, and because of you they're pressing us like in the old days. If you don't give it [shock work] up, then it'll be bad for you and your mug'll be smashed or we'll kill you altogether."[62]

At the beginning of Stalin's industrialization drive, the majority of young workers found themselves pressured by one side to conduct shock work and by the other to limit their activism. Radicals embraced the attack on cultural figures and undertook factory floor activism as a continuation of the revolutionary struggles of a decade before. They hoped that these actions would revitalize the Soviet Union's advance to socialism after the moderation of NEP. Stalinist leaders encouraged this protest not because they favored radical proletarianism as a principle, but because it was a means of mobilizing support against opponents who were skeptical about forced-pace industrialization. By endorsing shock work

---

58. RGASPI, f. 1m, op. 23, d. 926, l. 193.

59. RGASPI, f. 1m, op. 23, d. 925, ll. 6, 11–12.

60. RGASPI, f. 1m, op. 23, d. 964, ll. 17ob., 18.

61. Siegelbaum and Sokolov, *Stalinism as a Way of Life*, 45 (citing GARF, f. 1235, op, 4, d. 47, ll. 164–65).

62. Quoted in Rossman, *Worker Resistance under Stalin*, 130.

and Light Cavalry groups, though, the regime encouraged conflict, empowering youth as agents of Stalinist industrialization.[63] As Stalin's regime embarked on the second half of its plan to transform the country—the collectivization of agriculture—it again made young people its agents.

Youth to the Countryside

The Soviet Union of the 1920s was an overwhelmingly rural country. Nearly all the Bolsheviks believed that the country's industrialization would necessitate siphoning resources from the countryside to the cities. They disagreed over the timing and pace of industrialization, though. NEP had been a gradual approach, taxing the peasantry and establishing below-market purchasing of grain to pay for state-sponsored industrialization. In contrast, Stalin's turn toward forced industrialization in the First Five-Year Plan necessitated greater capital investment than the NEP framework could produce. Rather than seeing the grain crises of 1926–27 and 1927–28 as peasants' reactions to the state's below-market pricing, Stalin and his supporters believed that kulaks were intentionally starving industrialization efforts in the cities. Stalin broke with his moderate allies Nikolai Bukharin and Aleksei Rykov, accusing them of organizing a Right Opposition against his (and therefore the party's) policies of grain requisitions, collectivization, and dekulakization. As in industrialization, the politics of generation became a factor in the countryside as Stalin's regime granted youth authority in the collectivization campaign.

At the Eighth Komsomol Congress in May 1928, then Komsomol General Secretary Nikolai Chaplin called the organization of collective farms "the central task of the moment," and exhorted activists to go to the countryside in support of the policy.[64] Shortly after the meeting, the Komsomol Central Committee mobilized five hundred veteran youth workers from industrial centers to lead cells in the countryside.[65] Besides urban activists, central leaders counted on the support of the sizable number of young communists in the countryside. At the start of 1927, there were approximately 963,000 rural Komsomol members (49 percent of total membership) but only 307,000 rural party members (27 percent

---

63. See Neumann, "Revolutionizing Mind and Soul?," 252.
64. Quoted in Carr and Davies, *Foundations of a Planned Economy, 1926–1929*, vol. 1, 69.
65. RGASPI, f. 1m, op. 23, d. 804, l. 62.

of total membership).[66] At the end of 1931, a study of 412 villages in grain-surplus regions found that more than half (217) had a Komsomol cell but no party group.[67] The political demographics of the countryside gave party leaders hope that youth would assist the regime in the village.

Youth leaders did not think that all young people were capable of organizing collectivization, though. Within the Komsomol, there was increasing antagonism toward youth from the families of supposed kulaks and other class aliens. At the beginning of 1929, the Komsomol's Central Committee announced a verification of its ranks that would check the social composition of youth in the country-side.[68] The campaign became an occasion for "energetic class war" in Smolensk, where the provincial committee planned to send young workers to villages to hunt "Komsomol-kulaks." At the same time, Smolensk's Komsomol leader complained that a lack of resources made it impossible to pay workers to leave their jobs and undertake the campaign.[69]

Over the course of the year, the campaign against class aliens would continue as hostilities began to boil in the countryside. Central Komsomol leaders called for youth brigades in the countryside to inspect households for taxation and grain requisitions. They mobilized the Light Cavalry for this purpose, with predictable overenthusiasm. One cavalry group in a village in Bezhets district of Tver province surrounded the house of a kulak on horseback and confiscated three cows for the local collective farm.[70] Other local youth refused to assist outsiders in the grain requisitions. In a village in Lgov territory of the Central Black Earth province, one young man announced at a Komsomol meeting: "How can we put the peasant in his grave by taking grain? How can you take his grain when he has nothing to eat?" Another activist surrendered his Komsomol membership "because grain is more valuable than this card."[71] The leadership of Maikop region complained that young people "refused to spoil their 'neighborly' relationship with kulaks." Rather than taking the lead, Komsomol youth in the villages

---

66. This calculation considers youth placed in official categories of smallholding farmers (*edino-lichniki*), collective farmers, or agricultural workers (state farm and MTS workers) as rural. Industrial workers, white-collar workers, students, and other were urban. If anything, this calculation underestimates the number of Komsomol youth in the countryside, given that white-collar workers chaired village councils, students went to school in rural locations and youth listed as "other" could have been rural artisans. Komsomol figures from RGASPI, f. 1m, op. 126, d. 336, ll. 18–23. Party figures from Rigby, *Communist Party Membership*, 491.

67. RGASPI, f. 1m, op. 23, d. 997, l. 2.

68. RGASPI, f. 1m, op. 23, d. 804, l. 114.

69. RGASPI, f. 1m, op. 23, d. 822, ll. 31–33.

70. RGASPI, f. 1m, op. 23, d. 965, ll. 14–16, 70–72.

71. RGASPI, f. 1m, op. 5, d. 24a, l. 5.

often claimed that "grain requisitions are . . . the affair of outside authorities."[72] These conflicting reactions only increased tensions in the countryside.

The end of 1929 marked a turning point for the country. The number of peasant households belonging to collective farms had nearly doubled from June to October (to roughly 7.5 percent of households), while the total area sown for the autumn in the country was 6.5 percent higher than in 1928. Party leaders attributed the increase in area sown to the growth of collective farms, reaffirming their belief that collective agriculture was the solution to the country's grain crisis.[73] Despite increasing resistance from peasants, Stalin pushed for the wholesale collectivization of the country at the November 1929 Central Committee plenum.[74] Inseparable from the decision to collectivize was Stalin's December 1929 call for "the liquidation of the kulak as a class."[75] By January, the OGPU had prepared quotas by territory for the arrest and administrative exile of accused kulaks.[76] Although the term "kulak" had been a loose and malleable economic category, it soon came to be a term leveled at all opponents of collectivization.

The OGPU played an essential role in enforcing collectivization, but forging the collectivized countryside was possible only through the rapid mobilization of party and Komsomol workers from the cities. The movement of the state's agents to the countryside in the weeks and months following the November 1929 plenum dwarfed the deployment of activists in the previous two years. The best-known activists were the "twenty-five thousanders," veteran industrial workers sent to the village to organize new collective farms.[77] In virtually every province, though, especially those grain-surplus regions marked for wholesale collectivization, thousands of administrators and workers went to the countryside on behalf of the regime. The émigré Viktor Kravchenko was a ranking young factory specialist in Kharkov whom the party sent to organize collectivization. On the eve of his mobilization, Middle Volga province party secretary Mendel Khataevich appeared at a party meeting to exhort him and the other departing party activists, "Don't be afraid of taking extreme measures."[78]

72. RGASPI, f. 1m, op. 23, d. 940, l. 7.

73. Davies, *Socialist Offensive*, 133–35.

74. Lewin, *Russian Peasants and Soviet Power*, 446–81. For the record of the plenum, see Danilov, Khlevniuk, and Vatlin, eds., *Kak lomali NEP*, vol. 5.

75. I. V. Stalin, "K voprosam agrarnoi politiki v SSSR," *Pravda*, 29 December 1929, 3.

76. Danilov, Manning, and Viola, *Tragediia sovetskoi derevnii*, 2:143–47 (citing TsA FSB RF, f. 2, op. 8, d. 840, ll. 17–23).

77. See Viola, *Best Sons of the Fatherland*.

78. Kravchenko, *I Chose Freedom*, 92.

As in previous campaigns, youth organizers were supposed to assist authorities rather than act on their own. The Komsomol leadership of the Central Black Earth province, a grain-surplus region, mobilized 2,561 activists to villages in the first days of the collectivization campaign. Their chief goals were to persuade local young people to participate in grain requisitions, join collective farms, and become Komsomol members. In the town of Novokhopersk in Borisoglebskii territory, the local youth organization sent each neighboring village a troika (committee of three) to assign control figures to all the local youth for grain collections.[79] Other activists assisted OGPU agents as they searched for kulaks. In Balashovskii district of the Lower Volga province, the OGPU enlisted youth to "detain kulaks who attempted to run from the region."[80] In Zolotukhinskii district in Kursk territory, a brigade of 105 young people "discovered" fifteen kulak families the OGPU had yet to expropriate.[81]

The goals of the collectivization campaign and the coercion Stalin was willing to employ on its behalf were bound to spark violence. Contrary to Stalinist expectations that the village would break along class lines—with poor peasants supporting the campaign against the rich—peasants broadly resisted outside interference and lashed out with violence at the activists.[82] In Leninakan (today's Gyumri, Armenia), the local Komsomol mobilized the sixteen-year-old student Anastasyan Vairich to collectivize a village near the city. Sent with eight other young communists, his team gave speeches about the benefits of collective agriculture, especially the advantages of acquiring and sharing heavy machinery. When the peasants remained skeptical, the Komsomol leader of his university, Kalashyan, threatened, "It is obvious that some of those present do not understand the meaning of freedom. I am therefore forced to warn them that the Soviet regime is sufficiently strong to crush any resistance." Unmoved by the student's warning, the meeting dispersed.

The students' continued attempts to persuade peasants to collectivize created more hostility. After their first effort failed, the team contacted the party committee in Leninakan. Vairich later recalled, "The city committee replied that if the entire village was not collectivized by nightfall every local Communist and Komsomol member, as well as the members of the special team, would be immediately expelled from the Party and Komsomol." Kalashyan summoned the police to the village, but peasants surrounded the police truck

79. RGASPI, f. 1m, op. 23, d. 941, ll. 48–49.
80. RGASPI, f. 1m, op. 23, d. 938, ll. 116–19.
81. RGASPI, f. 1m, op. 23, d. 976, l. 5.
82. Viola, *Peasant Rebels under Stalin*, 100–131.

and set it ablaze. Shamefully returning to Leninakan, the party committee immediately sent the team to another village where the students went door-to-door rather than speaking to the entire community at once. When it seemed that one peasant was on the verge of joining the kolkhoz, a student in the group roped the farmer's cow and pulled it toward the building of the village council. Peasants viewed this act as coercion and began to riot. Chased and beaten by the villagers, the students barricaded themselves in the village council building until dawn.[83]

Although many youth activists went to the countryside as collectivizers, local organizers also used their authority to oppose outsiders. A future activist, Petr Kruzhin, remembered his Komsomol member older brother as one of the "fighters who had declared war on rural backwardness and ignorance." During collectivization, his brother's Komsomol group "literally took over the village. In those days they had a uniform—khaki jacket and breeches, broad belt and shoulder strap." Their presence in the village brought comfort to some peasants, although it made many others "uneasy." Nonetheless, the senior Kruzhin's Komsomol group helped peasants resist coercion into collective farms. A twenty-five thousander sent to Kruzhin's village convened a meeting to discuss collectivization in the autumn of 1930. When the outside activist produced a pistol as a threat to the peasants, the Komsomol members broke up the gathering. Kruzhin's brother paid for this act with expulsion from the Komsomol as a "follower of Bukharin" and a two-week stint in the district OGPU's holding cell. Later, he would rejoin the league.[84]

The authority activists possessed during collectivization and the campaign's radical goals encouraged aggression and exploitation. The repression of kulaks and the expropriation of their property provided many opportunities for organizers to enrich themselves. A Komsomol member who took part in Chanovskii district's (Siberian territory) commission for the confiscation of property was accused of taking and selling requisitioned goods and then drinking away the profits.[85] Other activists seemed to revel in the power they had over villagers. The secretary of the Komsomol cell in Novo-Aleksandrovka in Zinovevsk region of Ukraine put a noose around the head of a peasant and forced him to pull the end of it until he gasped for breath: "Here's some water," he jeered, "drink it."[86]

---

83. Anastasyan Vairich, "Youth It Was That Led Us," in *Soviet Youth*, ed. Novak-Deker, 65–67.
84. Petr Kruzhin, "False Dawn," in *Soviet Youth*, ed. Novak-Deker, 196–97.
85. RGASPI, f. 1m, op. 23, d. 975, l. 56.
86. Viola et al., *War against the Peasantry*, 281 (citing TsA FSB RF, f. 2, op. 8, d. 40, ll. 6–17).

Youth were far from the only perpetrators of "excesses" and OGPU reports only occasionally singled out young people as perpetrators.[87] Among activists of all ages, revolutionary enthusiasm and unfamiliarity with the countryside sparked violent clashes. Perhaps most important, Stalin and his allies pressured activists to take whatever measures necessary to realize collectivization, threatening retribution from above. Young activists were as susceptible as older party representatives to these factors and perhaps more prone to unrestrained zeal. In the radical vision of some organizers, collectivization would not only "remark the borders" of farms into collectives but "remake the life" of villagers. An article in *Komsomol'skaia pravda* from early in 1930 urged activists to "plow the human soil," turning peasants into rural proletariat.[88] These efforts were a type of civilizing mission—an attempt to colonize the countryside with urban ideas about how to live. The party's Central Committee had sanctioned the closure of churches primarily because they were a gathering place for peasant resistance to collectivization. Youth activists, however, gained a reputation not only for shutting churches but for the mockery and desecration of religion.[89] In Zolotukhinskii district (Central Black Earth province), Komsomol youth dug up the grave of a former tradeswoman, threw away the corpse and collected the zinc from the headstone as scrap metal. Provincial youth leaders lamented that activists insulted the religious but "undertook no measures to make the kolkhoz operate more effectively."[90]

When groups of activist youth did work toward organizing collective farms, their actions often exceeded their mandate to assist officials but not act on their own. In Ershovo, a village without communists in Zvenigorod district (Moscow province), the local Komsomol cell asserted that it was the true power in the village, commanding the OGPU to revise its tax for peasants.[91] In Okonoshnikov in Omsk region, groups of young people struck terror in local peasants with nighttime searches where they took "everything." In the same district, Komsomol members conducted a "demonstration" where they marched a half-naked kulak around their village.[92] In Kirsanov district (Central Black Earth province), the

---

87. Ibid., 216–18 (citing TsA FSB RF, f. 208, op. 8, d. 35, ll. 53–55).

88. "Perepakhivaem mezhi, perestraivaem byt: shturm komsomolii," *Komsomol'skaia pravda*, January 16, 1930, 3; "Podniat' liudskuiu tselinu" *Komsomol'skaia pravda*, February 28, 1930, 2.

89. Kravchenko, *I Chose Freedom*, 127.

90. RGASPI, f. 1m, op. 23, d. 976. In March 1930, the party's Central Committee would order lower-level party organizations to stop forced closures of churches. See Danilov, Manning, and Viola, *Tragediia sovetskoi derevni*, 2:303–5 (citing RGASPI, f. 17, op. 3, d. 779, ll. 18–20).

91. RGASPI, f. 1m, op. 23, d. 997, l. 2.

92. RGASPI, f. 1m, op. 23, d. 975, l. 25.

Komsomol cell issued a resolution to execute thirty kulaks, although the activists apparently did not follow through on the decision.[93]

The clash between peasants and the state reached crisis levels in the winter and early spring of 1930. Entire villages or even districts rose up against forced collectivization.[94] Moreover, although party leaders in the provinces maintained that huge numbers of villages had joined collective farms, reports from the OGPU to Stalin asserted that many were Potemkin kolkhozes. As soon as the state's representatives left the village, peasants tore up the collective farm charter and redistributed property as though nothing had occurred.[95] Whether Stalin feared a mass peasant rebellion or was displeased with the paper collective farms is unclear. In March, however, he released an article called "Dizzy with Success" that indicated a retreat from forced collectivization.[96] Stalin denounced activists as the source of excesses—failing to acknowledge that he and his ruling circle had effectively encouraged their aggression. Instead of continuing to press for collectivization, he signaled for activists to consolidate the collective farm economy they had created that winter. Rumors spread through the countryside of Stalin's supposed retreat, and millions of peasants left the collectives. In the spring of 1930, the OGPU registered thousands of anti-kolkhoz disturbances each month, the most at any time during the previous three years.[97] Despite the temporary retreat, Stalin and his followers never relinquished their plans to collectivize the countryside. In the fall of 1930, low rates of grain requisitions during a bumper harvest would lead to a renewed collectivization campaign, full of the same coercion as the "all-out drive" in the winter of 1929–30. There would be no retreat from the renewed campaign, and peasants either resigned themselves to the new collective farm economy or left for the cities.

During collectivization Stalin mobilized all those who supported his plans or whom he could coerce into soldiering in the village. Although the collectivization campaign was an attempt to extend Moscow's power in the countryside, it also lent the state's authority to those organizers sent to coerce the peasantry into collectives. Soviet youth were disproportionately drafted into collectivization for two reasons. First, the number of Komsomol members

93. RGASPI, f. 1m, op. 23, d. 976.

94. Viola, *Peasant Rebels under Stalin*; McDonald, *Face to the Village*, 259–97.

95. See for example, Danilov, Manning, and Viola, *Tragediia sovetskoi derevni*, 2:138–39 (citing TsA FSB RF, f. 2, op. 8, d. 653, ll. 14–16).

96. Stalin, *Sochineniia*, 12:197–205; Viola, *Peasant Rebels under Stalin*, 179. For the internal order of the party Central Committee that accompanied Stalin's article, see Danilov, Manning, and Viola, *Tragediia sovetskoi derevni*, 2:303–5.

97. Viola et al., *War against the Peasantry*, 342 (citing TsA FSB RF, f. 2, op. 9, d. 539, ll. 224–25)

(particularly in rural areas) exceeded the number of party members considerably and provided an organizational base for the regime to mobilize. Second, many were enthusiastic supporters of the renewal of revolutionary struggle and approached their task with relish. Often left alone in villages to fulfill the state's mission, one Komsomol leader claimed that "the lack of party leadership led to perversions and avant-gardism" among youth.[98] At the same time, young people's authority in the village could also lead to resistance, which party leaders decried as "kulak propaganda" from within the ranks of activists. In the midst of a catastrophe that would unfold in 1932–33, fears about the continuing influence of enemies in the countryside would lead to a witch hunt in the ranks of the Komsomol.

Expanding and Purging

Collectivization demanded activism from existing communists and Komsomol members, but it also spurred a campaign to recruit a large number of new members. From 1930 to the beginning of 1932, Soviet political organizations enlisted millions in an attempt to convert the population to the party's goals. Komsomol administrators announced a new slogan, "recruit 100 percent of worker youth." The targets of this "komsomolization" were class-based groups that the Bolsheviks believed were loyal to their goals in the countryside—workers, poor peasants, and peasant migrants to the cities. In 1930 and 1931, the youth league grew from roughly 2.5 million to almost 5.4 million members (Table 1 in appendix). Particularly after the "Dizzy with Success" article in the spring of 1930 and the temporary retreat from forced collectivization, youth leaders increased pressure to assimilate the countryside through league membership. In rural areas alone, the youth league expanded by a million members in the first six months of 1931. By July, nearly 80 percent of all young communists in the countryside had not been members before 1930.[99]

The recruiting campaign employed the planning and coercion characteristic of the First Five-Year Plan. Ukrainian Komsomol leader Aleksandr Boichenko announced that the republic alone needed to recruit 1.5 million members.[100] With quota in hand, activists rushed to realize it as they might complete production norms for pig iron. Just as shock workers received production bonuses, the

---

98. RGASPI, f. 1m, op. 23, d. 997, l. 2.
99. Ibid., l. 1.
100. TsDAHO, f. 7, op. 1, spr. 654, ark. 13, 15, 16, 24.

Komsomol of Krivoi Rog (Ukraine) offered a thousand-ruble prize for the cell that gained the most new members.[101] The youth leaders of Rusobrodskii district (Central Black Earth province) gave recruiting control figures for every local cell to fulfill.[102]

Local organizers were often skeptical about the new recruits. This doubt was especially prevalent in the cities, where peasant migrants had been arriving steadily for years and in even greater numbers since the start of collectivization. For urban youth organizers, the recruiting campaign challenged the meaning of Komsomol membership and changed the dynamic of their work. As young peasants became factory workers, they encountered a proletarian workplace culture that was not accepting of them and often not acceptable to them.[103] At a meeting of regional organizers in Ukraine, a Komsomol activist from a local group of coal miners in the Donbas expressed confusion—or perhaps incredulity—about the slogan "recruit 100 percent of worker youth." Previously, his group had only admitted industrial workers with work records longer than two years. Now his superiors in the league said that a peasant migrant with just six months of work experience could join the league as a member of the proletariat. How could a factory cell count a peasant as a worker without undermining its proletarian identity?[104] Other factory activists grumbled that new members were in fact hindering productivity. One organizer from Ukraine said, "We used to know that our Komsomol cell had firm discipline."[105]

Although central leaders pressed for increased recruiting, not all youth were viable members. A June 1930 article in *Komsomol'skaia pravda* denounced instances when local organizers recruited new members regardless of their background. The article was accompanied by a cartoon of a youth organizer dropping various anti-Soviet figures—kulaks, religious sectarians, and hooligans—into a fountain marked "complete komsomolization."[106]

In the sprint to "komsomolize" entire factories and collective farms, had youth organizers truly ensured that they excluded class enemies? Similar questions about kulak subversion motivated the end of the recruiting campaign by party

101. RGASPI, f. 1m, op. 23, d. 1006, l. 134.

102. RGASPI, f. 1m, op. 23, d. 979, l. 31.

103. Hoffmann, *Peasant Metropolis*, 33–42.

104. TsDAHO, f. 7, op. 1, spr. 655, ark. 11.

105. TsDAHO, f. 7, op 1., d. 1, spr. 617, ark. 133, 134.

106. "Sploshnaia ... Komsomolizatsiia vmesto regulirovaniia rosta," *Komsomol'skaia pravda*, June 18, 1930, 3. An earlier article had called for Komsomol youth to treat children of kulaks with respect but not to allow them to join the youth league. "O molodom pokolenii likvidiruemogo klassa," *Komsomol'skaia pravda*, April 5, 1930, 1.

FIGURE 1.2.   "Complete komsomolization." *Komsomol'skaia Pravda*, June 18, 1930.

decree in December 1931.[107] Supposed infiltrators would become party leaders' scapegoats for the disaster of collectivization.

The collectivization of agriculture and inflexible state grain requisitioning policies led to a deadly famine in the winter of 1932–33. The First Five-Year Plan

107. RGASPI, f. 1m, op. 23, d. 979, l. 31.

had assumed that collectivization would improve productivity, and plan figures for grain requisitions jumped accordingly. Instead, collectivization minimized peasants' incentives to sow more grain, compounding the shortfall of a bad harvest year in 1932. The combination of these factors meant that plan figures were so large that peasants often risked starvation by acceding to them. In contrast to realities in the countryside, police reports to Stalin insisted that peasants were hiding grain from the state.[108] Reports from party leaders in the provinces asserted that even party and Komsomol groups had been infected by enemy class elements.[109] A youth activist from a village in Ukholovo district (Moscow province) said, "The plan they gave us is big and we won't fulfill it. Let the people from the district committee fulfill the plan." His outburst was classified as an "opportunistic lack of belief in the feasibility of requisitioning plans."[110] Stalin readily accepted explanations like these for activists' inability to secure grain and threatened repression of those who would not produce their norms. The result was a ruthless campaign to pry the last stores of grain from peasants. Ukraine's party chief Stanislav Kosior even issued a directive for the confiscation of seed grain.[111] These policies led to a widespread famine in parts of Ukraine, the North Caucasus, and Kazakhstan. The Politburo ordered famine-afflicted regions to be cordoned off as peasants desperately searched for grain in areas far from their homes.[112] A reliable estimate suggests that between 5.5 and 6.5 million people perished from starvation and related effects.[113]

In the midst of the unfolding tragedy, party and Komsomol leaders initiated general membership verifications (*proverki*) as well as purges (*chistki*) targeting grain-surplus areas that had been the primary focus of collectivization. Like the Komsomol, the party had experienced a membership jump from 1.5 million in 1929 to 3.5 million in 1933.[114] In the purge, 18 percent of communists lost their membership, a similar proportion to previous membership cleansing operations before the revolution from above. Nearly a quarter of those removed from the party in the course of this verification were members

108. See, e.g., Danilov, Manning, and Viola, *Tragediia sovetskoi derevni*, 3:218, 472 (citing RGASPI, f. 82 op. 2, d. 138, ll. 80–97; TsA FSB RF, f. 2, op. 10, d. 520, ll. 699–708).

109. Ibid., 3:549 (citing RGASPI, f. 81, op. 3, d. 214, ll. 81–89).

110. RGASPI, f. 1m, op. 23, d. 1022, ll. 11, 31.

111. Danilov, Manning, and Viola, *Tragediia sovetskoi derevn*, 3:611 (citing RGASPI, f. 17, op. 26, d. 25, l. 214).

112. For the Politburo resolution and provincial reports about implementation, see ibid., 3:634–38 (citing RGASPI, f. 558, op. 11, d. 45, ll. 109–109ob.; f. 17, op. 42, d. 80, ll. 9–11; d. 72, ll. 109–11, 113.)

113. Wheatcroft and Davies, *Years of Hunger*, 401.

114. Rigby, *Communist Party Membership*, 52.

deemed passive but not enemies.[115] In contrast, in the targeted grain-growing regions the purges were a response to "massive attempts from district and rural organizations to deceive the state," in the words of the head of the Central Black Earth province.[116]

The purge in the Komsomol was as large or larger than in the party. The league's *proverka* in 1933 imitated the verification of party members. Youth activists even received instructions that they should participate in the party verification to learn how to conduct such an operation. In some cases, Komsomol members became too involved in the party verification. Organizers from several cells in Sverdlovsk formed commissions to investigate the private lives of communists.[117] According to Komsomol documents, the league's verification was planned "not as a purge [*chistka*]" but also not as a "simple technical measure." The result was a de facto purge of unwanted elements. The unnamed author of a report to central Komsomol leaders wrote that the verification had uncovered and expelled large numbers of alleged class-alien elements and their helpers. They had supposedly joined the Komsomol as a means of undermining the goals of the revolution from above. The league expelled roughly 20 percent of its membership, a figure on par with the party's verification.[118]

In addition to the verification, though, Komsomol members in grain-surplus regions were the targets of a membership purge. District youth committees in these regions appointed troikas of party members to visit each village in the district and conduct interviews in front of the entire cell. Troikas received instructions to judge youth on their "class face"—their social origins and activities during collectivization. After conducting the purge, the troika was supposed to send information on so-called socially dangerous expellees to the OGPU.[119] In total in the Kuban region and in the North Caucasus territory, troikas expelled more than half of the members—a figure that was probably matched in other grain-surplus regions.[120]

The purge inspired both mockery and fear, targeting those who had been leaders in areas that underfulfilled grain requisitions above all. In Kozeletskii district of Ukraine's Chernigov province, a troika expelled a village youth secretary for having allegedly told the district committee, "There is no grain in the

115. Getty and Naumov, *Road to Terror*, 125; Getty, *Origins of the Great Purges*, 54.

116. Danilov, Manning, and Viola, *Tragediia sovetskoi derevni*, 3:532–36 (citing TsA FSB RF, f. 2, op. 10, d. 355, ll. 25–26).

117. RGASPI, f. 1m, op. 23, d. 1029, l. 5.

118. RGASPI, f. 1m, op. 126, d. 310, ll. 15–25.

119. RGASPI, f. 1m, op. 23, d. 1028, ll. 1–2.

120. RGASPI, f. 1m, op. 23, d. 1028, ll. 49, 58; op. 126, d. 310, ll. 15–25.

village and therefore no need for our Komsomol meeting [to organize grain requisitions]."[121] "Sabotage" could take other forms, too. A troika in the North Caucasus uncovered that when peasants were late bringing grain to a young tractor driver, he "left his tractor, relieved himself, and went to sleep underneath the tractor."[122] Some youth refused to take the purge seriously, detracting from what central leaders called the class-economic goals of the operation. In Starominsk district of Krasnodar territory, village boys interrupted the proceedings to ask their peers questions like why they had cheated on their girlfriends.[123] In Eisk district, a member sighed, "It doesn't matter if I die of hunger in the Komsomol or outside it."[124] For others the question of membership was more important, though. Significant numbers of youth voluntarily forfeited their cards on the eve of the purge, hoping to avoid the troika and perhaps the OGPU. In one village of Krasnodar territory, only seven of seventy members appeared at the purge meeting, the others evading it out of fear.[125] Many of the urban workers ordered to the countryside under famine conditions refused to go to the village. Those who were already there sometimes left their posts without giving notice. In either case, these activists were typically expelled from the league as well.[126]

The campaign against supposed resisters in grain-growing regions bled over into membership practices in the cities and in other provinces. Factory youth committees in grain-surplus provinces also had to conduct the purge, although criteria for expulsion were different. Besides rooting out so-called class aliens, North Caucasus youth leaders instructed factory cells to judge members based on their history of norm fulfillment and absenteeism.[127] In nonsurplus Lopasne district (Moscow province), youth leaders at a December 1932 meeting applauded the expulsions of those Komsomol members who were accused of not fulfilling potato requisitions. During the "tense class war for potato requisitions," underfulfilling youth had become "the mouthpiece of the kulak in the Komsomol."[128] An article in the February 1933 issue of *Izvestiia TsK Komsomola*, the journal for youth organizers, explained that class enemies were still lurking even after collectivization, and Komsomol groups had to uncover them. Now enemies on

---

121. TsDAHO, f. 7, op. 1, spr. 818, ark. 44, 49.
122. RGASPI, f. 1m, op. 23, d. 1028, l. 6.
123. Ibid., l. 28.
124. Ibid., l. 26.
125. Ibid., ll. 49, 58.
126. TsDAHO, f. 7, op. 1, spr. 913, ark. 24, 34.
127. RGASPI, f. 1m, op. 23, d. 1028, l. 74.
128. OKhDOPIM, f. 648p, op. 1, d. 1, ll. 69–70.

collective farms were organizing "quiet sapping," takeovers of local leadership, and the misappropriation of socialist property.[129]

It is unclear what happened to the young people who were purged. Very few appealed their expulsion, and fewer still received reinstatement.[130] How many faced accusations that they were kulaks is unknown. Arrest was a distinct possibility in grain-growing regions, because party leaders issued a "final" round of quotas for the exile of kulaks after the party and Komsomol purges.[131] Many expelled members had joined only recently, and apathy or disillusionment seems to have spelled the end of their tenure in the youth league. Outside the meetings of leading Komsomol organizers, the reality was that few youth, no matter how loyal, were willing to starve to death to build socialism.

The purge of the Komsomol reinforced two trends that had intensified from 1927: the equation of youth activism with plan fulfillment and a wariness of "class alien elements" in political culture. In the aftermath of the purges of 1932–33, the party announced a moratorium on new members.[132] In contrast, Komsomol leaders never cut off membership entirely. They nonetheless instituted stringent standards for new members, including limitations on the admission of adolescents, and reaffirmed their commitment to the industrial proletariat as the Komsomol's core base. By 1935, the league's membership had fallen from 5.3 million, at the start of 1932, to just 3.5 million.

Stalin and his allies declared victory in 1933, announcing that the First Five-Year Plan had been completed in only four years and three months. In truth, the country had not achieved the plan's goals. Party leaders had expanded plan figures massively midway through its duration, but industrial growth had not even achieved the goals of its more moderate initial form.[133] Stalin's regime did realize an economic and political transformation in the country, though. It had produced significant industrial growth, and the war in the countryside placed the rural economy under the control of Moscow. Youth activists played an essential role in the factories as shock workers and in the villages as organizers of collective

---

129. "Boevaia proverka komsomol'skikh riadov," *Izvestiia TsK Komsomola*, no. 3–4 (1933): 2.

130. TsDAHO, f. 7, op. 1, spr. 924.

131. Danilov, Krasil'nikov, and Viola, *Politbiuro i krest'ianstvo*, 1:607–12 (citing RGASPI, f. 17, op. 163, d. 981, ll. 229–238).

132. Rigby, *Communist Party Membership*, 196.

133. R. W. Davies argues that heavy industry grew, but Soviet claims of fulfilling the plan in other sectors (especially light industry and consumer goods) were unfounded. Although Soviet leaders claimed that industrial production grew by 102 percent, Davies cites figures between 41 and 72 percent. Davies, *Crisis and Progress*, 238–39.

agriculture. At the demand of Komsomol and party leaders, activists became actors in the struggle to transform the country. There were radicals among Stalin's supporters who embraced the revolution they had awaited. Yet the regime's desperate need for activists to fulfill its plans meant that many young people unexpectedly found themselves the voice of authority in workshops or newly founded collective farms. Conflict was inevitable as Stalin steered the country toward radical policies. Nonetheless, youthful enthusiasm and the overturning of generational hierarchies also played a role in shaping and exacerbating clashes.

Political leaders were largely indifferent to the violence their activists committed, but the instability in the country gave them cause for concern. The USSR was reeling from a virtual civil war in the countryside. Millions of peasants had been displaced during collectivization, and contrary to the projections of the five-year plan, labor productivity had fallen. The bitter triumph of the revolution from above demanded a period of consolidation and stabilization. Among youth, the Komsomol's leaders embarked on another kind of revolution, one aimed at civilizing radical organizers along with the rest of the country, called communist upbringing.

CULTURAL REVOLUTION FROM ABOVE

Nineteen thirty-four was a year of change. At the Seventeenth Party Congress in January of that year, Stalin claimed victory against the forces of counterrevolution. The state had largely succeeded in collectivizing agriculture, defeating the supposed class enemies that had struggled against the campaign. Stalin asserted that in industry, the First Five-Year Plan had catapulted the Soviet Union forward as a modern industrial power and the first socialist state.[1] Amid these declarations of success, Soviet leaders worried about the social upheaval that collectivization and rapid industrialization had unleashed on the country. When millions of peasants had migrated to the cities, authorities had hoped to assimilate them into urban life. Instead, peasants frequently reproduced village culture in their new homes.[2] Although the regime could celebrate the growth of heavy industry, Soviet leaders acknowledged that the country still had a dearth of competent specialists. At a meeting of workers from metallurgical factories on December 29, 1934, Stalin said, "We need to cultivate [people] carefully and attentively, as a gardener cultivates his beloved fruit tree."[3] Building on this notion, Stalin soon

---

1. Davies, *Crisis and Progress*, 466–68.
2. Hoffmann, *Peasant Metropolis*, 159; Moshe Lewin suggests peasant migrants to cities caused the "ruralization" of urban life rather than the desired urbanization of rural life. Lewin, "Society, State, and Ideology during the First Five-Year Plan," in *Making of the Soviet System*, 218–22.
3. Stalin, *Sochineniia*, 14:40.

after unveiled the slogan, "cadres decide everything."[4] It would be people, not just industrial technology, that would define socialism's success.

Stalin's emphasis on cultivating people was at the heart of the transformation of Soviet youth culture in the mid-1930s. In the revolution from above of the First Five-Year Plan, activist youth had been a central force for economic mobilization. Prompted in late 1934 by Stalin himself, the center of Komsomol activism shifted from mobilizing activism in the economy to the moral upbringing of the first socialist generation. The Komsomol leader Aleksandr Kosarev termed the new policy communist upbringing—a cultural revolution from above meant to create a new society, just as the First Five-Year Plan had created a new economy. The main location of youth activism began to shift from workplace to schools, fitness programs, and civil defense as the league attempted to mold adolescents. It targeted young women as new members in the hopes of creating young socialist families. Although some radical organizers grumbled at the changes to their organizations, the core of Komsomol activism was no longer factory work. Now young communists were called on to turn youth into a cultured Soviet citizenry—one that did not explicitly exhibit a proletarian class identity but instead embodied socialist modes of morality, behavior and education.

This focus on developing youth in official culture under Stalin differed from the policies of NEP, even though youth leaders of the 1920s had also mobilized entertainment to influence youth. When Komsomol leaders after 1934 promoted "cultured" living, their notions of what culture meant and how to promote it were firmly rooted in the context of Stalin's 1930s. NEP-era idealists had hoped to inculcate youth with a sense of the proletariat's struggle that would allow them achieve the next stage of the Bolshevik Revolution.[5] Instead, the Stalinist definition of culture repurposed traditional notions of refinement for socialism. Cultured youth would have formal education and respect superiors. They would observe norms of cleanliness, maintain a polite demeanor, and demonstrate familiarity with the classics of Russian and Soviet culture.[6] In the 1920s, the Komsomol had been a community that radical organizers and the rank and file had played a significant role in constructing. In contrast, the main focus of Komsomol activity under Stalin was determined by top party and youth leaders. After the Stalin Revolution, the structure of the Komsomol became more hierarchical and centralized. Like associational life in the Soviet Union generally, the

---

4. Ibid., 95–96.

5. Fitzpatrick, *Education and Social Mobility*, 47.

6. For discussions of "culture" in the Soviet Union, see Kelly, *Refining Russia*, 192; and Hoffmann, *Stalinist Values*, 146–83.

youth league came under the control of the country's leaders.[7] Although Kosarev and other youth leaders had come from the league's radical milieu, from late 1934 onward they would use the Komsomol apparatus that emerged in the revolution from above to advocate for communist upbringing. Youth activists at once became the instruments and the targets of this transformation.

The Komsomol's turn toward developing cultured youth highlighted strengthening gender differences under Stalin. For some radicals of the 1920s, the Bolshevik Revolution had promised to overturn women's traditional roles, unleash sexual freedom, and end the family. Nonetheless, a tension existed during the years of NEP between those who believed that traditional gender relations between men and women would eventually disappear and those who supported customary gender relations out of principle or pragmatism.[8] Stalin's regime largely settled this friction by co-opting aspects of traditional gender relations as part of socialism.[9] In the Komsomol, activism for the ideal male organizer became tied to a military-style discipline and frequently to military training itself. As international tensions increased, youth leaders placed an emphasis on shaping young men as civilized soldiers. Although the majority of activists were still male, youth leaders gave tacit approval to "cultured" entertainment activities like dancing that they hoped would allow them to bring women into the league. Through these activities, the Komsomol aspired to make young women and, as the keepers of domestic life, their families into loyal Stalinist subjects. Conceptions of activism for men and women differed, yet for both sexes, the Komsomol's goals shifted from organizing economic production toward cultivating people.

Building Character in the Komsomol

In December 1934, Stalin called Komsomol General Secretary Aleksandr Kosarev and his top lieutenants to his office. According to Kosarev's retelling in the press, the *vozhd'* began by asking a series of Socratic questions about the work of youth activists. Learning that the Komsomol had an agricultural department, Stalin asked with mock surprise, "Why agricultural? Does the Komsomol finance or run agriculture?" The youth league, of course, had played an integral part in the

7. Mally, *Revolutionary Acts*, 182–83; Neumann, *Communist Youth League*, 217; Paperny, *Architecture in the Age of Stalin*, 82–104.

8. Gorsuch, *Youth in Revolutionary Russia*, 104–11; Bernstein, *Dictatorship of Sex*, 5–6, 28–30, 69–72.

9. Goldman, *Women, the State, and Revolution*, 296–335.

economy of the First Five-Year Plan, mobilizing youth in the countryside and on the factory floor. However, Stalin now demanded that the league turn away from organizing labor and turn toward youth itself—to provide moral socialization for the country.[10]

Stalin's intervention in youth culture occurred after a year of uncertainty in 1934. The dictator's announcement that socialism had been achieved pushed institutions throughout the USSR to reform themselves in anticipation of the needs of the new historical epoch. Yet it was not always clear what these needs would be. The Seventeenth Party Congress gave little indication of how youth culture would change under socialism. Nonetheless, Komsomol leaders announced a "reconstruction" of youth work soon after the congress. Without a program for significant changes, they introduced cosmetic alterations to the league. For instance, local groups stopped calling themselves "cells"—a holdover from the Bolshevik underground before the revolution—and became "local organizations." At a meeting of youth organizers in Donetsk, activists complained about the superficiality of the changes, "I haven't heard of anything new."[11]

Toward the end of 1934, Kosarev signaled a major shift in the Komsomol's mission under socialism—away from economic mobilization and toward the creation of cultured cadres. The emblematic young communists of the 1920s had been ungroomed young men clad in leather jackets who dismissed the received wisdom of the previous generation. During NEP, Kosarev himself had been one of these iconoclasts, asserting, "We frequently understand culture only by its outer appearance."[12]

Kosarev and his hard-boiled generation of activists had believed that culture was wrongfully associated with the frivolity of dances, fashion, and sophistication. They revolted against the perceived superficiality of this lifestyle and its embodiment in the "bourgeois" atmosphere of the universities and the cafés. For these rough-mannered young radicals, real culture lived among the workers on the factory floor.[13] By November 1934, Kosarev had changed his views entirely. At a meeting of provincial youth organizers, he chided activists for "idiotically" boasting of their lack of refinement. Instead, Kosarev asserted that activists must be the epitome of traditional notions of culture—of grooming, civility and conventional education. He linked the Komsomol's new emphasis on developing cultured people to concerns about social disorder after collectivization. In particular, he

10. "Doklad Tov. Kosareva," *Komsomol'skaia pravda*, June 28, 1935, 1.

11. TsDAHO, f. 7, op. 1, spr. 1031, ark. 8.

12. L. Gurvich, "Poiski i nakhodki," in *Aleksandr Kosarev*, ed. Mikhailova, 30.

13. Kelly, *Refining Russia*, 192; Gorsuch, *Youth in Revolutionary Russia*, 87–93.

FIGURE 2.1. Aleksandr Kosarev in 1925. RGASPI, f. 1m, op. 18, d. 2472, l. 29.

worried about hooliganism, a vague and variable category of criminal disobedience that encompassed acts of drunkenness, assault, and general disorderly public behavior.[14] Kosarev and other leaders viewed hooliganism not as sporadic outbursts but as a deliberate anti-Soviet program that could corrupt impressionable young people in the absence of wholesome alternatives. He asserted that it was necessary for the Komsomol to fill that role, becoming "a people's commissariat of cultured recreation" that would promote party-approved cultured lifestyles.[15]

The imperative to create refined young people was at the center of communist upbringing, the term Kosarev used in 1935 for the Komsomol's new goals. The changes to the youth league were introduced at the highest levels of the Soviet party-state. At a meeting of the Politburo on February 22, Stalin and Kosarev delivered speeches on the need to reform official youth culture. Toward that purpose, the Politburo formed a commission with a number of leaders from the party, state, and Komsomol, including Stalin himself.[16] Speaking on behalf of the party's Central Committee, the commission codified the criticisms Stalin had raised about the league in December of the previous year. A characteristic change was that the Komsomol's agricultural department became the department of rural youth.[17] Moves like these reflected a broader shift in the league's mission from channeling economic activism to the transformation of young people's behavior. When Kosarev spoke about the reorganization of the league at a meeting of provincial and republican youth leaders, he said that Komsomol workers would become "a type of professional for the upbringing of youth and children."[18] At a meeting of youth organizers in June 1935, Kosarev argued that the new focus of activism was cultured behavior: "The outer appearance of district and regional secretaries must change, so that they stop being provincial lads and become cultured people."[19] In order to cultivate young people, the unrefined, radical organizers of the cultural revolution themselves had to become worthy examples in appearance and deed. It was particularly important for these activists to become symbols of sophistication because Kosarev asserted

---

14. Solomon, *Soviet Criminal Justice under Stalin*, 224–25. Brian LaPierre makes the compelling argument that the definition of hooliganism encompassed only public disorderly behavior under Stalin. Under Khrushchev, the redefinition of hooliganism (under the term "domestic hooliganism") enabled authorities to police the home lives of citizens. LaPierre, *Hooligans in Khrushchev's Russia*, 59–95. On the politics and implementation of policing juveniles as hooligans under Stalin, see Shearer, *Policing Stalin's Socialism*, 219–42.

15. RGASPI, f. 1m, op. 5, d. 27, ll. 66–68.

16. RGASPI, f. 17, op. 3, d. 959, l. 4.

17. RGASPI, f. 17, op. 120, d. 114, ll. 32–36.

18. RGASPI, f. 1m, op. 5, d. 28b, ll. 1, 2–3.

19. RGASPI, f. 1m, op. 2, d. 115, l. 62.

that providing moral upbringing in schools would become a central aspect of the league's work.[20]

Youth leaders also placed a new emphasis on reaching another under-represented audience, young women. Kosarev established a women's secretariat in the league and appointed Tat'iana Vasil'eva as its first leader. Vasil'eva knew Kosarev from his time as youth leader of Moscow's Bauman district in the 1920s. Before Kosarev summoned her in 1935, Vasil'eva was studying at Moscow's Industrial Academy, a breeding ground for leading party figures. Only a few years before, the academy had launched Nikita Khrushchev's career.[21] In some ways, Vasil'eva's new secretariat resembled another Soviet institution, the Women's Department (Zhenotdel), the party section for women that had existed until January 1930. Like the Zhenotdel, Vasil'eva was charged with advocating on behalf of women's promotion and liberation, especially "among girls of national republics," code for women in Central Asia and the Caucasus.[22] In contrast to the activist-oriented Zhenotdel, though, the women's section in the Komsomol was also responsible for incorporating women into official culture through entertainment, combining "mass-political work, games, dances and so on."[23]

Although Kosarev and other youth leaders shaped the implementation of communist upbringing, Stalin and his inner circle were the initiators of the changes in official youth culture. Stalin intervened in the league directly only at key moments but was constantly present in Komsomol affairs through his agent, the party Central Committee secretary Andrei Andreev. A veteran member of Stalin's entourage, Andreev was the quintessential shapeless functionary. He was utterly loyal to Stalin and diligently moved from position to position—including playing a key organizing role in the dekulakization of the peasantry. In 1935, he joined the party's organizational bureau, which monitored party members and party-affiliated organizations like the Komsomol. At the June 1935 meeting of youth leaders where Kosarev unveiled the concept of communist upbringing, Andreev instructed: "If we raised economic questions before, now we will put forward questions like how to lead a meeting. We will educate guys [activists] on

---

20. Ibid., l. 69.

21. Taubman, *Khrushchev*, 72–113.

22. For an examination of the broader Soviet efforts to "liberate" women from the veil in Central Asia, see Northrop, *Veiled Empire*, 3–4.

23. RGASPI, f. 1m, op. 2, d. 116, l. 157. Local Zhenotdel cells had also been a venue for "*bab'i bunty*" (peasant women's protests) against collectivization. These protests led party leaders, already skeptical about the role of activism by and on behalf of women, to eliminate the organization. Goldman, "Industrial Politics," 60–61.

how to run a district committee according to the wishes of Comrade Stalin."[24] As Andreev envisioned youth activists, they were not rough-and-ready revolutionaries but polished bureaucrats capable of the disciplined implementation of Stalin's plans.

Youth leaders faced resistance as they explained the Komsomol's transition to an organization for character building. To some activists, the goal of making themselves and others into cultured people seemed less important than the class warfare and worker-heroism of the First Five-Year Plan had been. At Ukraine's Komsomol plenum in July 1935, the republican youth secretary Sergei Andreev suggested that a mix of nostalgia and alarm drove resistance among these activists, "A few will say, 'How can it be? The economy will sink.' The economy won't sink."[25] Enacting communist upbringing seemed like a demotion—a characterization that Kosarev described as a "deep and dangerous error." His comrade Evgenii Fainberg, the Komsomol secretary in charge of the youth press, also reacted to activists' complaints about their shifting function, "Now the gigantic task of working in the schools stands before us. Could this be the depreciation of the Komsomol's role?"[26] How many youth activists resented their new task is unclear, although the number was likely to have been significant if leading figures like Kosarev felt obliged to address their protesting voices. Over the objections of radical organizers, though, league leaders pressed activists into a more engaged role in the schools, sports, and civil defense.

The expansion of Komsomol participation in formal schooling created friction with education officials. Since the 1920s, youth activists had engaged in a competitive and sometimes acrimonious relationship with administrators from Narkompros, the ministry in charge of education. Under NEP, youth leaders had supported vocational education as a means of training a new generation of proletarians while education officials promoted the traditional general curriculum.[27] At the beginning of the Stalin Revolution, Komsomol educational policies won out. Vocational training became the norm in secondary education, in part because state economic institutions could use adolescent apprentice workers to feed the enormous labor hunger of the First Five-Year Plan. By 1931, regime leaders shifted approaches again, however, giving the traditional curriculum

24. RGASPI, f. 73, op. 1, d. 133, l. 135.

25. TsDAHO, f. 7, op. 1, spr. 1208, ark. 4, 55, 104, 212.

26. RGASPI, f. 6m, op. 10, d. 1, l. 13; d. 6, l. 35.

27. On Narkompros from the revolution to the end of the cultural revolution, see Fitzpatrick, *Commissariat of Enlightenment*; and Holmes, *Kremlin and the Schoolhouse*. On the teaching profession under Stalin, see Ewing, *Teachers of Stalinism*.

preference over the factory apprentice system.[28] At the same time that conventional instruction was reinstated, the school system expanded markedly. In the five years from 1930 to 1935, Soviet schools grew by ten million pupils (some 40 percent).[29] In conjunction with this expansion, youth organizers were asked to cooperate with Narkompros, assuming new roles in schools as mediums of moral and cultural upbringing.

Unlike the 1920s, when Komsomol and Narkompros figures had held substantially different conceptions about education, the tension between the organizations' leaders in 1935 was largely territorial. Komsomol leaders, in particular, worried about how to separate general education from communist upbringing. At a rancorous meeting between Kosarev and education officials, the youth leader accused Andrei Bubnov, the head of Narkompros, of allowing the schools to appropriate the Komsomol's role in self-governance among students. At the end of the meeting, though, Kosarev made a proposal for collaboration: Officials from Narkompros and the youth league would create a special Komsomol position in schools in major cities.[30]

The new position of *komsorg* (an abbreviation of "Komsomol organizer" sometimes used in an informal sense to describe activists more broadly) marked the border between Narkompros and the Komsomol. Approving the recommendation of the Narkompros-Komsomol commission, Kosarev hired fifteen hundred Komsomol workers to become "assistants to school directors for political-upbringing work" in Kharkov, Kiev, Leningrad, and Moscow. Because the title seemed to suggest that the Komsomol organizer in the school would be the deputy school director, Kosarev renamed the position komsorg. The komsorg would be in charge of "political, cultural-upbringing and extracurricular work among students," and the Komsomol Central Committee itself reserved the right to approve appointees. After beginning in four cities, posts expanded to other places soon after, and the new position became a significant intervention in the everyday life of schools.[31] In some cases, the arrival of the komsorgs disrupted power dynamics within schools. A common theme in reports to party leaders was that Komsomol organizers were "too commanding," treading on the authority of school administrators.[32] Despite these problems at the local level, the youth league had become a partner in general education, rather than its competitor.

28. Fitzpatrick, *Education and Social Mobility*, 209–10, 221–25.
29. Ewing, *Teachers of Stalinism*, 60.
30. RGASPI, f. 1m, op. 3, d. 131, ll. 73–122.
31. RGASPI, f. 1m, op. 3, d. 133, ll. 14–15, 22; d. 135, 99–104.
32. RGASPI, f. 17, op. 120, d. 237, ll. 1–5, 6–23; d. 238, ll. 51–59.

The Komsomol's role in moral upbringing became inseparable from physical and military education as youth leaders occupied key posts in sports and defense organizations. In January 1935, Kosarev nominated Ivan Kharchenko to join the state sports committee as "responsible secretary" and asked Stalin to make Kharchenko its chair after a year.[33] Before his appointment, Kharchenko had headed the semiautonomous Komsomol organization for railroad workers. Under Kharchenko's auspices, the railroad organization conducted large-scale and apparently effective policing activities along transit lines.[34] Kharchenko had previously headed the Komsomol's military department, responsible for overseeing the youth organization's physical and military training. Kharchenko's new assistant in the sports administration was Boris Kal'pus, who had before been the Red Army's head of physical preparation and sport. These appointments both tied the sports administration tightly to the Komsomol and infused it with military personnel.

Kosarev and his leadership group also established authority over the civil defense organization, Union of Societies for Aid to Defense and Aviation-Chemical Development of the USSR (Osoaviakhim). An amalgamation of several 1920s-era voluntary defense organizations, Osoaviakhim inherited a wide range of functions related to civil defense: preconscription training for young men, civilian firearms training, air and chemical defense. It also was responsible for the production and distribution of defense products (e.g., gas masks) and pest extermination. So wide ranging were its responsibilities that in August 1935, the Soviet government accused its leaders of forgetting its main duty: providing preconscription training.[35] Facing a barrage of criticism, the longtime Osoaviakhim leader Robert Eideman submitted his resignation to Commissar of Defense Kliment Voroshilov in November 1935.[36] Although Voroshilov rejected the resignation, party leaders called on Kosarev to exert increasing oversight over Osoaviakhim.

The Komsomol's involvement in civil defense was a natural outgrowth in the development of both administrations. The Red Army expanded considerably from the mid-1930s onward, and large numbers of youth undertook preconscription training in Osoaviakhim.[37] Another step in the entanglement of the

---

33. RGASPI, f. 1m, op. 23, d. 1155, l. 11.

34. RGASPI, f. 1m, op. 23, d. 1072, ll. 92–96, 97–98. Kharchenko was responsible for organizing the kind of civilian collaboration with police that David Shearer has examined. See Shearer, *Policing Stalin's Socialism*, 184.

35. GARF, f. 8355, op. 1, d. 102, ll. 203–10.

36. RGASPI, f. 74, op. 2, d. 107, ll. 89–92.

37. Reese, *Stalin's Reluctant Soldiers*, 147.

league with civil defense was when Pavel Gorshenin, the Komsomol's military secretary, introduced Osoaviakhim positions for work among youth at every hierarchical level.[38] The new civil defense post was co-appointed and supervised by corresponding youth committees. At the upper levels of the administration, Kosarev and Gorshenin became the leaders of its network of civil aviation clubs. The flagship Central Air Club in Moscow was renamed in honor of Kosarev. After Eideman was arrested in the spring of 1937 as part of the broader purge of the military, Gorshenin would become the head of Osoaviakhim.

Communist upbringing created new opportunities, resentments, and requirements for young communists. The shift in the league's mission was pushed by the country's top leaders, above all by Stalin. While many ordinary activists accepted the new direction in the Komsomol, a vocal group of organizers resented their new calling as character builders. Nonetheless, it transformed Kosarev, a former radical, into a key figure in the production of state-sponsored cultured entertainment, and turned the youth league itself into the center of moral and physical education in the USSR. The socialization the Komsomol sought to provide was increasingly divided along gender lines. As komsorgs entered the schools and activists organized groups of young communist women, they grappled with how the Komsomol should shape men and women in a socialist society.

Boys into Men

The Komsomol did not cater explicitly to a male audience. In many respects, the conception of ideal youth—loyal, disciplined, and refined—spanned the sexes. But though the league had no "men's secretary" as it had a "women's secretary," it nonetheless sought to shape male activists as men. The urban activist milieu of the 1920s and early 1930s, dominated in numbers and spirit by young men, had promoted a rough proletarian ethos. They cultivated egalitarianism, a working-class identity, and spontaneous enthusiasm for fulfilling factory norms. As party leaders sought domestic social stability and defense from external enemies in the mid-1930s, Komsomol work among young men increasingly centered on disciplined outward behavior and military training.

The komsorg became a key instrument of character building among school-age young men. Although the position involved political education, its main task was to influence the social behavior of students. Through local Komsomol

---

38. GARF, f. 8355, op. 1, d. 89, l. 92.

groups, komsorgs created an honors society of sorts within schools. Their personal example was supposed to demonstrate how pupils should dress and what media they should consume. Oleg Krasovsky was a student at a Moscow school where a komsorg named Vorobev arrived during the 1934–35 academic year. Decades after he graduated, Krasovsky still described Vorobev reverently as a figure of authority: "He often came to our class and talked about sports and new movies. He was an ardent hunter and would sometimes spend an entire half-hour recess telling us hunting stories." Vorobev restarted both the student council and the Komsomol committee at the school. He urged Krasovsky to join both organizations because of the student's exceptional grades. As a member of the student council, Krasovsky met Komsomol Education Secretary Sergei Saltanov. In his memoirs, Krasovsky did not recall the speech Saltanov made but instead commented on his refined appearance: "I literally devoured him with my eyes. I can remember his smooth, pink, clean-shaven cheeks which proclaimed good health and good living . . . Saltanov was smoking long aromatic cigarettes; he smelt of fine scent and he said very little."[39]

Vorobev and Saltanov made their mark on Krasovsky based on their sophistication and social influence rather than their espousal of Marxist doctrine. Vorobev befriended Krasovsky and his classmates by organizing events and treating them as chums, addressing them informally (*ty*) rather than formally (*vy*), as a teacher would. When Vorobev later reprimanded members of the school's Komsomol for creating a satirical newspaper, Krasovsky noted how odd it seemed when the komsorg shifted discursive registers from school society to party policy. He wrote, "One could feel that Vorobev was repeating somebody else's words and not expressing his own views." Krasovsky found the reprimand strange because Vorobev's role had not typically involved overt political indoctrination.[40] He was an agent of central Komsomol policy that aimed to fashion loyal and cultured young men.

Like komsorgs, Pioneer counselors were Komsomol-affiliated mentors within the school who worked outside the academic process. Although every school with a Pioneer organization should have had a counselor, in practice many brigades were largely unsupervised or even unofficial, especially in the countryside.[41] At large schools, though, the position of counselor was important enough

---

39. Oleg Krasovsky, "Early Years," in *Soviet Youth*, ed. Novak-Deker, 136–37.

40. Ibid., 145.

41. For example, Catriona Kelly questions whether the famed Pioneer martyr Pavlik Morozov was even formally in the organization, which may not have had an officially approved group at his school. Kelly, *Comrade Pavlik*, 237.

that district Komsomol committees made the appointment. Indeed, the biggest schools had senior counselors who organized a team. Pioneer counselors organized extracurricular activities, social life, and moral upbringing outside the confines of the classroom. Like komsorgs, counselors were expected to be an example of correct behavior for children. In 1935, the Komsomol's Central Committee issued a resolution criticizing counselors who came to school with "dirty shoes and smoking." Instead of using proper Russian, they used phrases like "thumbs up" instead of "good," or "tromp" instead of "walk."[42]

Models of cultured behavior for boys in the Pioneers became militarized in the mid-1930s, a shift that was the product of the tense international environment. Japan's invasion of Manchuria in 1931 alarmed Soviet leaders with the possibility that an invasion of the Far East would follow.[43] Although war with Japan did not materialize in 1931, the threat of conflict deepened in the following years. The ascendance of Adolf Hitler in Germany in 1933 raised new fears, including the possibility of a two-front war with Japan in the east and Germany and Poland in the west.[44] Voroshilov warned the Red Army's military council in December 1934 that Germany and Poland were "serious antagonists" who were "reaching out their hands to the Japanese."[45] Although youth culture had long glorified the Red Army, Komsomol leaders increasingly undertook practical training to acculturate children for a future of war.

In the Pioneer organization, games, field trips and other activities took on a martial character. In 1935, the Komsomol Central Committee named Vasilii Muskin as the new Pioneer leader. As secretary of the Donetsk province youth committee in Ukraine, Muskin had been known for his eloquence and his activity in paramilitary work. In a Komsomol military training campaign, he completed extensive pilot training for which he received several awards.[46] Like the appointment of Kharchenko in the sports committee, Muskin's assignment was indicative of a wider influx of military values into recreational culture. On revolutionary holidays like Red Army Day (February 23), Komsomol and Pioneer leaders expected youth to give a ceremonial gift of extra productivity or paramilitary training to the regime.[47] The February 1936 edition of the Pioneer counselor journal *Vozhatyi*

42. "O nepravil'nom povedenii vozhatykh pionerskikh otriadov," *Komsomol'skaia pravda*, January 5, 1935, 1.

43. Stone, *Hammer and Rifle*, 209.

44. Harris, "Encircled by Enemies," 533.

45. *Voennyi Sovet pri NKO SSSR. Dekabr' 1934 g.*, 361–62.

46. TsDAHO, f. 7, op. 1, spr. 654, ark. 59; spr. 1004, ark. 36.

47. The ceremonial gift had a symbolic meaning that reinforced the legitimacy of the Soviet order as well as promoting themes (like militarization) within that system. On the symbolic value

FIGURE 2.2. Children at an equipped Osoaviakhim corner, 1934. Rossiiskii Gosudarstvennyi Arkhiv Kino-Foto Dokumentov (RGAKFD), 2-70541.

(Counselor) was dedicated entirely to Red Army Day. One article used illustrations to advise counselors on how to train Pioneers for military style marches, including how to wear gas masks and crawl on the ground with rifles.

The author explained the connection between the Pioneers and the military, "The very understanding of the words 'brigade' and 'squad' is that they are organized and disciplined collectives." The stress on discipline extended into Pioneer life generally. Readers wrote to the journal to ask if a Pioneer could give the organization's official salute to a member who was not wearing the emblematic red kerchief (an item that suffered from chronic shortages). The journal answered that an undisciplined Pioneer out of uniform was not worthy of the salute.[48] Pioneer work was supposed to be fun but also to teach discipline and the rudiments of military organization.

The Komsomol's use of paramilitary training reflected a broader expansion of defense education among youth. As the youth league incorporated more military

---

of gifts to the motherland and Stalin, see Brooks, *Thank You, Comrade Stalin*, 83–105. On the use of parades and public holidays to legitimize the Soviet regime, see Rolf, *Soviet Mass Festivals*, 31–154.

48. M. Zanegin, "Otriad v stroiu," *Vozhatyi*, no. 2 (1936): 7–11; "Voprosy i otvety," *Vozhatyi*, no. 4 (1936): 58–59.

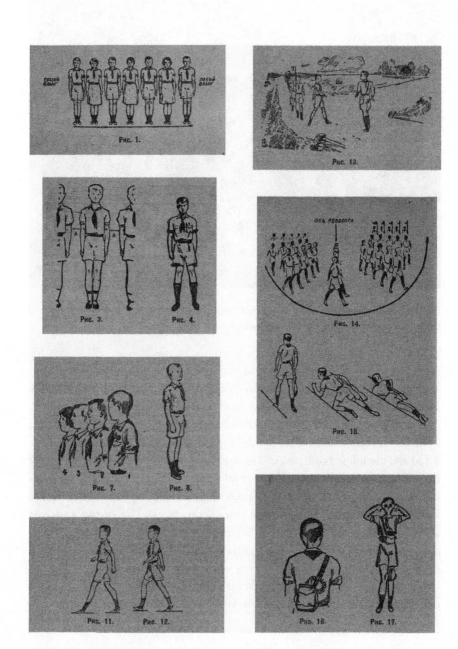

FIGURE 2.3. Pioneers in formation. *Vozhatyi*, February 1936.

training into its programs, the Red Army attempted to increase its role in the general curriculum. The school system already included compulsory defense education for older students, and Red Army statistics from 1935 showed that Narkompros sent roughly half of students in grades eight through ten (about 400,000) to some form of military training. The program included general fitness; military skills like marching, shooting, and grenade throwing; and classes on military history and the contemporary army. These programs, however, faced a lack of qualified instructors and contemporary equipment. In February 1935, Voroshilov asked Premier Viacheslav Molotov for state investment in school military training to prepare teachers, construct new facilities like firing ranges, and create an up-to-date textbook for courses. It appears that Voroshilov and the military did not get the increased funding they wanted. Nonetheless, the proposals demonstrate that the Red Army increasingly sought out schools and higher education as partners in military training.[49]

Among young adults outside the school system, the Komsomol began to invest significant resources in paramilitary training. At the same time that the Japanese threat emerged in 1931, the Komsomol initiated the Ready for Labor and Defense (GTO) program—a physical fitness system that would continue until the end of the Soviet Union.[50] The program was a set of athletic, skill, and knowledge-based tests that ranged from running and swimming to first aid. In 1934 the league organized a Military-Technical Examination based primarily on the GTO. In addition to completing the fitness test, participants who wanted to pass the exam in full had to finish the Voroshilov Shooter firearms training program, plus courses in topography and parachuting. For men, the exam also included thirty hours of instruction in automobile or tractor driving, while women had to complete the Red Cross and Crescent's first-aid program Ready for Sanitation Defense (GSO). Few participants finished the entire exam, but Komsomol reports showed that from July 1934 to February 1935, over 1.2 million did at least one of its components. Parachuting was especially popular— most likely, as a form of entertainment as much as training. Komsomol statistics claimed that nearly 700,000 youth passed the GTO program, 500,000 young women met the GSO norms, and 800,000 finished driving training.[51]

The impact of the examination is difficult to assess. Certainly, it was more successful in the cities than the countryside. Almost all the participants were from towns, because infrastructure and personnel often did not exist in rural

49. RGASPI, f. 1m, op. 23, d. 1134, ll. 2, 20–25.
50. RGASPI, f. 1m, op. 23, d. 1005, l. 17. On the GTO, see Grant, *Physical Culture and Sport*, 37–41.
51. "Nagrada udarniki oborony," *Komsomol'skaia pravda*, February 20, 1935, 2.

areas.[52] Even in places where the youth league reported large numbers of participants, it is possible that local leaders embellished their results. For example,
local activists might have included an entire youth group when only a handful of members completed the norms—although youth leaders did not record
such incidents. In contrast, Komsomol leaders in charge of the examination
were pleased with its results. A tangential consequence they applauded was that
the campaign had provided a reason to build infrastructure like firing ranges
and parachute jump points that could be used in the future.[53] The main result,
though, according to Osoaviakhim's head of youth training in Ukraine, Nek-
horoshev, was that the examination had "infected youth with military enthusiasm." The defense activist even claimed that participation in the exam had provided the cultured recreation that prevented several Komsomol members from
turning to hooliganism.[54]

Although programs like the Military-Technical Examination were supposed
to teach young men concrete skills, the more important goal was to inculcate a
sense of military discipline. In the 1920s, radical Komsomol youth had advocated
revolutionary enthusiasm. The poet Vladimir Mayakovsky wrote a tribute to the
league and its enthusiasts in 1929 called "Perekop Enthusiasm!" The Red Army
had defeated the White Army in southern Russia at Perekop in Crimea, and the
poem urged youth to overturn the stability of the NEP period with the spontaneous fervor of the battle: "Take up little things with barricade energy, pour
Perekop enthusiasm into the construction site." The mission of the Komsomol
in the 1930s had shifted. Leaders now hoped to instill regimented discipline in
youth.[55] The case of a Ukrainian factory activist named Ivan Serikov is illustrative of the difference. Serikov was an enthusiast of defense training who wrote
about his passion to Ukrainian Komsomol Secretary Sergei Andreev in September 1935. The semiliterate Serikov wanted to create a "Komsomol segnal" that
would alert all young communists to gather at a predetermined location as a way
to "mobilize the fighting spirit" of youth. Serikov finished his letter by saying that
it would be best to "keip the segnal a secret so no one knows whot is happening."
To a youth leader like Andreev, who had just overseen a purge of "enemies" from
the Ukrainian Komsomol, the secret "Komsomol segnal" must have resembled an
uprising. In his response, Andreev dismissed the idea and instead pushed Serikov

---

52. OKhDOPIM, f. 648p, op. 1, d. 3, l. 44.
53. TsDAHO, f. 7, op. 1, spr. 1192, ark. 106; spr. 1198, ark. 30.
54. TsDAHO, f. 7, op. 1, spr. 1198, ark. 37.
55. For more on the broader shift in Stalinism to discipline and hierarchy, see Paperny, *Architecture in the Age of Stalin*.

to put his energy into organized training for "parachutists, riflemen, and pilots."[56] What Andreev and others wanted from youth like Serikov was not spontaneous enthusiasm but regular military training.

Komsomol leaders expected leading activists to provide examples of paramilitary training. Toward this end, the league's Central Committee organized an intensive training program for mid-level organizers in the autumn of 1935. All male Komsomol secretaries or heads of Marxist-Leninist education at the district level were supposed to participate. Initially planned for forty-five days, the final program included thirty days in an Osoaviakhim military camp, where life would "be militarized completely from start to finish," according to planning documents.[57] In addition to military training, the program included an equal number of hours spent on party history. The camps also made time for training in youth group organization, geography, and agriculture.[58]

When the camps opened in the autumn, Komsomol leaders found that some activists balked at the role they were asked to play as would-be military organizers. A report from Voronezh described an "unhealthy attitude" spreading among even the leaders of the province's camp. In the wake of several participants' expulsion for drinking and making anti-Soviet remarks, the head of the party committee in the camp said, "Discipline in the Red Army is one thing, but it's another thing in Osoaviakhim." Undoubtedly, he was correct that the atmosphere in Osoaviakhim camps was less regimented and hierarchical than in the Red Army. Nonetheless, his complacency about the environment undermined the purpose of the camps—the temporary militarization of Osoaviakhim and the Komsomol. Young pacifists also presented an impediment to the camps' goals. At one training center in the Far East, a schoolteacher and Komsomol organizer said: "The camp forces teachers to learn military affairs. They [Soviet leaders] talk about the politics of peace, but at the same time they demand military training from childhood until old age." At a Moscow-area camp, an incoming participant asked to be sent home because of his pacifism: "I am against war. I will not fight and am going nowhere. Brother, this fratricidal war is not for us." The local Osoaviakhim committee released him from this responsibility—but also forwarded the NKVD information about the "counterrevolutionary."[59]

---

56. TsDAHO, f. 7, op. 12, spr. 658, ark. 11, 12.

57. RGASPI, f. 1m, op. 23, d. 1133, ll. 9, 11–13.

58. Ibid., l. 59.

59. Ibid., ll. 55–58. On the broader conflict of Stalin's regime with pacifism, see Petrone, *Great War in Russian Memory*, 134–38, 251–52.

FIGURE 2.4. Kosarev (second row, center) and Gorshenin (fourth row, center) in uniform with delegates from the Azov-Chernomor territory at the Tenth Komsomol Congress, 1936. RGASPI, f. 1m, op. 18, d. 2472, l. 83.

The camps reflected a turn in the Komsomol's conception of the ideal youth organizer. The examples that activists were supposed to set for young men were increasingly entangled with discipline and paramilitary training. A particularly revealing aspect of the training camps was that they included the district heads of Marxist-Leninist education. These youth activists were usually the de facto deputy youth leader of their district, but their title also implied a key role in promoting the values of Soviet political culture. Part of this role meant supervising education in the Marxist-Leninist canon, although it mainly meant knowing the recent policies of the party and its interpretation of current events. The inclusion of these cadres demonstrated how moral education in the Komsomol was increasingly connected to military discipline. Stalinism was a culture of violence. It was not the uncontrolled violence of class war in the countryside that radicalism and the conditions of collectivization had created, though. Instead, the ideal socialist young man was capable of committing violence within a controlled hierarchy.

Aleksandr Kosarev himself embodied the shift in the league's goals for young men. At the 1936 Komsomol congress, Kosarev gave the keynote speech that solidified communist upbringing as the central task of the youth organization. It was not his words alone, however, that symbolized the change in the league. After speaking in a gray suit, he changed into an air force uniform that he could wear as head of the Central Air Club. Alternating between these outfits, Kosarev personified the radical proletarian turned into a cultivated official-officer hybrid.[60] Komsomol leaders hoped that young men—through education, cultured entertainment, and military training—would follow Kosarev's lead.

Dancing with Komsomol Mothers

As the youth league incorporated military discipline into its program for young men, it also became interested in recruiting young women as members. The league, especially its leadership, had been dominated by men since its founding. These male activists believed that the best way to integrate young women was to appeal to traditional conceptions of women's demands such as dancing, fashion, and motherhood. This gendered discourse, common in much of Europe at the time, represented a dominant but not universal understanding of women's role under Stalinism.[61] The women's section of the Komsomol, for example, called for the promotion of women into leadership positions, above all in Central Asia. There party authorities hoped to create a foundation of Soviet supporters by empowering the disenfranchised female population.[62] Another role for women was as settlers in distant areas of the USSR. The Komsomol organized parties of adventurous women to populate the Far East in the Khetagurovite movement of the late 1930s.[63] Meanwhile, female enthusiasts of paramilitary training volunteered for Osoaviakhim campaigns.[64] Despite these alternative roles for women, Komsomol leaders primarily envisioned female young communists in a traditional role as future mothers.

The youth league's embrace of conventional gender roles was part of Stalinism's broader turn to the family as a pillar of socialism. Many early Bolshevik policy makers had assumed that social structures like the family would eventually fade away as the country progressed toward communism. Based on this notion, they enacted laws that made getting a divorce simple, while conditions in the country made getting child support difficult. For this reason, women in the 1920s were often left alone with children when their husbands disappeared.[65] In the

---

60. RGASPI, f. 1m, op. 23, d. 1193, ll. 28–31.

61. For a comparison of Soviet and European pronatalism, see Hoffmann, "Mothers in the Motherland," 40–42.

62. See Northrop, *Veiled Empire*.

63. Shulman, *Stalinism on the Frontier of Empire*, 17–18.

64. Krylova, *Soviet Women in Combat*, 37; Nikonova, *Vospitanie patriotov*.

65. Goldman, *Women, the State, and Revolution*, 1–3.

search for social stability, Stalinist leaders asserted that the family would become socialist. In 1934, Kosarev stated: "The stronger and more harmonious a family is, the better it serves the common cause. . . . We are for serious, stable marriages and large families. In short, we need a new generation that is healthy both physically and morally."[66] In 1936, Stalin's regime criminalized abortion and made obtaining a divorce more difficult. These policies found support among many women who wanted men to share responsibility for families. Stalinist leaders were not intent on easing the burden of women, though. The Soviet economy depended on the continuing presence of women workers who had been a significant driver of industrialization during the Stalin Revolution. For many women, mobilization as mothers and laborers created a double burden of home life and the workplace.[67]

Women's marginal place in official youth culture had created tensions during the 1920s and into the 1930s. They made up a relatively small percentage of young communists until the end of the 1920s, when large numbers of women who entered the factories simultaneously joined the league (see Table 1 in Appendix). The Komsomol was a preserve of masculine values, where radical activists denounced "bourgeois" women for wearing long hair and dresses, or for showing an interest in dancing. At the same time, male activists were uncomfortable when women attempted to reduce signs of visible gender differences by adopting masculine clothing and mannerisms.[68] Male organizers at the lower levels had little interest in incorporating women into the league, and central youth leaders did little to encourage gender parity among young communists.

In 1935, the Komsomol's leadership placed a significant emphasis on addressing women's issues through its new women's secretariat. Like the party's Zhenotdel, the Komsomol women's secretariat attempted to elevate women into leadership positions. In contrast to the Zhenotdel, though, the Komsomol's efforts in the 1930s focused on sponsoring individual women in party and state organizations rather than promoting the interests of women as a group.[69] Youth administrators wanted to produce female organizers because women were an underrepresented and underdeveloped section of the population. This goal was especially relevant in Central Asia and the Caucasus, where Tat'iana Vasil'eva's first major task as women's secretary was to organize affirmative action programs

---

66. Quoted in Hoffmann, "Mothers in the Motherland," 45.
67. Goldman, *Women, the State, and Revolution*, 342–43.
68. Gorsuch, *Youth in Revolutionary Russia*, 114; Guillory, "We Shall Refashion Life on Earth!," 32.
69. Goldman, "Industrial Politics," 75–76.

for women as part of the regime's broader campaign to Sovietize the non-Slavic ethnic periphery.[70] In other regions, however, programs to promote women as leaders also existed. In July 1935, the Ukrainian Komsomol's Central Committee conducted training courses for seventy-five young women marked to become district-level youth secretaries. These courses were not only organized for young women, though. Similar programs existed to train people from other groups that made up a disproportionately small percentage of cadres in the youth league. A contemporaneous course promoted ethnic Ukrainians, another underrepresented group among Komsomol activists.[71]

The male-dominated culture of the Komsomol stymied efforts to promote women. In the Ukrainian program, only a handful of the trainees went on to work as district-level leaders. Instead, many became activists in the Pioneer organization—a less prestigious landing spot. Iakov Geiro, the Ukrainian youth leader in charge of cadres, interviewed subordinates about the lack women in significant posts, "Are there really no qualified women?" One administrator responded, plausibly, that some female activists preferred to stay in the Pioneer administration where the background in pedagogy that many had might be useful.[72] In a case in the Far East, a young woman named Ol'ga Mel'nikova clashed with her male counterparts after she went to work as a district-level Komsomol secretary. The conflict between Mel'nikova and male administrators in the district went so far that NKVD officers arrested Mel'nikova's detractors.[73] Few cases were so extreme, but it appears that there were significant hindrances to promotion for young women in the Komsomol, even as central leaders dictated that local groups recruit more female administrators.

Skepticism about women's capacity as activists in paramilitary training was prevalent among both ordinary activists and youth leaders. In August 1935, an all-female flight team undertook an experimental flight from Moscow to Leningrad to test how women endured high altitudes. During the flight, the plane experienced mechanical difficulties and had to make an emergency landing. Although the team eventually completed the trip unharmed, the experiment shocked Komsomol leaders, who supervised civil aviation. Kosarev and Eideman canceled prospective experiments involving the team and demanded that future research be vetted through the Komsomol. The flight team's supervisor,

---

70. Vasil'eva, "Nachalo puti," in *Aleksandr Kosarev*, ed. Mikhailova, 18.

71. TsDAHO, f. 7, op. 1, spr. 1218, ark. 62, 78; spr. 1219, ark. 166–68.

72. TsDAHO, f. 7, op. 12, spr. 671, ark. 62, 66.

73. Shulman, *Stalinism on the Frontier of Empire*, 199.

Pavel Grokhovskii, wrote to Voroshilov and then to Stalin himself. The pilots deserved another chance, he said: "They fly planes not one bit worse than male pilots." Stalin summoned both Grokhovskii and Kosarev to discuss the issue.[74] It is unclear what the outcome of this meeting was, although Grokhovskii continued to work in the aviation industry into World War II. Nonetheless, Kosarev's reaction to the incident reflected his view that conducting such an experiment with women was an unnecessary risk. After all, the difficulties the flight had faced were hardly the worst that Soviet aviation had experienced. A particularly notorious accident occurred on May 18, 1935, when the giant plane the *Maksim Gorkii* crashed during an air show, killing dozens on board. In total, Osoaviakhim counted twenty-three air accidents in 1935 and eleven in 1936.[75] For Kosarev and his associates in Osoaviakhim, these crashes highlighted the pointlessness of sending women on experimental flights. Female pilots would risk their lives but would never serve as military pilots. Nikolai Uvarov, head of Osoaviakhim's aviation department, said in December 1936 that women might become reserve instructors but "of course, they will not fly a fighter plane."[76] The view of women as a reserve force at most was common in Komsomol leadership circles.

Activists and researchers involved in physical education for youth also argued for limiting the activities that women could undertake. At a meeting of Ukrainian Komsomol workers in October 1934, the head of Ukraine's Institute of Physical Culture, Vladimir Bliakh, claimed that sports like soccer and weightlifting were unsuitable for "the particularities of the female body." In some activities, including gymnastics, he said, "After several years of training in this sport, a woman will lose her female particularities and will begin to turn partly into a mannish type."[77] Bliakh prescribed only those physical activities that he believed would protect the femininity of women. Some Komsomol organizers opposed women's participation in sports altogether. At the Komsomol's June 1935 plenum, an organizer named Lisogurskaia described a typical case when a group of girls asked the local Komsomol organizer to arrange a shooting contest. The organizer responded, "It looks like a *baba* wants to become a Voroshilov Shooter. What kind of Voroshilov Shooter would you be?" In general, Lisogurskaia found that women who wanted

---

74. RGASPI, f. 1m, op. 23, d. 1154, ll. 75–79, 80–81.
75. RGASPI, f. 1m, op. 23, d. 1190, ll. 93.
76. Ibid., l. 65.
77. TsDAHO, f. 7, op. 1, spr. 1263, ark. 419, 420. For more Soviet views of the ideal female form in the 1920s, see Grant, *Physical Culture and Sport*, 73–79.

to play sports met the response that physical culture was "not for women."[78] Press accounts promoted images of women in sport and paramilitary activity.[79] In real life, their ability to take part was far more limited.[80]

Leaders in the Komsomol promoted a traditionalist program, believing that these activities were what would please women. At a Central Committee meeting of the Ukrainian Komsomol, its head Sergei Andreev reprimanded Kiev organizers for allowing a local group to expel a young woman whom they claimed was "impossible to mold in the communist spirit." Andreev assured the audience that "girls have a number of particularities" that required a different kind of upbringing.[81] This approach meant providing cultured entertainment laced with political information. In a report on Komsomol recruiting practices among young women, Kosarev informed Andrei Andreev about the league's attempts to satisfy women's demands—more sewing circles and other groups that youth organizers would infuse with political content.[82] At a meeting of Komsomol leaders in 1937, Kosarev amused the other activists when he said, "Even though I am not a woman, I know a little something about women." Drawing on his expertise, Kosarev explained that political work among women could not be too serious. A pregnant woman was interested in her health and her family, not in a lecture on Marx's *Capital*.[83]

The Ukrainian Komsomol followed Kosarev's thinking in its attempts to include women in the organization. At a meeting of Kiev's women activists in June 1935, Pavel Kravchenko, Ukraine's chief activist in charge of female organizers, emphasized the need to remove "the remnants of bourgeois culture" among women. But what was bourgeois culture? A worker at a clothing factory in Kiev equated it with notions of frivolity that had been common among radical Komsomol organizers in the 1920s. The girls at her factory, especially those who came from the villages, were only interested in "dances, the foxtrot, and manicures." Many of her peers disagreed, though. They welcomed the opportunity to organize activities like dances that they believed would attract women into Soviet political culture. An organizer named Krakovskaia, the head of the department of student youth in Kiev city and one of the more senior female youth leaders in Ukraine, believed that "girls don't want to be out of fashion." For her, the new period of

---

78. RGASPI, f. 1m, op. 2, d. 116, l. 117.
79. Krylova, *Soviet Women in Combat*, 60.
80. Grant, *Physical Culture and Sport*, 96.
81. TsDAHO, f. 7, op. 1, spr. 1208, ark. 49.
82. RGASPI, f. 1m, op. 23, d. 1096, ll. 66–76.
83. RGASPI, f. 1m, op. 5, d. 52, l. 53.

socialism had muddled the boundaries of frivolity and good taste. "We ourselves do not know the border between being bourgeois and being cultured," she said.[84]

Of course, there were still borders between culture and politically inappropriate behavior. When a female Komsomol organizer mentioned that her organization had not punished a woman who baptized her child, Kravchenko demanded that the mother be expelled from the group.[85] For Komsomol leaders, religion was at the core of the anti-Soviet worldview rather than just an element fit to disregard or appropriate. Kravchenko also asserted that dances were dangerous if political content was absent: "The body will move forward but the mind will stay put."[86] Not all dances were equal, too. A contemporary manual on how to organize a carnival for youth instructed readers to allow classical and folk dances—the Pas de Quatre, the Vengerka, or the Pas de Partner. Indecent dances like the foxtrot were not among the approved repertoire.[87] Leaders like Kravchenko pushed the female activists to Sovietize traditional dances and other activities to entice women into official culture.

Kravchenko and other organizers envisioned women's primary role as being mothers, which now equaled or superseded their status as laborers. Kravchenko asserted that unlike men, female young communists bore an extra burden of being "an exemplary, cultured mother."[88] One activist expressed relief that her work as a mother was now being recognized. Before, Komsomol members had accused her of selfishness for being a mother, not understanding that she was "raising [her] child for socialist society and by doing so fulfilling the task of molding youth."[89] Komsomol leaders hoped to keep young women in the league's orbit as they had children so they could shape families into cultured subjects. Because youth leaders expected that the duties of motherhood would supplant activity in the league, they sought to keep young mothers involved rather than allowing them to withdraw into family life. Groups often assigned an activist to visit and update the mother about goings-on in the organization, a practice that had gained support in the Komsomol Central Committee.[90]

---

84. TsDAHO, f. 7 op. 1, spr. 1238, ark. 5, 17.

85. Ibid., 26.

86. Kravchenko also suggested that dances should not be held before Komsomol meetings, "Otherwise when everyone leaves they don't discuss what they heard at the meeting . . . but only talk about how so-and-so danced." Ibid., 37.

87. *Detskii karnaval*, 2.

88. TsDAHO, f. 7 op. 1, spr. 1238, ark. 6, 7.

89. Ibid., 11. Physicians of the 1920s cast motherhood as a normative part of women's lives, which Francis Bernstein asserts was a precursor to the Stalinist turn to traditional gender norms in the 1930s. Bernstein, *Dictatorship of Sex*, 171.

90. TsDAHO, f. 7 op. 1, spr. 1238, ark. 15, 18; RGASPI, f. 1m, op. 2, d. 116, l. 157.

Many women activists embraced the Komsomol's turn toward traditional gender norms. Nina Kosterina imbibed communist upbringing in the Komsomol for five years from 1936 to 1941. In 1938, she divided the girls in her school class into "the swamp," "the baronesses," and the Komsomol girls. The girls of the swamp studied poorly and had no interests, and the baronesses were interested only in boys. Kosterina approvingly said that the Komsomol girls "were more like the boys," but even some of the Komsomol girls were turning into baronesses. "Dolginskaia [a Komsomol girl] is straightforward and smart but she loves her perm, her nail polish and her narrow skirts too much." When Nina finished school and went to a geological institute, though, her attitude changed. She became interested in boys, meeting with potential partners ("but of course, not making the first move") and dismissing them all as uncultured. A promising young man named Zhora disqualified himself with his faux-revolutionary questioning of institutional hierarchy and formal education: "What can the institute give us today . . . ? Can't a person become cultured without it?" Finally, in the spring of 1941, she found happiness with a boy named Sergei. Before leaving for summer vacation in Moscow—and as it turned out, for war—she had a parting, final conversation with him, "I told him the truth, 'I want a baby.'"[91] Kosterina, like many young women raised in the Komsomol, equated the climax of her upbringing with becoming a mother.

As they attempted to encourage women to become cultured parents, youth officials also monitored sexual activity that supposedly posed a threat to this goal. In the Commissariat of Defense Komsomol organization, a scandal erupted over the "distribution of parnography [sic]" by several young women. In the cafeteria of the commissariat, a former worker produced what the committee described simply as a "letter." The document—probably a drawing or an erotic limerick—was passed from hand to hand. Several young people, including Komsomol members, read it aloud in the dormitory. Eventually, the letter got to a dorm dweller who worked in a print office and made copies for the whole dormitory. When the local youth group learned of the note, its leaders summoned the letter's readers and producers—all young women—before the commissariat's Komsomol committee. The women claimed that they knew little about the letter, but their youth organizers dismissed this excuse because they were "literate people" who should have known better. Five young women faced varying levels of discipline. One was fired from her job. The commissariat's Komsomol circulated a resolution demanding that lower-level groups "mercilessly excise obscene

---

91. Kosterina, *Diaries*, October 25, 1938; May 22, 1940; June 20, 1941.

and ugly jokes." The attention the commissariat's Komsomol gave the case was characteristic of official culture's relationship to female sexuality. During the disciplinary hearing, one member of the youth committee remarked, "It's bad that this case happened among girls." If young men had distributed the lurid materials, the incident would have probably been unwelcome, too. But it was especially scandalous because those involved were women.[92]

Venereal disease, divorce, and abortion among women were also topics of concern for youth leaders. The women workers of Odessa, with its reputation as an unseemly city, were the subject of an alarmist 1935 report to the leaders of the Ukrainian Komsomol. The city's local venereal disease institute had diagnosed 1,556 young women with gonorrhea or sores from January 1933 to September 1935. At a local factory where 95 percent of workers were women, city youth leaders had taken a survey of their relationship history. Of the ninety-nine married women who were league members, the report claimed that fifty-five had been divorced twice or more. The author asserted that the factory's young communists had procured a combined 118 abortions. Odessa's youth leaders maintained that the situation at the factory was representative of women in the city overall. They blamed the sexual depravity among the city's young women on economic conditions and lamented Odessans' belief that "sexual degeneracy is normal."[93] Sergei Andreev found the report so shocking that he forwarded it to Ukrainian Party Secretary Pavel Postyshev. He explained that the popular opinion was that venereal disease was the product of prostitution, itself the product of foreigners coming through the port town. Andreev did not fully discredit this reasoning—it would have been convenient to believe that foreigners were to blame for venereal disease—but he also faulted the local youth committee with tolerating prostitution and divorce. Underlying the Odessa report, though, was the implicit blame it placed on women for promiscuity rather than men.[94]

Accusations against male sexual impropriety tended to draw a lesser response and typically arose when the man's action threatened to break up a marriage or was a sign of corruption. When a group of administrators in the Far East took advantage of their positions as managers to exploit young women searching for work, police became involved because it was an abuse of power.[95] In Donetsk, the secretary of a mine's youth committee named Lakhtereva described how she had fought a hospital administrator's improprieties. A hospital worker whose

92. RGVA, f. 9, op., 30, d. 8, ll. 56–57; d. 9, ll. 128, 129.
93. TsDAHO, f. 7, op. 1, spr. 1241, ark. 30–39.
94. Ibid., 50–53.
95. Shulman, *Stalinism on the Frontier of Empire*, 184.

husband was away in the army became the target of harassment by the new head of the hospital. At midnight he would come to her apartment for "surprise checks." At first she said nothing, but eventually she went to the Komsomol group organizer to complain. Lakhtereva and another young woman pressed the hospital chief until he admitted to harassment. The hospital removed him from his position, and the Komsomol organization gave him a warning that he would be punished for subsequent incidents. Kravchenko, the Ukrainian organizer working on women's issues, heard Lakhtereva's speech and said her actions had gone too far, "You are pressing guys there." According to Kravchenko, the hospital director had harassed his subordinate, potentially threatening her marriage, and needed to be stopped. The damage had been limited, though, and there was no need to press the hospital chief. Lakhtereva replied that she had fulfilled the mandate of the Komsomol Central Committee as she had understood it.[96]

Komsomol leaders considered promiscuity among both sexes undesirable because their objective was to encourage strong, Soviet-loyal families. They believed that transient sexual relationships of any kind undermined this goal.[97] When promiscuity occurred, though, it was women who were more often accused of impropriety as the gatekeepers of sexuality. In contrast, male urges were understood implicitly as inescapable. There were no reports to the Komsomol's leadership about male venereal disease or about high rates of divorce among men. In the league, female promiscuity was the supposed source of social instability and threats to public health.[98] The treatment of women as responsible for morality in family and sexual life was the primary motivation for Komsomol leaders' attempts to enlist them in official culture. However, the activities that radical activists had earlier labeled as bourgeois did not just become lures to entice women into official culture. For many a love of dancing or sewing or fashion became a key way that women could distinguish themselves as cultured under socialism.

Kosarev presented communist upbringing in 1935 as an answer to Stalin's demand to generate cultured youth. It was a program that emphasized discipline over enthusiasm, a refined appearance over asceticism, and obedience to

---

96. TsDAHO, f. 7, op. 1, spr. 1239, ark. 108–11.

97. Shulman, *Stalinism on the Frontier of Empire*, 161. Along these lines, Shulman finds that marriages that dissolved quickly (and especially those that ultimately resulted in single mothers) were just as undesirable as other passing sexual liaisons.

98. Similarly, Bernstein, *Dictatorship of Sex*, 99, asserts that physicians were uninterested in studying the causes of women's sexual pleasure because it was superfluous to procreation.

authority over generational rebellion. Although the Komsomol had a mandate to raise all young Soviets for socialism, it also distinguished the ways that organizers should treat men and women. Youth leaders placed a particular emphasis on physical and military training for men. In contrast, the league hoped to develop young women as the core of regime-loyal families. For all youth, the Komsomol's new program was a turn inward for activism. Instead of youth acting as an organized political force in the country as a whole, the Komsomol asked young communists to embrace and promote a code of behavior.

Some youth organizers protested their new role as character builders because they believed it marginalized their importance. They were correct that party leaders wanted to decouple youth activism from the direct implementation of political and economic campaigns. The transformation of the Komsomol instead directed youth activists' responsibilities into the realms of entertainment and education. To the chagrin of young proletarians, the new emphasis on creating cultured youth symbolized a shift in the center of youth activism away from the factory floor and toward schools and the professions. The aim of cultivating youth extended to new social groups—even to class groups beyond workers, who had been the chief constituency of the youth league. Meritocratic measures now appeared to outweigh class identity in defining the ideal youth of socialism. With socialism achieved, organizers emphasized the goal of molding *Soviet* youth, a category that was supposed to supersede class boundaries. As Komsomol leaders attempted to spread communist upbringing to the entire younger generation, though, they pondered what the role of young "enemies of the people" would be in official youth culture. Optimism about the socialist future and fears about the present would determine who would find a place in Stalinist political society.

CLASS DISMISSED?

When Stalin declared socialism's victory in the USSR, Soviet leaders believed this epoch would herald not only a new form of economic organization but a new type of society. One of the signature changes expected as the country moved from socialism to communism was that class antagonisms—classes themselves—would fade away. Anticipating this change, the new Soviet constitution adopted in 1936 (the Stalin constitution) guaranteed voting rights to all people regardless of their social origin. The two-and-a-half classes of Soviet people that leaders claimed remained (workers, peasants, and a stratum of intelligentsia) would enjoy equal privileges and equal civic burdens.[1] Stalin himself seemingly rejected the notion that people inherited their parents' social status in his famous formulation, "a son does not answer for his father."[2] Despite proclamations of class leveling, though, the advent of socialism did not end hereditary social categorization. Instead, it complicated how state and society would group Soviet people, introducing new tensions in political culture over what a socialist society would be.

---

1. Fitzpatrick, *Russian Revolution*, 154–55. On the development of the constitution see Wimberg, "Socialism, Democratism, and Criticism," 313–32. On the process of implementing the constitution's promise of free elections, see Getty, "State and Society under Stalin, 18–35.
2. For this statement and a broader discussion of class in the mid-1930s see Fitzpatrick, *Everyday Stalinism*, 130–32.

The continuing use of heredity to define the place of young people in the body politic was not just a failure of Stalinist realities to live up to Stalinist rhetoric. In the Komsomol, the tension over who could join demonstrated the uncertainty among ordinary citizens and Soviet officials—even ranking leaders—about the form of socialist society. In the 1920s, proletarian youth had held a dominant position in the Komsomol's identity, although students and white-collar workers had also been members and even leading activists.[3] The process of creating socialism was supposed to transform the Komsomol into a classless organization of the "best" Soviet youth, based on personal achievement rather than class identity. The league's new admissions policies made it possible for large numbers of educated youth to join Soviet political society. Their increasingly dominant position within the league became both a sign of their elite status and a mechanism of continuing social mobility.

Despite Stalin's promise, inherited social status continued to play a role in children's lives, especially among the children of "enemies." The murder of the Leningrad party leader Sergei Kirov in December 1934 sparked a campaign of repression against former party oppositionists like Grigorii Zinov'ev and Lev Kamenev, who admitted under coercion to "moral responsibility" for the assassination. In the following years, thousands of their former supporters faced arrest in the early stages of the Great Terror, and millions of Soviets would face repression by the end of the decade. As the NKVD arrested these supposed enemies, it often persecuted their children as well.[4]

A popular misconception about Stalinism is that it sought to destroy families. Revolutionary radicals of the 1920s may have envisioned the breakdown of the family, but Stalinist leaders from the early 1930s onward hoped to leverage it as the building block of a strong socialist society; children of Soviet loyalists would become regime supporters. The counterpart to Stalinist belief in the socialist family, though, was the conviction that the relatives of the regime's enemies were also likely to become enemies.[5] Party and youth leaders demanded that the children of enemies of the people cut ties with their parents, creating a moral dilemma for young loyalists who had allegiances both to their families and to the Soviet regime. In Komsomol meetings, it was unusual for young people to defend relatives, but it was also unusual for them to renounce beloved enemies altogether. Some lost their status as members or could not join the league. Others

---

3. Gorsuch, *Youth in Revolutionary Russia*, 46–48.

4. See Kuhr, "Children of 'Enemies of the People.'"

5. See Alexopoulos, "Stalin and the Politics of Kinship"; Hooper, "Terror of Intimacy"; Goldman, *Inventing the Enemy*, 140–250.

faced arrest or de facto detainment in children's colonies. Many, however, escaped the years of Stalinist repression physically unharmed, learning to reconcile their loyalties through silence or omission.

For the children of another repressed group—special settlers—there was little hope of escaping their families' status as dekulakized peasants. Although they lived in exile settlements often far from population centers, many nonetheless took up the idea of joining the "best" youth, pressing for the privileges that the Stalin constitution promised them. In their efforts to join the Komsomol and integrate into Soviet society more broadly, they faced discrimination. The bias against class-enemy children reflected both a prejudice with roots in revolutionary class categorization and in contemporary fears of marginalized groups that the state itself had created.

The rise of educated elites and the precarious place of children of various enemies complicated notions of class and heredity in Stalin's USSR. While ordinary youth and leaders voiced unanimous, broad support for the regime's march toward socialism, they frequently questioned—or simply did not know—what the ideal youth would be in the new epoch. Processing this uncertainty, youth leaders and activists negotiated the boundaries between pragmatism, anxiety, and their own interpretations of doctrine, reconfiguring and reinforcing the role of class in the Soviet Union.

Elites in a Classless Society

The use of class categories was a hallmark of the first years of Soviet rule. When the Bolsheviks came into power, they used Marxist class designations to distinguish their enemies from their allies in society. Unlike Marx, who had defined classes by their relationship to other groups in society, the Bolsheviks created a set of categories that defined these groups' relationship to the party-state. In a sense, the system resembled an inversion of tsarist *sosloviia*, similar to estates in the Western European context.[6] The Bolsheviks supported groups they believed had been disadvantaged under the imperial state, while opposing groups they believed had been privileged and therefore ill-disposed toward the new regime.[7] In addition, Bolshevik policies established new social-legal categories like special

---

6. On *sosloviia* and mobility between tsarist estates, see Smith, *For the Common Good.*

7. The previously privileged included former nobles, wealthy peasants, merchants, educated elites, clergy, and others. The newly privileged included workers and poor peasants. For a detailed analysis of this issue, see Fitzpatrick, "Ascribing Class." On policies of social promotion for proletarians, see

settlers, created from dekulakized peasants and other groups exiled to distant set-tlements. Although the Bolshevik state initially placed people into classes, these categories became social realities, central elements of people's communal and legal identity.[8] Young people who were too young to work before 1917 inherited their parents' class. In spite of what their current position in society was, they had to recite their parents' background in virtually every interaction with the party-state.

From the founding of the Komsomol, class discrimination existed with vary-ing degrees of strength in its official and informal practices. In the 1920s, the Komsomol promoted a proletarian identity in its ranks, with its regulations explicitly giving preference to workers and their children.[9] Despite this prefer-ence, youth not born into proletarian or peasant families still made up roughly 10 percent of the league (Table 2 in appendix), and in some regions educated workers and students were roughly equal to the proletarian contingent.[10] The discrepancy between the league's proletarian aspirations and the reality that the Komsomol contained a sizable number of nonproletarians became a source of anxiety. Proletarian members feared the influx of nonworkers—not only class aliens but also peasants and white-collar workers. The Komsomol had under-taken a massive membership campaign from 1929 to 1932 that led to the recruit-ment of millions, mostly young peasants. When youth leaders initiated a massive purge of supposed class aliens in 1932 and 1933, however, they reinforced dis-criminatory practices against nonworkers.

As the country emerged from the upheaval of the First Five-Year Plan into socialism, Komsomol members and leaders maintained their obsession with class. In a meeting in April 1935, Aleksandr Kosarev upbraided provincial and district committees for admitting too many nonproletarian youth. In the early 1920s, Kosarev had been the youth secretary of Moscow's Bauman district. He claimed that if a local factory's youth cell had admitted thirty white-collar workers out of a hundred new members, he would have called an extraordinary

Fitzpatrick, *Education and Social Mobility*, 181–208. On the history of class aliens in the first two decades of Soviet rule, see Alexopoulos, *Stalin's Outcasts*.

8. On class identity among Soviet people in the 1930s, see Fitzpatrick, *Tear off the Masks!*, 51–70. On class categories as a reality among rank-and-file Komsomol members, see Neumann, *Communist Youth League*, 83–102.

9. Workers and poor peasants could join the Komsomol without a period of candidacy, whereas white-collar workers and intelligentsia could join as candidate members (who could not vote or run for office in Komsomol elections) and then become full members later. Komsomol organizations were not supposed to admit youth from any other categories. *Tovarishch Komsomol*, 1:248.

10. Gorsuch, *Youth in Revolutionary Russia*, 46.

meeting to discuss the issue. Kosarev stressed that monitoring membership was at the center of youth leaders' work and that class was the most important factor in assessing membership.[11]

At the local level, cases of otherwise outstanding youth from undesirable class origins complicated admissions policies. In the Administrative-Economic Department of the Commissariat of Defense, a shock worker named Bystritskii applied for admission to the Komsomol for the third time in January 1935. Two different local cells had admitted him, but because his father was a priest, the commissariat's Komsomol bureau had effectively rejected his application by tabling it indefinitely both times. The third time, he applied through yet another cell. This group approved him nearly unanimously, except for a member named Konovalov, who said, "If Bystritskii is admitted to the organization, then I will turn in my Komsomol card, because his social origin makes him a class alien to us."[12] Konovalov lost his membership card soon after when the commissariat's Komsomol bureau expelled him for his outburst.

Konovalov's expulsion did not mean that the bureau would admit Bystritskii, though. At the next meeting, the youth bureau discussed Bystritskii's candidacy. Bureau members were careful to ask him about his connections to his priest father, whom he claimed he had not seen since he was eighteen. Bystritskii presented the Komsomol bureau with a difficult decision. He was the child of class-alien elements, but he was also an excellent worker who desperately wanted to join the league. The bureau found a way out of its predicament: Bystritskii had recently turned twenty-four and therefore exceeded the age limit of twenty-three for new members. Bystritskii was at a loss and understood his rejection as based on his father: "Why can't I be a Komsomol member? I have worked since I was sixteen years old. I was raised among worker youth. . . . Where can I go now that I cannot be a Komsomol member?" The head of the Komsomol bureau suggested that Bystritskii apply for party membership. This suggestion was likely to offer little solace. Not only had the party placed a moratorium on new members since 1933, but given Bystritskii's experience with the Komsomol, could he expect the party's doors to open for someone with his background?[13] Bystritskii appeared to be everything a politically active youth was supposed to be—except a proletarian.

The case revealed a tension between merit and class origin. Most members of Bystritskii's local youth groups seem to have had little trouble approving his applications. He was an outstanding worker (perhaps even their supervisor) who

---

11. RGASPI, f. 1m, op. 3, d. 136, l. 88.

12. RGVA, f. 9, op. 30, d. 5, ll. 16–24.

13. RGVA, f. 9, op. 30, d. 5, ll. 34–37; d. 6, ll. 1–12, 16–24.

claimed to have no contact with his class-alien parents. The notable exception was Konovalov's strident opposition to Bystritskii's admission, which represented a segment in the Komsomol that still maintained intense, radical class convictions. Ultimately, authorities in the case made the safe decision to reject Bystritskii on technical grounds. In all likelihood, though, the Komsomol bureau rejected his application because of his class origin, undermining the notion that accomplishment could outweigh class as a factor in admission.

Bystritskii and other children of class aliens who considered joining the Komsomol were aware of the precariousness of their situation. Ivan Tvardovskii and his immediate family, except for his poet brother Aleksandr, the future editor of *Novyi mir*, were dekulakized and sent to a special settlement during collectivization. Ivan eventually escaped the settlement and went to work at various factories. At one, the Komsomol organizer suggested that Ivan, an excellent worker, join the league. Tvardovskii instead surprised the local organizer and quietly ignored the suggestion, fearing that membership in the Komsomol would expose him to further repression.[14]

In contrast to youth from marginalized backgrounds, proletarian youth enjoyed disproportionate advantages in the Komsomol. In July 1935, the bureau of the Commissariat of Defense Komsomol organization, the same that had denied the application of Bystritskii, expelled a young worker named Dovgaliuk for embezzling money at work. Nonetheless, the Komsomol bureau resolved, "Dovgaliuk by his origin is one of us; his brothers are fine people of our motherland." Its members left open the possibility that he would be able to rejoin the league with good behavior.[15] The informal indulgence Dovgaliuk received was an extension of official discriminatory practices. Komsomol regulations in place from 1926 to 1936 mandated that a local committee wishing to expel any worker or peasant from the organization needed confirmation from the provincial youth committee (whose leaders were usually on the Komsomol's Central Committee). District committees could expel all other members without higher confirmation.[16]

As class discrimination persisted into 1935 and beyond, party leaders moved toward a conception of political culture that was more inclusive of nonproletarians. In February 1935, Stalin initiated the rewriting of the Soviet constitution, and a Constitutional Commission composed of party leaders created multiple drafts over the course of 1935 and early 1936. The evolution of these drafts

14. Tvardovskii, *Rodina i chuzhbina*, 139.
15. RGVA, f. 9, op. 30, d. 7, l. 15.
16. *Tovarishch Komsomol*, 1:248.

revealed that party leaders were becoming more open to a broader body politic in the USSR. In the first version of the section on elections, those Soviet people disenfranchised by the old constitution because of their class origin remained unable to vote. However, the commission, which Stalin chaired, revised it to grant universal suffrage, asserting that even former class aliens had the right to vote.[17] The change in the electorate reflected the leveling of class difference that was supposed to occur under socialism.

The constitution accompanied other pronouncements that indicated an easing of class struggle in the Soviet Union. Stalin famously declared in late 1935 that "a son does not answer for his father" in response to an outstanding worker who had asked why he faced continuing discrimination for his father's being a kulak.[18] Some Soviet citizens would accept Stalin's assertions that class differences were ending (especially when citing the speech to their own benefit), while others would look on these pronouncements cynically.[19] Stalin's main point seems to have been that exemplary workers would earn a place in the USSR, regardless of their parents' history. In one case, for example, the Politburo in 1936 backed L. A. Oboznaia, a seventeen-year-old collective farmer from the North Caucasus who petitioned to the party after she was rejected from tractor-driver courses because she was the child of a kulak.[20]

As party leaders signaled changes in the status of class aliens and other nonproletarian groups, their position in society nonetheless remained unclear. Abram Room's film *A Strict Young Man* (Strogii iunosha), produced between 1934 and 1936, reflected these uncertainties. The film's eponymous hero is Grisha Fokin, a young engineer, athlete, and ideal Komsomol member. Grisha falls in love with Masha Stepanov, the young wife of a renowned, innovative physician. Although Grisha fights with Doctor Stepanov over Masha, the real conflict is for Doctor Stepanov himself. The future clearly belongs to Grisha and the younger generation, but will Doctor Stepanov and the old intelligentsia have a place, too? Ultimately, Doctor Stepanov shows his willingness to work toward the Soviet future, using his medical genius to save the life of a seemingly fatally ill Komsomol Central Committee member. Although the original conflict over Masha goes unresolved, Stepanov throws in his lot with the new generation, showing that the intelligentsia—even the prerevolutionary bourgeois—could have a place in Soviet society.

---

17. Getty, "State and Society under Stalin," 21–22.
18. Fitzpatrick, *Everyday Stalinism*, 130–32.
19. Davies, *Popular Opinion in Stalin's Russia*, 102–8. Fitzpatrick, *Everyday Stalinism*, 179–80.
20. Khlevniuk, *Politbiuro*, 155.

When the film was initially commissioned, it was hotly anticipated. In addition to its large budget (the biggest of 1936), the key figures in its production were high-profile intellectuals like Room and the writer Iurii Olesha, who wrote the original play and the screen adaptation. On the film's completion, Ukrainfilm banned it, citing several ideological problems in the portrayals of its characters. The young people in the film were stiff, humorless, and pretentious. The film also never showed Grisha working and thus did not reflect the realities of young Soviet laborers.[21] Perhaps the greatest problem, though, was that the head of Ukrainfilm called Doctor Stepanov "an arrogant and boastful man, alien to Soviet reality."[22] How could the conceited bourgeois *intelligent* have an honored place in the classless future that the Komsomol represented? The film's fate revealed how ambiguous and treacherous the task of envisioning a classless society would be. At the same time, the film's attempt to reconcile the classless future with current social realities highlighted the significance of the issue and its association with young people.

Based on these broader trends, Komsomol leaders raised the possibility of admitting youth from nonproletarian or peasant backgrounds in larger numbers. At the June 1935 meeting of the Komsomol Central Committee, Kosarev declared that the league was for the "best youth of the country." Defining the best youth, Kosarev singled out young engineers, shock workers, and excellent students. He notably ignored social origin as a factor. His emphasis on workplace accomplishment for defining the best youth did not mean the end of class distinction, though. In the reader response section of *Izvestiia TsK Komsomola* from October 1935, the first letter asked, "How can we correctly organize admission to the Komsomol?" The response was that organizers needed to record young people's social origin in detail: "They write: 'peasant.' What kind of peasant? There are well-off peasants, middle, poor. It needs to be shown."[23] The league was becoming more open to youth from a variety of social origins (except class aliens), especially those who were recognized as leaders at their workplace or school. Youth leaders nonetheless demanded that social origin be precisely

---

21. Milena Michalski argues that Room was perhaps satirizing the overly serious youth of the Komsomol at the time, portraying Grisha as a caricature of the code of ethics in the Komsomol. Michalski, "Promises Broken, Promise Fulfilled," 835.

22. Ibid., 836. Belodubrovskaya, "Abram Room, *A Strict Young Man*, and the 1936 Campaign against Formalism," 320, argues that the film was banned not because of its ideological message but because of Room's formalism. However, Belodubrovskaya also contradicts this argument by saying that for its content "it is likely that *Strogii iunosha* would have been banned regardless of Room's formal treatment."

23. "V apelliatsionnoi komissii TsK VLKSM," *Izvestiia TsK Komsomola*, no. 8 (1935): 25–27.

recorded because they believed that it continued to be a meaningful way of differentiating the population.

Public treatment of class as a factor in political society became more explicit and more public at the Komsomol's Tenth Congress in April 1936. Creating a new set of regulations was a major purpose of the congress, the only body with the right to approve these changes. Although the Komsomol's regulations mandated at least one congress per year, the 1936 congress was the first since 1931. The infrequency of congresses meant that they were supposed to inaugurate major changes in the league's mission. In this case, Komsomol leaders asserted that communist upbringing in the epoch of socialism demanded a new set of regulations for the youth league.

The drafting of the new Komsomol regulations coincided with and reflected the same concerns as the drafting of the new constitution. In the youth league's regulations, too, Stalin's role was key for revising its treatment of class. Much like the previous regulations, the first draft (written by Komsomol leaders) continued to promote the interests of workers and peasants above other classes. It divided youth in two groups: children of workers and peasants, and all others. Youth from the first group could join the Komsomol with two recommendations and a six-month candidacy period. Those from the second category could join the organization with three recommendations and a year-long candidacy.[24] Kosarev sent this draft to party leaders, including Stalin, who edited it himself. Stalin's revision focused primarily on admissions policies, particularly those related to class. He replaced the divisions between classes with a policy admitting all youth equally based on political literacy, regardless of social origin.[25]

Although confined to a more limited public, the campaign surrounding the proposed Komsomol regulations was similar to the later "all-union discussion" of the constitution. The public dissemination of the draft constitution both gauged popular opinion and mobilized support behind the new constitution.[26] In the same way, Komsomol leaders pored over summary reports of meetings about the proposed regulations to assess young people's reactions and published selected letters and articles in the youth press to inform the league's members and generate support among them. Because the changes in the Komsomol regulations reflected the same broad goals as the constitution (indeed, Stalin's hand guided the writing of both documents), the Komsomol regulations can be seen as a trial run for the discussion of the themes that would appear in the constitution.

24. RGASPI, f. 1m, op. 23, d. 1153, ll. 49–50.
25. RGASPI, f. 1m, op. 23, d. 1157, passim.
26. Getty, "State and Society under Stalin," 28.

Members from local cells largely ratified the new regulations pro forma or with minor suggestions for changes. The Komsomol group in Velikaia Guba (Karelia province), for example, "fully agreed" with the program with the proviso that the section on military training in the Komsomol should mention the leading role of Osoaviakhim in civilian military training.[27] Other youth demanded that the league's official name change from the Leninist Komsomol to the Leninist-Stalinist Komsomol.[28] When youth did speak out against the proposed regulations, though, they frequently criticized the treatment of class. Ivan Sapozhnikov, the secretary of a youth group from a railroad station, complained that the new regulations would enable large numbers of white-collar workers to join: "How will we regulate the increase in white-collar workers if admission is based only on young people's political literacy? It seems to me that white-collar workers are much more literate than worker and kolkhoz youth."[29] Similarly, youth activists in Azov-Chernomor territory questioned why a factory worker with five or more years of experience would receive the same treatment as a white-collar worker.[30] These muted protests echoed the views of young radicals of the 1920s, who saw the Komsomol as an organization of young proletarians above all—a vision the new regulations contradicted.

The regulations were approved at the Tenth Komsomol Congress (April 11–21, 1936), a major event for the league. Stalin and most major political leaders attended, as did Soviet heroes like the arctic explorer Otto Shmidt, the soccer impresario Nikolai Starostin, and the chess champion Mikhail Botvinnik. The congress inspired hundreds of preparatory activities. Most often, committees would pledge a "gift" in honor of the congress—frequently preparing a certain number of youth for the GTO or Voroshilov Shooters programs, or overfulfilling workplace norms. Youth also marked the congress with uniformed marches through the streets of Moscow. The marches and promises of defense training symbolized the link between Komsomol and a more militarized Soviet youth. At the same time, the pageantry of the congress also lent weight to the new rules that it would codify.

In a sense, Kosarev's speech at the congress confirmed worker youth's suspicions about the changing class dynamics in the league. He characterized the regulations as a product of socialism, under which class would have less meaning than

---

27. NARK, f. 4070p, op. 1, d. 30, l. 17.
28. RGASPI, f. 1m, op. 23, d. 1159, l. 58.
29. "Regulirovat′ priem v Komsomol," *Komsomol′skaia pravda*, March 22, 1936.
30. RGASPI, f. 1m, op. 23, d. 1159, ll. 43–48. On popular opinion of the new constitution and related initiatives, see also Davies, *Popular Opinion in Stalin's Russia*, 102–8.

FIGURE 3.1. Kosarev, Joseph Stalin, and Andrei Andreev. RGASPI, f. 1m, op. 18, d. 2472, l. 87.

young people's subscription to a broader Soviet identity and their usefulness to the state. For that reason the Komsomol, too, needed new criteria for admissions: "The Komsomol is becoming a broader Soviet organization, I emphasize, of Soviet youth, in contrast to an organization of worker-peasant youth, which it was in the past." Kosarev insisted Soviet youth did not include just students or white-collar workers and their offspring, but class-alien youth as well. Citing Stalin's statement that "a son doesn't answer for his father," he said that even class aliens, "the best of them, those verified and loyal to Soviet power, can be admitted to the Komsomol in individual cases."[31]

Central Committee Secretary Andrei Andreev appeared at the congress in his role as party overseer of the Komsomol. He, too, asserted that members needed to be "verified" and have basic knowledge of current politics. However, Andreev—citing the wishes of Stalin—insisted that the organization should incorporate a more diverse cross-section of society: "There is no reason to limit admission to the Komsomol as admission to the party is limited."[32] It would seem that Kosarev and Andreev's statements opened the doors for all Soviet youth to join

---

31. RGASPI, f. 6m, op. 10, d. 1, ll. 103, 105–6; Fitzpatrick, *Education and Social Mobility*, 235–36.
32. RGASPI, f. 6m, op. 10, d. 4, ll. 222–25.

the Komsomol. Yet they had couched their statements in ambiguous terms. What made a young person part of the best youth? Were the offspring of proletarians still more likely to be exemplary? Could the child of a kulak ever be verified?

Stenographic records of youth leaders' postcongress meetings show that the primary beneficiaries of the Komsomol's new membership policies were intended to be white-collar workers and students. In the months after the congress, Komsomol Central Committee workers went to the provinces to investigate how local committees were fulfilling its decisions on the new regulations. In Minsk, the Pioneer leader Vasilii Muskin discovered that opportunities had opened up for students: "Before they were afraid to admit students, and now those youth [students] are moving up. . . . One district secretary asked a tenth-grade student [at the standard admissions interview], what books have you read? He named so many that it was more than even the secretary had read." Muskin later found out that the student had applied to the Komsomol before but had been rejected under its old policies.[33] The change in the Komsomol's orientation had been accepted so readily in some locations that the youth worker who went to Kursk found, to his dismay, that district secretaries now were only interested in applicants' achievements in formal education.[34]

Although they were pleased that white-collar and student youth were now joining the league in greater numbers, investigators were alarmed when the new policies enabled class aliens to join. One worker, Abramov, who had gone to Omsk, discovered that a new member's parents had been deprived of voting rights and exiled. When Abramov questioned the local organizers about the young man, they admitted that he had only come to the factory five months ago, and that no one really knew him. Not surprisingly, no one could recommending him to the Komsomol.[35] Another instructor who went to Azov-Chernomor region found a similar reason for concern: "One girl (from a kulak family) read Comrade Kosarev's speech, went to the Komsomol organization, and announced that she had the right to be in the Komsomol. . . . The cell was flustered because [the local youth organizers] themselves had not managed to read the speech as closely as they should have."[36] Of course, it was just as likely that the organizers had read and understood Kosarev's speech but were unsure how to reconcile its seeming inclusivity with the continuing need to exclude class aliens whom they perceived as genuine threats. The investigator suggested that Kosarev issue a

---

33. RGASPI, f. 1m, op. 5, d. 32, l. 9.
34. Ibid., l. 42.
35. Ibid., l. 15.
36. Ibid., l. 79.

directive that would clarify the organization's position on class-alien youth and prevent similar incidents in the future.

The Komsomol Central Committee soon after did release a resolution "About Violations of Regulations during Admission to the Komsomol." The widely distributed resolution proclaimed that white-collar and student youth were now welcome in the league. It was less explicit about what kinds of youth had been mistakenly accepted but implied that youth from social groups previously considered hostile to the regime still were not to be considered among the best youth.[37] The local youth press was often more explicit about the continuing need to exclude class aliens. In an article in the Karelian youth newspaper, the head of the province's appeals commission, Kirillov, wrote about various cases where local cells had admitted unfit youth. In two instances, young people who supposedly had remained in contact with their kulak parents were improperly admitted.[38]

As youth groups read the new regulations and explanatory articles that followed, white-collar youth and students would become the dominant groups in the league (see Tables 2 and 3 in appendix). In 1936, students and youth in the professions made up approximately 35 percent of Komsomol members. By 1938, this figure grew to 44 percent, and by 1940, to 57 percent. Moreover, summary statistics in those years became increasingly detailed about the precise nature of the work white-collar and student youth were doing. In 1936, league statistics gave only the total numbers for white-collar workers and students. By 1939, Komsomol statisticians were collecting data on the different types of students and professionals in the league. They included, for example, a separate category for engineers. The influx of professionals and students, as well as the concern among Komsomol leaders with tracking these youth, reflected the regime's emphasis on creating and rewarding an educated elite.[39]

The Komsomol's reporting showed not only an intense interest in cultivating youth from white-collar professions but also less interest in social origin. It is possible that many of the new white-collar and student members were the children of party members who themselves had been promoted as workers into administrative positions in the 1920s and early 1930s. Moreover, many of the young industrial workers of the late 1930s were peasants who had arrived from

37. See the explanatory article "Ob oshibkakh pri prieme uchashchikhsia v Komsomole," *Izvestiia TsK Komsomola*, no. 13 (1936): 18–19.

38. Kirillov, "Ne narushat' ustav," *Komsomolets Karelii*, September 30, 1936.

39. RGASPI, f. 1m, op. 126, d. 336, ll. 6, 18–23; d. 344, ll. 14, 16, 17; d. 358, ll. 11–12, 25–26, 38–39, 42–43; d. 372, ll. 9–10, 20–21, 32–33, 40–41.

the village.[40] The imprecision of available evidence makes it impossible to measure the exact footprint of worker progeny. After the middle of 1936—following the dissemination of the Stalin constitution and the league's congress—summary statistics that grouped youth by social origin were no longer kept. It was as though Komsomol leaders truly had stopped caring about the class origins of members. Despite this turn in official policy, the concerned reactions of youth leaders to "incorrect understandings" of admissions policies and the ubiquitous demand to disclose parents' social status revealed that inherited class was still a factor in many cases of admission.

The conception of the best Soviet youth was filled with ambiguity. Above all, organizers faced a difficult decision when young people from marginalized groups applied for membership. Over the course of the 1930s, millions of people turned into enemies of the people, some instantly transforming from party loyalists into political criminals. In the mid- to late 1930s, the children of "unmasked" political enemies confronted official youth culture. Ordinary young people, activists, and even Komsomol leaders harbored doubts about what impact these potentially hostile elements would have on political culture. For the children of enemies themselves, the shift in their fortunes created a crisis that pitted family loyalties against their devotion to the state and desire not to join their parents in an NKVD cell.

Children of the Enemy

Stalin's regime had a penchant for devising enemies. During collectivization, leaders turned a culture of peasant resistance to authority into a world of class conflict in the countryside.[41] Out of Zinov'ev, Kamenev, and Bukharin's once-real opposition to Stalin, the show trials of 1936–38 created wild fantasies of terrorism against party leaders. These campaigns gave rise to new and malleable sociopolitical categories beyond those inherited from Marxism. Accused Trotskyists in Stalin's 1930s were rarely supporters of Trotsky's political program, just as kulaks had not exclusively included rich peasants during collectivization.

The broadest and perhaps most infamous term was enemy of the people. It encompassed people who had undertaken any form of supposed hostile activity against the state. Their families, too, became the targets of state repression. Some

---

40. Hoffmann, *Peasant Metropolis*, 42.
41. Viola, *Peasant Rebels under Stalin*, 29–44.

young people were arrested immediately after their relatives, although repression was not a certainty. On learning about the arrest of family members, Komsomol youth were supposed to disclose this news to their group and renounce their relatives. Some youth, very rarely, defended them openly. Most often, though, young people practiced dissimulation. Refusing to reveal their parents' status or avoiding denunciation by pleading ignorance provided a means for youth to appease their loyalties to the family and to the regime.[42]

Some youth escaped their parents' status by denouncing their family. The most famous Soviet child denouncer was Pavlik Morozov, the Pioneer martyr from a village in Siberia. Pavlik allegedly informed on his father in 1932 and was murdered for his treachery by relatives. Post-Soviet archival evidence has cast doubt on the reality of the story, showing that Pavlik may not have denounced his father. Indeed, he may not have even belonged to the Pioneers. Nonetheless, the story became a Soviet legend—the subject of books and an aborted film by Sergei Eisenstein.[43] Some emulated Pavlik and denounced their relatives. In Kuntsevo district of Moscow province, a young man wrote to his Komsomol organization, "The sordid past of my father, as well as his current suspicious activity, makes me believe that he is an *enemy of the people*." The denunciation made its way to NKVD investigators, who arrested the father.[44]

In spite of such cases, there were not "millions of Pavliks," as the youth press of the time stated. In contrast, for many people young and old, the conception of the family as a tiny political clan was fatal.[45] When the NKVD made arrests in the terror, it was common practice to use the family principle—accusing relatives of an arrestee to fill quotas for repression.[46] A characteristic case was the Donetsk NKVD's "Sprouts" investigation in June 1937. Investigators arrested three young men—two children of kulaks and the son of a man arrested for Trotskyism. Supposedly, they had concocted a conspiracy to cross the Polish border, obtain weapons, and murder Soviet officials. With Donetsk several hundred kilometers from the Polish border, though, it seems more likely that their true crime was their parents' status.[47]

42. See Goldman, *Inventing the Enemy*, 190–98. Goldman asserts that the third strategy was the "refusal to choose," which only encompasses part of the way that youth reacted to relatives' arrest in official culture.

43. Kelly, *Comrade Pavlik*.

44. Vatlin, *Agents of Terror*, 82.

45. Alexopoulos, "Stalin and the Politics of Kinship."

46. Vatlin, *Agents of Terror*, 108–13.

47. HDA SBU, f. 16, op. 1, spr. 83, ark. 148–50.

In the summer of 1937, NKVD Commissar Nikolai Ezhov issued Order no. 00486 that called for the repression of the families of "traitors, members of right-Trotskyist organizations, and those indicted by military tribunals"—categories that included those caught up in the repression of Zinov'ev, Kamenev, and their supposed co-conspirators. Relatives fifteen and older faced arrest depending on the NKVD's assessment of the "social danger" they posed.[48] The children of enemies who ended up in an orphanage found themselves subjected to a range of abuses. In Odessa province, a procuracy investigation found that orphanage personnel were beating children and depriving them of food. For the children of enemies, psychological cruelty accompanied physical harm: "[One teacher] scared children with [threats of being taken in] a 'black vorona' (the closed car for transferring arrestees) and deceiving them by sending them to the police or a closed orphanage outside the city instead of on the field trip he had promised."[49]

Although the NKVD targeted the children of enemies, arrests and detainments were sporadic.[50] Even the particularly vulnerable relatives of notable Bolsheviks could sometimes escape repression. Valerii Bronshtein, a grandnephew of Trotsky, found himself orphaned at the infamous Danilovskii House orphanage in Moscow province after the NKVD arrested both his parents in rapid succession. Desperate to escape placement in an NKVD colony for orphans, the thirteen-year-old stealthily phoned his grandmother, who rescued him through adoption.[51] The son of the famous revolutionary Vladimir Antonov-Ovseenko, Anton, was a university student when his father was arrested in 1937. Anton refused to denounce his father to his Komsomol organization, although he apparently also did not defend him. For the next two years he occupied a liminal place in Soviet society. His youth group and university, not knowing whether the son of a major enemy of the people should answer for his father, expelled and then reinstated him. He was finally arrested in 1940, only partially in connection with his father.[52] The future linguist Iurii Lotman wrote that at least ten students in his Moscow school had arrested parents. One of them, Borka (Boris) Lakhman, was left alone in his apartment after his father, a visible party leader in the economy, was arrested and shot.[53]

48. Vilenskii et al., *Deti GULAGa*, 234–38.
49. GARF, f. 8131, op. 14, d. 47, l. 26.
50. Kuhr, "Children of 'Enemies of the People,'" 213.
51. Bronshtein, *Preodolenie*, 25–26.
52. Antonov-Ovseenko, *Vragi naroda*, 17–43.
53. Lotman, "Ne-memuary," 3–7.

Most children of enemies of the people did not have (in)famous Bolsheviks for parents. This relative anonymity offered them the chance to hide, but they risked the accusation that they had masked their intentions. Grade school student Oleg Krasovsky's father had been arrested as an alleged spy in February 1934, and Oleg moved to Moscow with relatives. A year later, his excellent grades drew the attention of the local *komsorg*, who pressed him to join the league. Krasovsky stalled, fearful that his father's status would earn him an expulsion from school, but he could not avoid the organizer forever. When he applied for membership, he said his father's whereabouts were unknown. His lie was never found out—and he was fortunate.[54]

In many situations, though, young relatives of arrestees faced a complicated choice when the reality of an intimate enemy faced them. At a meeting of the Petrozavodsk Komsomol in November 1938, a member of the city's youth leadership named Iakovlev spoke out against the "dozens of youth with arrested relatives." Iakovlev singled out one of them, a young man named Ionin whose father was arrested. Made to explain himself, Ionin claimed, "He [father] was in Leningrad when he wrote [about his arrest], and I responded and asked why he had been arrested. I didn't write him again."[55] Ionin's response was common. The path of least resistance was to deny having contact with arrested parents. This strategy allowed young people to reject their relatives without actively denouncing them. It seems that by denying contact, Ionin and many others in the city were able to escape expulsion from the Komsomol or worse.

The dedicated schoolgirl-activist Nina Kosterina could not lie to the Komsomol, though. She wrote in her diary about a friend, Lora, whose parents had been arrested in September 1937. A month earlier she had written, "If my father turns out to be a Trotskyist and an enemy of his people, I won't be sorry for him!" Nonetheless, when her Moscow school's Komsomol secretary approached her about voting to expel Lora from the school's youth group, Kosterina at first refused. He convinced her by saying that Lora was no longer a minor and had refused to denounce her parents. Additionally, Kosterina consented to vote against Lora because she did not want to lose her membership. After all, she liked her work in the Komsomol—it had just assigned her to be counselor for the Pioneers in the fifth grade. After the meeting where she voted to expel Lora, she wrote a letter to her father in her diary: "The girl was crying. She wanted to stay in

---

54. Krasovsky, "Early Years," in *Soviet Youth*, ed. Novak-Deker, 134–35, 137, 139.
55. NARK, f. 779, op. 21, d. 37, l. 8.

the Komsomol so badly but at the same time said that she loved her mother and father and would not renounce them. It was so hard on me that after the meeting I went home and cried for a long time. Is she to blame because her parents were arrested for something?"[56]

Kosterina's heartfelt reaction to her friend's misfortune caused only a slight change in her attitude. When her own father was arrested in September 1938, she privately refused to accept it, writing, "I haven't a shadow of a doubt that father is innocent." She recognized that her father's arrest had real consequences, though, and she could not hide it from the Komsomol. She "informed her komsorg about her family affairs," although it is unclear whether she renounced her father or not. It seems likely that she remained silent, refusing to denounce or support him. The komsorg let Nina stay in the Komsomol and gave her a Pioneer brigade to work with, even though Kosterina "fervently protested" that her father's arrest had made this impossible. Despite this comparably positive outcome, she still decried the hypocrisy of Stalin's statement that "a son does not answer for his father" after her new institute denied her a stipend when she enrolled in the following fall. Only a few weeks later, though, her mother successfully petitioned to Stalin personally in a letter citing that famous phrase. Her loyalties torn, Kosterina never gave up her belief in Stalin's system. Paradoxically, her participation in Stalinist youth culture often saved her from the "dark thoughts and moods" that were a result of the Stalinist system of repression.[57]

Not everyone who was forthright was so lucky, though. After the student Vadim Iasnyi's father was arrested in 1937, he did not attempt to hide the repression of his family from his Komsomol organization at a Leningrad institute. Other members of his youth group also had parents arrested. They approached the local secretary to ask, "What will happen to us—to children with arrested parents?" The secretary smiled as he gave a vague but threatening reply, "I don't know yet. I haven't received any directive. Maybe nothing will happen. You might get a reprimand, or they might expel you from the Komsomol or even from the institute. Or maybe even more . . ." The Komsomol group soon after expelled Iasnyi for his father, but he remained a student for another year. Iasnyi would attribute his eventual downfall to his search for sympathetic ears. Two friends from the institute had arrested parents as well. "Alas, it was clear to everyone," he later wrote, "You needed to keep your mouth shut, especially in the [university] hallways when your parents were arrested. . . . Still, we dared to talk about

---

56. Kosterina, *Diaries*, September 10 and 13, 1937.

57. Ibid., September 5 and 7, October 30, 1938, August 29 and December 5, 1939.

'it' among ourselves." In 1938, the NKVD arrested him in conjunction with the arrest of his friends.[58]

Iasnyi's Komsomol organizer was right. No one knew if the children of enemies were also enemies who should face exclusion, if not arrest. Children of disgraced party members were often well educated and loyal—previously among the best youth in the country. Iasnyi's retrospective insight was also correct, though. He might have escaped arrest if he had thrown himself into activism and retained his place among the best Soviet youth. If he had dedicated his thoughts to a diary rather than confiding in the other children of enemies, he might have remained free. Indeed, he might have been able to claim with authority that he had rejected his father, that he had cut off contact. Iasnyi was unable to keep silent about the arrest, though, unlike others who managed to lead a dual life, like Kosterina. It is impossible to say how many were able to disassociate their family loyalty from their loyalty to the regime. It is even less possible to say how many were true adherents of Stalin's regime and how many simply feared their own arrest. In both cases, though, the problem they faced made young people downplay or conceal their anti-Soviet personal loyalties while maintaining their public status as good young Soviet people.

Special Settlers and the Komsomol

There was a group whose members could not hide. They were the special settlers, one of the most marginalized populations in the interwar Soviet Union. Their children formed a sizable cohort of youth, a loathed byproduct of Stalin's campaign of collectivization and dekulakization. Nearly two million people from alleged kulak families who were accusing of obstructing the process of collectivization were uprooted and deported to so-called special settlements, some in the peasants' home provinces, but many in the least habitable areas of the USSR. How long this exile would last, and whether any possibility of rehabilitation existed, was unclear even at the highest levels of the party and state apparatus. Initial plans from 1931 to rehabilitate special settlers after five years, and their children at age eighteen, were dashed at Stalin's insistence. Nonetheless, the easing of restrictions on rehabilitation in the first half of the 1930s allowed some special settlers to shed their status partially—by 1936, nearly 150,000 had been rehabilitated in this manner. Yet legislation from 1935 bound even rehabilitated

---

58. Iasnyi, *God rozhdeniia—deviat' sot semnadtsatyi*, 38–41.

special settlers to their place of exile. Like the children of other enemies, parents passed on an informal stigma to children. In addition to this stigma, though, special settlers and their children (even with rehabilitation) also had legal restrictions on mobility and civil rights.[59]

The Stalin constitution and the introduction of the Komsomol's more inclusive program in 1936 only added more uncertainty to special settlers' status. In February 1936, Stalin approved NKVD Commissar Genrikh Iagoda's suggestion that limited numbers of young shock workers and activists among special settlers be allowed in the Komsomol with the approval of the territory's youth committee. This privilege did not apply in all regions, though, nor was it clear which special settlers would be eligible.[60] In Igarka, a town in Siberia, the party head petitioned Stalin and Molotov in 1936 to ask whether the local party committee could rehabilitate the most heavily vetted of the local special settlers who wanted to receive admission to higher education. The secretary had received an explanation from the territory's NKVD office that it was only possible with the approval of the NKVD and that the special settlers could travel no farther than the territory's capital, Krasnoiarsk. The Politburo decided that Igarka's secretary was in the right, and the party committee could send special-settler youth to universities throughout the Soviet Union at its discretion.[61]

Reading or hearing of these inclusionary developments, youth in special settlements started to ask for admission to the Komsomol and for other rights and privileges. The first motions from below in the Komsomol began in 1936. At the April 1937 meeting of the Komsomol Central Committee, Mariniushkin, the leader of the Karelian youth committee, remarked that six hundred special settlers had applied for membership in the region's Komsomol during the last half of 1936, but that only nine had been admitted because it was unclear to organizers (including Mariniushkin) whether these young people were eligible. Even more problematic were the issues these young people were raising when they came into contact with activists. What were the limits of the Stalin constitution? Could they leave the settlement with an internal passport? Would the Red Army recruit them? Karelia had eighteen thousand Komsomol-age special settlers in twenty-one labor colonies, and Mariniushkin anticipated that these incidents would only multiply in the future. Mariniushkin asked Kosarev to speak on the

59. Viola, *Unknown Gulag*, 155–57.

60. Danilov, Krasil'nikov, and Viola, *Politbiuro i krestianstvo* vol. 1, 698–99, 699–700 (citing GARF, f. 5446, op. 18a, d. 905, ll. 3–4; APRF, f. 3, op. 30, d. 197, ll. 93–94).

61. Khlevniuk, *Politbiuro*, 155.

issue—to say whether special-settler youth could enter the Komsomol or if the stain of their parents' status still precluded admission.[62]

Activists often balked at the idea of including class enemies. At another Komsomol Central Committee meeting in 1938, the head of the league in the Komi republic—another region with many special settlers—announced that its youth committees had been accepting special settlers "who have no connection with relatives, have no parents, and work honestly." Some organizers objected, though, saying that class aliens would endanger the youth organization by exposing it to subversion from within. The Komi youth leader, too, asked Kosarev to settle the matter, to no avail. Provincial leaders broached the idea that the best of special-settler youth had a place in official youth culture. Yet ranking leaders' hesitation and the outright opposition of some activists revealed ambivalence about including special settlers in political society.[63]

At the local level, the Stalin constitution left the question of special settlers' status in society just as unclear.[64] Two activists, the secretary and propagandist of a local committee in Northern province, wrote to Kosarev on May 22, 1938, to ask how they should handle special settlers who wanted to join the Komsomol. They had turned to their district and provincial youth committees for clarification but received no firm answer. "In the majority of cases," they explained, special-settler children "set good examples at work, are activists, are interested in the Komsomol organization." The league's regulations should have allowed them to become members, and the authors themselves believed that some special settlers belonged to the ranks of the best youth. What made the organizers uncomfortable was special settlers' legal status. If the league accepted special settlers, the activists believed that this would create a "free" and an "exile" Komsomol: "How would we explain to Komsomol members who are in that unusual situation the logic and correctness of their exile?"[65]

The authors exercised caution in their letter. After all, by supporting the admission of class aliens into the Komsomol, they could be accused of abetting the enemy. Unbeknownst to them, Iagoda's secret proposal for the Komsomol to admit limited numbers of special settlers had excluded Northern province.[66] All the same, writing the letter itself was more than likely an appeal meant to benefit

---

62. RGASPI, f. 1m, op. 2, d. 129, ll. 8–9.

63. RGASPI, f. 1m, op. 2, d. 136, l. 97.

64. Viola, *Unknown Gulag*, 158–59.

65. RGASPI, f. 1m, op. 23, d. 1291, l. 58.

66. Danilov, Krasil'nikov, and Viola, *Politbiuro i krest'ianstvo*, 1:698–99, 699–700 (citing GARF, f. 5446, op. 18a, d. 905, ll. 3–4; APRF, f. 3, op. 30, d. 197, ll. 93–94).

special-settler youth. The activists' motivations were unclear. Perhaps they had personal connections with special settlers whom they wanted to help. Or perhaps they were just tired of rejecting applications without an authoritative justification. No matter the inspiration, their argument for admitting special-settler youth was significant for deploying the language of universal rights for citizens found in the Stalin constitution.

These signals from activists and provincial leaders apparently had little effect on Kosarev and his leadership circle, though. No official policy discussions occurred. This silence was possibly deliberate. Kosarev had made explicit remarks about other types of class aliens who could join the Komsomol if they were verified. In a closed meeting of the Komsomol Central Committee's bureau in 1938, the general secretary reprimanded two regional youth leaders for having supported the expulsion of a sixteen-year-old as a class alien: "I can't imagine what kind of kulak he is. He was eight when we did away with the kulaks." Even if his father was a kulak, Kosarev continued, "He hardly considers himself a kulak and he is offended. You have created a tragedy in his life."[67]

The children of special settlers, especially those exiled along with their families, were another case. Kosarev remained silent on the issue, leaving local committees to decide on their own how to proceed. The difference between special settlers and other class aliens was probably that, in addition to the lasting stigma of their origin, special settlers faced significant legal obstacles to their physical and social mobility. Additionally, it is likely that Kosarev and other youth leaders knew about Order no. 00447, the largest of the NKVD's so-called mass operations that began in August 1937 and specifically targeted hundreds of thousands of former kulaks (along with whole groups of civil war-era class enemies and other anti-Soviet elements) for arrest and execution.[68] To admit special-settler youth to the Komsomol would mean accepting the kinds of people who were potential NKVD targets.

Youth leaders revisited their policies toward special settlers at the end of 1938, when the mass operations were winding down, and the Komsomol leadership had undergone a change. In late 1938, *Komsomol'skaia pravda*'s editor, Nikolai Mikhailov, would succeed Kosarev as Komsomol first secretary. A month after he assumed leadership, he became alarmed at the number of special settlers attempting to join the league and the lack of a clear policy regarding their admission. In December 1938 alone, the Komsomol Central Committee received over

67. RGASPI, f. 1m, op. 23, d. 1291, ll. 49–52.
68. Hagenloh, *Stalin's Police*; Shearer, *Policing Stalin's Socialism*; Binner and Junge, *Kak terror stal bol'shim*; Vatlin, *Agents of Terror*.

sixty letters about the issue. Like Kosarev, though, Mikhailov was unwilling to make a decision on his own authority, so he instead wrote directly to Stalin for advice in January 1939. Mikhailov painted a picture where confusion abounded at all levels, with admission for special-settler youth varying even within a single district. It seems that the sense of alarm in Mikhailov's letter stemmed more than anything from the lack of central control over the issue, that some committees were deciding "on their own." Although Mikhailov called on Stalin to resolve the matter, he cautiously expressed his own opinion: "I believe that the practice of indiscriminately denying children of repressed parents admission to the Komsomol is extremely dangerous and could create anger among those youths who want to work honestly for the people." He suggested a policy of "strict individual admission." Stalin apparently read the notice immediately and underlined the sentence with the words "extremely dangerous." He wrote beside the paragraph with Mikhailov's recommendation, "Correct!"[69]

What pushed Stalin and Mikhailov to allow controlled numbers of special settlers into the Komsomol was mostly pragmatism rather than dogma. Mikhailov emphasized in his letter the danger of blocking admission of this segment of the population, and it is not surprising that the Soviet leader picked up on this argument. By offering the chance, slight as it was, of acceptance into official political culture, they hoped to open a safety valve on the dissatisfaction of a potential enemy. The end of mass repression (or at least of Order no. 00447) also allowed the possibility for special-settler children to be drawn into official youth culture.[70] Mikhailov, like Kosarev before him, was familiar with the arguments of lower-level activists who asserted that the new conditions of socialism could allow class-alien youth to join the league. However, Stalin and Mikhailov appear to have seen the issue not as a matter of principle but primarily as a question of security and order. Despite Mikhailov and Stalin's agreement about the decision, news of special-settler youth's altered status seems to have passed by word of mouth among Komsomol leaders, rather than through a public resolution. Mikhailov sent a draft resolution on the issue to party secretaries Andreev and Malenkov, but the Komsomol bureau appears never to have approved it.[71]

Amid this uncertainty, special-settler youth were slowly joining the Komsomol. Karelia was one of the places where special settlers had been admitted in 1938. That year, youth organizations in eight districts accepted a total of sixty-three special settlers. What process special-settler youth went through to join

69. RGASPI, f. 1m, op. 23, d. 1327, ll. 21–25, 46.
70. Shearer, *Policing Stalin's Socialism*, 368.
71. RGASPI, f. 1m, op. 23, d. 1327, ll. 65, 97.

is unclear, but the meticulous paper trail left behind suggests that leaders there were monitoring admissions. In 1939, acceptance of special settlers was more common but just as stringent. Every special settler who joined the Komsomol had to interview at the local level, with the district committee, and then with the province's youth leaders. Simultaneously, youth leaders would soon do away with all but the local interview for admissions of all other youth. The league did not keep statistics on the total number of special settlers who joined in Karelia for 1939–41, but the figure was probably several hundred.[72] This group was only a fraction of the eighteen thousand special-settler youth Mariniushkin had cited in 1937 and made up a far smaller proportion than league members among eligible youth at the time (nearing 30 percent).[73]

In spite of limited inclusion in the Komsomol, young special settlers would continue to face discrimination. Ivan Tvardovskii partially escaped his own status but married a special settler. In May 1939, his wife gave birth to a son. When he went to register the child with authorities, the clerk at the registration office said: "No, no! What are you doing! Registration of newborn special settlers is through the NKVD." Desperate that his child not be branded as a special settler, Tvardovskii sent Stalin a protesting letter that referenced the idea that "a son does not answer for his father." Three weeks later, Tvardovskii received a summons to appear at the local NKVD office. The officer, waiting with registration papers for the child, said, "Here's something you probably didn't expect." He showed Tvardovskii his own letter, forwarded from the party's Central Committee, and registered the boy as a special settler.[74]

The secrecy and wariness surrounding special-settler youth reflected the broader uncertainty of class categorization in Stalinist socialism. Officials themselves faced a contradiction from the mid-1930s onward: they believed that socialism had been achieved, yet class aliens remained, broken but not entirely disarmed. The whole system of class categorization continued to have significance as Komsomol leaders demanded that youth from all backgrounds note their social origin on applications for admission, in disciplinary appeals, and for work in the league. At the same time, youth leaders and activists, as well as the country's leadership, believed that the USSR was still on a trajectory toward a classless society. As they pointed to the new, "most democratic" constitution, Soviet leaders could also present class inclusiveness as one more proof of their

72. NARK, f. 779, op. 20, d. 60, ll. 15–17; op. 22, d. 25.
73. RGASPI, f. 1m, op. 126, d. 393, ll. 5–6, 11, 20.
74. Tvardovskii, *Rodina i chuzhbina*, 155–57.

political system's superiority to that of capitalist states.[75] To reject class aliens publicly as members of the Soviet body politic would cast doubt on the USSR's progression from socialism to communism. In light of these tensions, Komsomol leaders opted to make cryptic, semipublic statements about the ability of class aliens to join the youth league but issued no specific directives about who would be eligible. Proclamations of class unity effectively allowed the appearance of inclusion, but practices of class categorization persisted as youth leaders hoped to prevent large numbers of supposedly dangerous elements from joining the ranks of the league.

The factors that made a model young person in Soviet political culture underwent a transformation in the mid-1930s. Youth leaders re-envisioned the best youth to include people whose educational accomplishments were at least as important as their class origin. This change in focus, accompanied by a shift from the factory toward the classroom, marked a fundamental change in the conception of youth culture in the Soviet Union, allowing students and educated workers to displace industrial workers decisively as the most valued groups among Soviet youth. At the same time, the conception of the best youth effectively continued to incorporate the social origin of would-be Komsomol members. Inherited social class, in particular, precluded the inclusion of a large number of class-alien children in official culture.

Rather than eliminating inherited class groupings altogether, the advent of socialism created confusion about the social hierarchy of the USSR. Administrators and activists at every level in the Komsomol experienced considerable doubts about who would be an exemplary young person in the formative period of socialism. In Soviet political culture, the idea that classes would disappear someday met and mixed with Stalinist realities in the historical juncture of the mid- to late 1930s—when supposed enemies internal and external abounded. The conclusion that leaders and organizers drew from the persistence of both privileged and hostile class groupings was not that the Soviet Union had deviated from the path to communism. Instead, it was that class groupings might change but would still have significance. While nationality was becoming an increasingly meaningful category for Stalin's state to differentiate elements of the population, class groups retained their importance.

It was hardest of all for youth to shake enemy status inherited from parents who became the targets of state repression. Youth from class-alien origins

---

75. Getty, "State and Society under Stalin," 19. On the broader Stalinist "superiority complex," see David-Fox, *Showcasing the Great Experiment*, 285–311.

became lumped in with their parents in arrest campaigns like dekulakization and NKVD Order no. 00447. For those young people with favorable class origins, their parents' downfall posed a quandary. It demanded that they implicitly reject, if not outright denounce, their loved ones or risk their place in society. Family catastrophe less often resulted in open denunciations than it became a disciplinary process that taught young people to be wary about how they discussed their private loyalties in public. Repression would discipline youth in other ways, too. Entering the Komsomol in the late 1930s meant exposing one's personal life to the inspection of local youth groups. Even leaders in the Komsomol faced accusations that they adhered to "old lifestyles" of degeneracy rather than to the new ways of cultured Soviet youth. In the Great Terror, the behavior of young people would become the object of a state-sponsored moral panic.

THE GREAT TERROR AS A MORAL PANIC

The years 1936–38 were the apex of Stalinist repression. In August 1936, Stalin instigated the first Moscow show trial of his former opponents, headlined by Grigorii Zinov'ev and Lev Kamenev. Soon after, in the fall of 1936 and spring of 1937, NKVD Commissar Nikolai Ezhov attacked the entrenched bureaucratic "families" of provincial party chiefs and military leaders, whose supposed intransigence Stalin viewed as potential sources of opposition.[1] At the February–March 1937 party Central Committee plenum, Stalin announced that the party was filled with hidden Trotskyist enemies whom loyalists had to uproot.[2] Panic gripped local party cells as members denounced their peers, fearing that they might themselves be denounced for their lack of vigilance.[3] Meanwhile, in July 1937 Stalin demanded the NKVD undertake a series of secret mass operations to arrest and execute hundreds of thousands of dekulakized peasants, recidivist criminals, "hostile nationalities," and other supposed anti-Soviet elements. These

---

1. See Solomon, "Local Political Power," 305–29; Rigby, "Was Stalin a Disloyal Patron?" 322; Gill, *Origins of the Stalinist Political System*; Getty, *Origins of the Great Purges*, 196–97; Getty and Naumov, *Road to Terror*; Easter, *Reconstructing the State*. Historians who have embraced the cultural turn tend to see the Great Purge as a Bolshevik auto-da-fé spurred by genuine belief in the Soviet project. See Kotkin, *Magnetic Mountain*, 286; and Halfin, *Stalinist Confessions*.

2. I. V. Stalin, "O nedostatkakh partinnoi raboty i merakh likvidatsii trotskistskikh i inykh dvurushnikov," *Pravda*, March 29, 1937.

3. See Goldman, *Terror and Democracy*.

operations would make up the majority of those arrested and executed in the Great Terror. In the years 1937–38 alone, Soviet police arrested over 1.5 million people, of whom more than 700,000 were killed.

Youth became targets of the terror just like adults, and yet mass repression among youth was also distinctive for its emphasis on problems of social disorder. Like party members, ranking Komsomol organizers were vulnerable for their connections with supposed enemies of the people. Young people also faced arrest as members of the various categories in the mass operations. Political repression among youth had effects beyond arrest and execution, though. Authorities sought to create social discipline in society through the terror. Even before the start of mass repression in 1937, officials in the NKVD and Komsomol had engaged in a war with hooliganism. It was a war fought with anxious newspaper articles and a large-scale campaign of arrests beginning in 1935. The drive against social disorder also struck the highest ranks of the Komsomol. In July and August 1937, nearly all of the top youth leaders were removed from their positions and arrested soon after. Only Aleksandr Kosarev and a handful of his closest allies remained in the leadership. In many ways, the campaign in the youth league was similar to any other Stalin initiated against entrenched bureaucratic families in the USSR. The distinctive charge in the Komsomol's purge, though, was that its leaders were "Trotskyist degenerates"—drunks, philanderers, and reprobates—who had used their authority to corrupt the young.

The narrative of the Komsomol's purge reflected anxieties about the conduct of the new generation of cultured youth through the lens of repression. When Kosarev promoted communist upbringing among youth activists, he envisioned a generation that would observe traditional manners, be familiar with the classics of Soviet and Russian culture, and not drink to excess. Adherence to these norms symbolized the achievements of Soviet socialism and, youth leaders argued, would contribute to productivity.[4] The accusation of degeneracy effectively charged leading Komsomol organizers of sabotaging the central task of providing and exemplifying a cultured upbringing. The connection between degeneracy and terror in the youth league also exposed increasing tensions over the aging group of organizers, called *pererostki* (overgrown people). Impeded from joining the Communist Party by a moratorium that had been in place since 1933, their presence created a clash in the Komsomol between the old, rough proletarian activism and the new refinement of communist upbringing.

---

4. On notions of cultured behavior, see Fitzpatrick, "Becoming Cultured," in *Cultural Front*; Kelly, *Refining Russia*, chapter 4; and Hoffmann, *Stalinist Values*, 57–87.

Fears about hooligans, Trotskyist degenerates, and pererostki were aspects of a broader Stalinist moral panic about social discipline and cohesion among youth. During such moral panics in liberal democracies, the media identify supposed deviant behavior as a way of attracting the interest of a public that fears abnormality.[5] In Stalin's Soviet Union, political leaders directed the moral panic through the media and Komsomol groups as an attempt to enforce restrained behavior among the younger generation. Although Stalin's campaign against degeneracy was directed from above, it was not cynical. Among concerned organizers, the goal was not only to excise hooligans and degenerates but to recover those young people on the cusp of deviancy, embedding the politics of terror in the private lives of youth.

Hooligans and Social Disorder

The ambiguous category of hooliganism had appeared in Russia at the end of the empire. Characterized by alcohol abuse and public disorder, the popular press published fear-mongering accounts of brazen murders and other scandals that alarmed affluent citizens. Nonetheless, hooliganism also reflected real lower-class unrest created by the socioeconomic transformation of urbanization and industrialization.[6] Hooliganism continued in the Soviet Union as working-class young men, more often than not outside the ranks of the Komsomol, disrupted social order. Stalinist leaders did not see hooliganism as the product of frustration and boredom, though, but as a subculture of anti-Soviet rabble who shared a collective identity based on their love of alcohol, cards, and fighting. Moreover, party leaders viewed hooligans as a self-conscious anti-Soviet group that wanted to corrupt the souls of youth. At a 1935 meeting of provincial activists, Kosarev moaned that hooliganism was endemic among young factory workers. Rather than blame workers for their behavior, the Komsomol leader argued, "A small number of hooligans, but the active organizing core, are class enemies . . . for whom hooliganism is a form of political activity."[7]

Even in the late 1920s, Komsomol leaders had received sporadic reports about "organized hooliganism."[8] Although youth from factories occasionally got in drunken fights with police, it was in the countryside where violent incidents

---

5. Cohen, *Folk Devils and Moral Panics*.
6. Neuberger, *Hooliganism*, 217–18.
7. RGASPI, f. 1m, op. 5, d. 27, ll. 66–68.
8. RGASPI, f. 1m, op. 23, d. 749, l. 61.

flourished. The combination of moonshine and rivalries between villages led to gang fights that police were unable to stop. Komsomol leaders and OGPU investigators also identified a crime called "political hooliganism," public disorder that occurred at official gatherings or was directed at administrators. In a village in Kirsanov district (Tambov province), a group of drunken young people broke up the celebration of International Youth Day in 1926 and beat up the leader of the district council. Another incident labeled as hooliganism occurred on the same holiday in Krasivskaia district (Voronezh province). A young villager interrupted an official's speech, jumping on the podium and announcing: "Why are you propagandizing Marxism and Leninism. Nothing good will come of them. Better to get a ticket to hell [svintsovyi bilet] than a Komsomol card."[9]

Political police increasingly became involved in monitoring hooliganism in the 1930s. In 1932 in Orenburg district, the OGPU uncovered a conspiracy of hooligan youth supposedly called the Central Society of Non-Party Youth. The assistant head of the OGPU's secret-political department, Georgii Molchanov, claimed that dissatisfied Komsomol members in the village Krasnokholmskaia had formed the organization as an alternative to their youth cell, whose despised leader had "introduced strict discipline in the Komsomol." Apparently, the young woman in question had forbidden drinking, given that the society's chief rule was that "drinking would not be considered shameful but rather should be welcomed when it doesn't hinder work." After the investigator questioned the frightened teenagers—mostly boys, but some girls—he reported that their "program" called for members to gather weapons. One of the boys claimed he told friends that they needed to "put [Nesmeianovaia, the local youth leader] on ice." The interrogator also had them recite a drinking song that had spread from their group to other villages:

> In the pub, on the road, at the bazaar,
> Drunken death's walking and singing,
> Drink to the bottom, drink a bit more,
> Even the chickens are drinking.
>
> Tear up the papers and spit on the books,
> That say that your boozing should end,
> Hey shirkers, hey soakers, hey foul mouths and crooks,
> All of these guys are my friends.
>
> Drink to the bottom, the ball-and-chain's nagging,
> And raising a deafening row,

---

9. RGASPI, f. 1m, op. 23, d. 743, ll. 22ob., 23ob.–24ob.

Why put up so long with your old lady's haggling,
Grab the axe there from the stove.

Out on the run, you have nothing to lose,
If they catch you then it is fate,
What do you care if a snakebite or booze,
Finally makes you croak, mate?

Your empress, your Tsarina stands at the fore,
Your laughing lady death,
Hey shirker, you'll serve as my true knight of honor,
Nobly here we have met.

Hey Mishka, hey Volodka, and Stepka, too,
Get to the pub now all right,
I'll give you a bit of my own special brew,
And then a whole drum like each night.

The ode was only explicitly anti-Soviet insofar as drunken death railed against official condemnations of drinking. However, the investigator read the violence and alcohol abuse in the song as anti-Soviet hooliganism. It is uncertain if the investigator imposed political motivations on the case or if the society's members truly opposed the regime. It seems clear that young people in Krasnokholmskaia were dissatisfied with their youth organization's strictures against alcohol. In all likelihood, the investigator's conclusion demonstrated how Stalinist conceptions of hooliganism could transform a local squabble into plans for an armed, politically motivated attack on local leaders.[10]

NKVD investigators made a similar accusation against political hooligans in Dnepropetrovsk in 1934. Police claimed that an organized group of fifteen hooligans had broken into a dormitory of newcomers. The group, apparently made up of ethnic Ukrainians, yelled, "*Katsapy* [a derogatory term for Russians] have arrived in Ukraine." The investigators did not see these typical conflicts between locals and newcomers as such but instead as the rise of groups "whose hooliganism has taken on political tones."[11]

By the mid-1930s, leaders in the NKVD (which inherited and expanded the functions of the OGPU in 1934) were broadening their definition of hooliganism to include juvenile crime. In the 1920s, police leaders had treated juvenile

10. RGASPI, f. 1m, op 23, d. 1008, ll. 2–6.
11. HDA SBU, f. 16, op. 1, spr. 9, ark. 29, 131.

delinquency as a holdover from the capitalist past. They hoped that education and social relief organizations would solve the problem of theft and vagrancy among the Soviet Union's many homeless and abandoned children.[12] As the country entered the period of socialism, though, social disorder did not decrease. Instead, the triple crisis of collectivization, dekulakization, and famine unleashed mass chaos in the country as peasants perished or fled to the cities to find work, and thousands of children found themselves without parents. As NKVD officials grappled with social disorder more broadly, they began to use prophylactic policing—mass sweeps of cities to get rid of so-called socially hostile elements, including vagrant children. They came to see juvenile delinquency as a serious problem and, from 1935, a form of hooliganism.[13] Komsomol youth became involved in these campaigns through auxiliary battalions for policing hooliganism. On the Western train line, 120 brigades comprising 707 young people stopped 8,145 people in June 1934 alone. Of them, 1,556 were branded hooligans, and 2,538 were abandoned children.[14]

Meanwhile, hooliganism itself came to encompass not only disorderly public behavior like drinking but also serious assaults. By Stalin's edict in March 1935, the Soviet government created a new crime, "aggravated hooliganism," an offense that included armed attacks. This conflation of violence and disorder led to harsher punishments for all kinds of hooliganism. While simple hooliganism had carried a noncustodial sentence, conviction on aggravated hooliganism now could result in five years of incarceration.[15] The introduction of the new crime served as a call to action against social disorder. In 1934, authorities arrested 95,071 people for hooliganism, sending 15,438 to labor camps. The next year, authorities arrested 136,521 hooligans and sent 58,045 into incarceration. By 1937, aggravated hooliganism was a far more common charge than ordinary hooliganism and incarceration a more common fate for convicts.[16]

As arrests against hooligans mounted, articles in the youth press bewailed the dangers that hooligans posed to a good society. At the ski factory in Petrozavodsk, hooligans barged into the "anti-Christmas" party at the end of 1934, hitting the Komsomol secretary in the face as he and an auxiliary brigade attempted to eject them. The local newspaper commented that "the hand of the class enemy" had been behind previous incidents of hooliganism and concluded: "We need to teach

---

12. Ball, *And Now My Soul Is Hardened*.
13. Shearer, *Policing Stalin's Socialism*, 219–22, 229, 231.
14. RGASPI, f. 1m, op. 23, d. 1072, ll. 92–96.
15. Solomon, *Soviet Criminal Justice under Stalin*, 225.
16. GARF, f. 9474, op. 10, d. 49, l. 6.

the hooligans a lesson. The police must do more than hand out fines."[17] Similar articles appeared throughout the country at the beginning of 1935. An article in *Za industrializatsiiu* from April 1935 profiled a group of teenagers at School no. 2 in Voroshilovsk (today's Stavropol). The seventh graders supposedly bullied classmates, interrupted lessons, and carried knives. The parents of the group's leaders, who included the commercial director of the local factory, took no steps to curtail their activity. Eventually the children were expelled from school. The article led to a procuracy investigation of the group, particularly its leader Petrovskii. The procurator of Voroshilovsk, named Basha, asserted that Petrovskii's actions were criminal but lamented that action could not be taken unless the new law on aggravated hooliganism was given retroactive power. Whether Basha or other authorities ultimately managed to prosecute the boy is unknown.[18]

Following the escalation of political repression after the first Moscow show trial in August 1936, the NKVD increasingly linked hooliganism to enemies of the people. An NKVD report on cases of political crime among youth in Kiev province included the "absolutely representative" investigation of a fifteen-year-old student, Daniil, for hooligan activity. It is unclear how the seventh grader came to the attention of the authorities, but in early 1937, they gathered testimony about him from his school's director and the local schoolboard inspector. The director asserted that Daniil led a group of hooligans and instructed them to beat up other students. When the director called Daniil to his office, he improbably claimed, "He [Daniil] admitted that his hooligan activities were organized with the goal of undermining school discipline and discrediting the Soviet school. He shares Trotsky's views, and his diversionary activity is a method of Trotskyist sabotage in school." The inspector added, "[Daniil] explained that he carries out hooligan activity consciously and that 'it is the tactic of the enemy.'"

It is possible, but hard to imagine, that the fifteen-year-old truly had maintained that his bullying and classroom disruptions were Trotskyism. A more likely scenario is that the school administrators gave NKVD investigators the politically charged testimony they wanted, and the police helped them dispose of a troublesome student. The only evidence the NKVD put forward from Daniil himself was a collection of his forlorn poems that he had let classmates read. His poem "Everything Is Gone" concluded:

> All life is boring, believe me,
> Joy is for asses and the dumb,

---

17. "Prouchit′ khuliganov," *Komsomolets Karelii*, January 3, 1935.

18. GARF, f. 8131, op. 12, d. 29, ll. 8–11.

> To set things right all you need,
> Is a bullet and a gun.

In another verse, Daniil cited the influence of the poet Sergei Esenin, whose troubling work, torrid affairs, and 1925 suicide had struck fear in party leaders who worried that youth would follow the poet's example.[19] For NKVD officials, though, Daniil's story was not one of depression and potential suicide but of intentional sabotage of the school.[20]

The link between hooliganism and enemies of the people also appeared in the youth press. One article from the town Kandalaksha in Karelia from January 1937 depicted a typical hooligan night—drinking, crashing a respectable dance, and a raid on the women's dormitory at the local factory. A month earlier, there had been a murder in the town, and the police had not yet identified the killer. The author asserted (without evidence) that the murderer was a hooligan, and therefore the police were at fault not only for treating social disorder lightly but also for ignoring how hooliganism could spawn serious crimes. At the same time, youth leaders in the town were also at fault for not providing alternative activities and standing up to hooligans at those events they sponsored.[21] Another article charged two hooligans at the dormitory of the Onezhskii factory in Petrozavodsk with taking vulnerable Komsomol members and corrupting them with card games and alcohol. The youth group should have intervened. Instead, the leaders of the group "built a Great Wall of China around the personal life of youth."[22]

In unpublished reports, justice officials expressed discomfort about the expanded use of repression against hooliganism. In 1938, an official from the Soviet Supreme Court named Grachev claimed that violent crime perpetrated with a weapon had fallen between 1934 and 1938 while arrests for aggravated hooliganism had only increased. Three neighbors—a man and a couple—were charged with aggravated hooliganism after they had a succession of loud arguments. The case was atypical in that a woman was charged with hooliganism. All three received an eighteen-month sentence. Grachev concluded that verdicts like these were unduly harsh. In his view, punishment should have represented the offender's threat to society, because first-time hooligans "can be reformed faster and more easily than recidivist hooligans."[23]

---

19. Pinnow, *Lost to the Collective*, 224–25.
20. HDA SBU, f. 16, op. 1, spr. 153, ark. 79.
21. V. Shcheglov, "Khuligan—vrag naroda! O Kandalakshskikh nravakh," *Komsomolets Karelii*, January 3, 1937.
22. "Byt ne chastnoe delo," *Komsomolets Karelii*, December 8, 1938.
23. GARF, f. 9474, op. 10, d. 49, l. 6.

Another common claim was that hooligans themselves were not to blame, but rather that the influence of criminal elements had turned good youth bad. When the hooligans were teenagers or preteens, authorities often saw the influence of adult criminals. In Odessa province, the procurator blamed the police for not "uncovering the true source" of child hooliganism in the town of Niko-laev. Three adults, including a twice-indicted thief and two "déclassé elements," allegedly organized a group of children to "terrorize Pioneers and Komsomol members," particularly targeting Jewish children. Another group was a "den" for homeless children led by a pair of adult sisters. "The children gave the stolen money and items to the sisters, who organized nighttime drinking sessions for the children."[24] The procurator thus suggested that arresting children would not address the real problem, which lay with adults. Soviet justice and policing officials were split on the role that administrative repression should play. NKVD administrators believed that sweeps of marginal populations were an effective method of cleansing urban areas of crime, whereas legal officials suggested that reform and discipline were more effective.[25]

Hysterical articles in the youth press reflected this split as well, both justifying repression against social disorder and demanding that youth leaders do more to protect good youth from hooliganism. Moreover, in portraying drunk and disorderly youth as enemies of the people, the authors suggested there was political intent behind hooliganism, even a subculture united by outlaw songs and violence. Disorderly behavior existed in the Soviet Union, of course. Ordinary workers and peasants drank, gambled on cards, and told supposed anti-Soviet jokes. Some young people perhaps saw their reverie as resistance to the discipline of local authorities. There was even political hooliganism, when alcohol loosened people's lips enough for them to interrupt a party meeting or when teenagers vandalized the portraits of party leaders at their schools.[26] Nonetheless, hooliganism as conceived by Soviet leaders was a fiction. There was no conspiratorial anti-Soviet subculture working at the direction of class-alien elements. What motivated exposés in the Komsomol, and in the NKVD to a lesser degree, was fear that cultured Soviet young people would become corrupted. The dissemination of this panic in the youth press led to disciplinary proceedings in the Komsomol and formal charges in the procuracy.

Party leaders believed that hooliganism was largely a form of working-class opposition. Its home was in the factory dormitory and in the kolkhoz tavern, and

---

24. GARF, f. 8131, op. 14, d. 47, ll. 18–19.

25. Shearer, *Policing Stalin's Socialism*, 233–37.

26. HDA SBU, f. 16, op. 1, spr. 47, ark. 91–92.

it posed a threat to Komsomol youth. The panic over young people's behavior extended into the ranks of the youth league as well, though. In the purge of the Komsomol, accusations of organized degeneracy against leaders would become another means of spreading the alarm over the supposed corruption of youth.

Degeneracy and Terror

At the end of August 1937, the Komsomol's Central Committee convened an extraordinary meeting in the guise of a regular plenary gathering. In the previous two months, the NKVD had arrested almost the entirety of the youth league's leadership. One of the lone survivors, Kosarev, made the shocking public announcement that his former colleagues had not only been enemies of the people but that they had used degeneracy as their main weapon. The central figure among the Trotskyist degenerates was Sergei Saltanov, the former educational secretary now turned into the leader of the Komsomol's counterrevolutionaries. According to Kosarev, former Komsomol First Secretary Lazar' Shatskin had recruited Saltanov into an oppositionist conspiracy. Shatskin had truly opposed Stalin's increasing domination of politics in the late 1920s and early 1930s and had been arrested in 1935. Stalinist accusations turned Shatskin's opposition into participation in a "united Trotskyist-Zinov'evite rightist organization" that Saltanov had supposedly joined.[27]

After their recruitment, Saltanov and the others were alleged to have enlisted followers from the Komsomol at drunken parties in their apartments, using alcohol as a lubricant for anti-Soviet discussions. Amid lurid tales of Trotskyist drinking Kosarev summarized, "Through drinking bouts they broke down the weak-willed; they worked over and recruited followers for their efforts." Kosarev, a product of the radical proletarian Komsomol of the 1920s, had his own reputation as a drinker and explained his actions in a speech called "My Drinking Bouts."[28] Kosarev chastised himself for not seeing the fundamental contradiction between this degeneracy and work in the Komsomol. "Lifestyle cannot be separate from politics," he said. "Lifestyle, especially of leading Komsomol workers, is entirely political."[29]

The accusation leveled at the deviants was *bytovoe razlozhenie* (literally, everyday corruption), which included domestic violence and adultery but above all

---

27. RGASPI, f. 1m, op. 2, d. 133, l. 79.
28. Ibid., l. 94.
29. Ibid., l. 81.

drinking. Komsomol leaders had never welcomed drinking, although it was often tolerated and even encouraged in some circles. In the 1920s, some local youth committees had attempted to fight drinking and philandering in their midst. A few groups had even expelled their leaders for various forms of degeneracy in the late 1920s. Nonetheless, Komsomol members and leaders viewed alcohol abuse as a form of social misconduct rather than a political crime.[30] Accusations of alcohol abuse were also leveled at party members and leaders during the campaign of repression in 1937–38, as well as in the party's previous purges. In contrast to the Komsomol, though, drinking in the party was unpleasant but truly dangerous only as a symptom of more significant abuses of power. Party members faced an amalgam of allegations, but degeneracy, as a nonpolitical activity, was nonetheless distinct from the most important charges of political conspiracy.[31]

During the terror, Stalin and his inner circle were aware of smoldering dissatisfaction in the country. The repression against local grandees—always driven from above with the main goal of removing supposed enemies—channeled the resentment of the disaffected toward the privilege of local authorities and away from central leaders.[32] The campaign against Trotskyist degenerates, too, tied into dissatisfaction with the privilege of young bureaucrats. Its main function, though, was as a moral panic, a campaign to save youth from becoming degenerates and therefore enemies.

Until the summer of 1937, the Komsomol's purge was similar to the purge in the party, where political allegiances and class background were the most important factors. In August 1936, Kosarev sacked the Voronezh Komsomol leader, Mikhail Grubman, after he was caught holding drunken parties in his headquarters. Kosarev characterized Grubman's boozing not as a serious crime in itself but as a sign of a political offense—"familyness" and abuse of power that had allowed his underlings to keep silent about offensive behavior.[33] In November 1936, NKVD commissar Nikolai Ezhov launched a major campaign of repression against supposedly intransigent provincial party leaders and their clans, beginning

---

30. Expulsion from the Komsomol for personal behavior was relatively rare in the early 1920s but became a more important factor in membership politics as the Komsomol set up conflict commissions to oversee expulsion and reinstatement. Guillory, "We Shall Refashion Life on Earth!," 268. Unlike the case of the demonized Trotskyist degenerates, the Komsomol Central Committee dedicated a meeting to understanding and preventing alcohol abuse in late 1928. The lead organizer opened the session by saying, "We gathered you here today to chat about why we drink and what might make you stop drinking." RGASPI, f. 1m, op. 5, d. 18, l. 1.

31. Getty, *Origins of the Great Purges*, 83–85.

32. See Fitzpatrick, "How the Mice Buried the Cat"; and Goldman, *Terror and Democracy*, 217–21.

33. "Ser'eznoe preduprezhdenie," *Izvestiia TsK VLKSM*, no. 18 (1936): 12–14; RGASPI, f. 1m, op. 23, d. 1172, ll. 18–50.

with the political group in Azov-Chernomor province. Virtually the entire clan in the province was removed and arrested, including the province's youth leader, Erofitskii, and his Komsomol subgroup. During a meeting of the Komsomol Central Committee convened principally to denounce Erofitskii and other supposed enemies, Kosarev singled out a fallen district youth leader from the clique whom he called with bemusement the "Pulverizer" because of his reputation for womanizing. After listing the Pulverizer's many faults, Kosarev finally came to the main reason for his expulsion: he was the son of a prerevolutionary gendarme.[34]

Local Komsomol organizations had also cared about their members' conduct but had not considered behavioral transgressions a threat to Soviet rule. In the Moscow-based Commissariat of Defense youth organization, organizers were active in policing their members' drinking and sexual improprieties. In a typical case from 1936, the commissariat's Komsomol bureau summoned and reprimanded a young activist when police found him at the railway station "not behaving like a Komsomol member" after four mugs of beer.[35] The bureau also investigated an activist husband whose wife accused him of beating her, eventually removing the activist from his position but not from the league.[36] Another young man came before the bureau in October 1936 to answer for allegations that he "lives with many girls, telling each he would marry them and lying to all." Challenging these accusations, the young man claimed he had just gotten married. A week later the committee checked his marital status, revealing that he had lied: "He never proposed to anyone and he has different women each day." The bureau removed him from the Komsomol, as much for his deception as for his philandering.[37]

After the Komsomol Central Committee's August 1937 purge plenum, the work of ordinary youth groups was consumed by discussions about the disgraced youth leaders. Many of the gatherings resembled purge meetings at factory party committees, where accusations of political disloyalty or connections with enemies also dominated.[38] In Komsomol groups, though, the lesson of the August purge was not just to avoid and root out Trotskyists but to recognize these enemies through their drinking habits and sexual behavior. The Komsomol Central Committee sent instructors to the provinces to lead purge meetings

34. RGASPI, f. 1m, op. 2, d. 126, l. 39; d. 127, l. 6.
35. RGVA, f. 9, op. 30, d. 8, ll. 19–21; d. 81, ll. 261–62.
36. RGVA, f. 9, op. 30, d. 8, l. 4.
37. Ibid., ll. 18, 19–22.
38. Goldman, *Terror and Democracy*, 186–91.

in local committees. Before they left, Kosarev told the instructors that local organizers would claim that drinking had occurred in the Komsomol's Central Committee but not in their provinces. Mimicking a local activist, he said, "We don't have that here, especially because I myself don't drink."[39] Although they would hide, Kosarev insisted that degenerate organizers were there and had to be uprooted.

Even before the instructors arrived, early rumors may have spread about the fate of the purged Komsomol leaders. In the summer of 1937 in Moscow, two members of the Komsomol organization of the Central School for Staff Commander Preparation in Moscow beat a man severely while drunk, resulting in a police investigation and a disciplinary hearing. Particularly damning for the accused men was that they supposedly had access to military secrets. One member of the disciplinary committee remarked, "When a person is drunk, he could fall into the trap of the enemy and give away a military secret. The enemy recruits just these kinds of people, who are already corrupted by systematic drinking."[40] The assertion that drinking could lead to the disclosure of national secrets was not unique to the military and reflected an obsession among party elites with perceived foreign conspiracies. The same conspiratorial logic that allowed NKVD agents to treat foreignness as a sign of disloyalty allowed Komsomol groups to see drinking as a precursor to the transformation of cultured young Soviets into deviants ready to betray the motherland.

In Lopasne (Moscow province), the district youth committee held a meeting in advance of the Komsomol's purge plenum. In the previous months, the committee had expelled 7 of the district's 691 members for degeneracy in addition to the 10 it expelled for connections with enemies of the people. Explaining these expulsions, the committee came close to Kosarev's formulation from the purge plenum later that month: "We cannot skate around incidents of drinking binges and degeneracy or explain them as 'coincidences.' Our mission is to unmask infections, to show the political meaning of this behavior." In drinking, the committee asserted that the Komsomol "must see the hand of the class enemy." The district committee considered the possibility that a lack of culture was the cause of drinking but dismissed this possibility because "in Moscow there is culture but there is [also] degeneracy."[41]

When local youth committees discussed the Komsomol's purge plenum itself, degeneracy was a major focus. In Lukhovitsy district (Moscow province),

---

39. RGASPI, f. 1m, op. 5, d. 41, l. 12.
40. RGVA, f. 9, op. 30, d. 81, ll. 339–40.
41. OKhDOPIM, f. 648p, op. 1, d. 6, l. 9.

activists wavered between characterizing alcohol abuse as "enemy work" and as merely an unsavory alternative to better forms of entertainment. "Drinking and degeneracy . . . are the enemies' methods of work," said Kozlov, a local youth secretary from the district center. He then moderated his statement by adding that some of the local deviants "began to drink because leisure time is not organized." Several other youth leaders echoed these remarks, suggesting a strong connection between drinking and boredom rather than Trotskyism.[42]

The purge of the so-called Trotskyist degenerates resonated in the everyday life of Komsomol members. In September 1937, the Central House of the Red Army (TsDKA, the army's cultural wing) accused an activist of having "inappropriate relations" with a young woman, ultimately resulting in an illegal abortion. Pronina, the head of the youth organization, accused the activist of willfully ignoring the lessons of the August 1937 plenum. "To this day," she said, "he believes that his personal life is not the affair of the Komsomol organization." Soon after that, he received an audience before the entire group, dozens of peers, where he declared that the August purge plenum had shown him the light: "Until the decision of the plenum . . . I couldn't put together behavior and politics." Countering his testimony, a friend of the woman blamed him for the abortion.[43] Against the wishes of the group's leadership, its membership voted twenty-eight to eight for a reprimand rather than expulsion. The leniency the majority male group showed was probably based on gendered notions of misbehavior that placed the burden of promiscuity with the woman. But even the group's organizers, who saw the accusations of Trotskyist degeneracy as a mandate to expel the young man, did not call for his arrest as an enemy of the people.

The purge of high-ranking Komsomol leaders as deviants represented a hard line against the old culture of youth activism. However, the result was not the expulsion of all Komsomol members who drank or were promiscuous but an awareness of these issues and an urgency to correct them. The impetus to discipline was itself problematic. It begged the question—where did social malfeasances end and degeneracy as a political crime begin? The moral panic over degeneracy pressured organizers to fight for young people through discipline, rather than outright expulsion, before enemies exploited moral weaknesses to fill their ranks and sap the strength of the young generation.

Although the scale of repression subsided over the course of 1938, discussions of degeneracy would continue. A year later in TsDKA, its new secretary,

42. OKhDOPIM, f. 648p, op. 1, d. 7, l. 31.
43. RGVA, f. 9, op. 30, d. 81, ll. 56–57, 58–60.

Bernmenson, asserted that Komsomol organizers' laissez-faire attitude toward conduct in daily life was allowing ordinary youth to become degenerates. A case in the organization involved an activist caught drinking and stealing. Bernmenson insisted that the young man was in political danger: "The contemptible 'enemies of the people,' the Trotskyist-Bukharinite bandits are attempting with their chief method—the degeneracy of youth and above all through drinking bouts—to break apart the harmonious life of the Komsomol." In spite of these problems, Bernmenson argued that the activist should receive a reprimand but stay in the league.[44] At a December 1938 meeting of the Komsomol group in the Commissariat of Defense's clerical office, members took turns criticizing the behavior of their peers. One said, "Not all of us are exemplars in our behavior, like Comrade X. He wanted to divorce his wife." Another speaker chose a different target: "What kind of example could a Komsomol member like Comrade Z. be when he gets drunk and ends up at the police station?"[45]

In late 1938, the nine-member-strong youth organization of the newspaper *Boevaia podgotovka* held a meeting where a local party organizer spoke about the Komsomol's failure to unmask enemies following another significant purge of the league's leadership. When the speaker mentioned degeneracy, the secretary of the group asked what exactly this meant. A peer responded, "Degeneracy starts with small things. Today a person has one extra drink, tomorrow a little more, and so on. And enemies catch on to this, study the weak side of people, and play on that." When the secretary stepped in to put his spin on the purge and how it applied to his small organization, he was interrupted by another member, who said, "Degeneracy is the behavior of [the secretary] himself." His colleague claimed that the secretary got into fistfights with his wife and broke glasses at home, showing up to work with blood on his clothes. He concluded self-critically: "As for me, once I was hit by a car when I was drunk. That is also degeneracy."[46]

Accusations of degeneracy against women were unusual. Indeed, female Komsomol members made up a disproportionately small percentage of expulsions overall. By the end of 1938, women were nearly 35 percent of the Komsomol's membership but only 20 percent of its expellees.[47] The relative infrequency of accusations against women was likely to have been a product of several factors.

44. RGVA, f. 9, op. 30, d. 177, ll. 46–47, 125.
45. Ibid., ll. 64, 65. I anonymized the names of the people involved in the case.
46. Ibid., l. 29.
47. RGASPI, f. 1m, op. 126, d. 344, ll. 14, 16, 17, 28, 29, 32, 33, 36, 37, 40, 41; d. 358, ll. 11–12, 12–13, 14–15, 25–26, 36–37, 38–39, 42–43, 46, 47.

Soviet leaders did not consider women to be serious political actors, and for this reason women were less likely than men to face repression during the Great Terror.[48] In addition, female members were less frequently targeted because they were underrepresented in high-ranking, paid activist positions.

With few cases to draw on, making a categorical conclusion about the effects of the antidegeneracy campaign among female young communists is difficult. Komsomol records did not provide separate statistics listing the reasons for women's expulsion. Of the thirty-seven cases of female activists the Smolensk province Komsomol committee reviewed in early 1938, just two cases involved degeneracy.[49] Cases with women Komsomol members that came to the attention of the league's Central Committee at a plenary meeting in 1938 concerned accusations of sexual misconduct exclusively. In Gorkii province, one woman faced the charge that she had been "physically connected with the enemy" because she had been the assistant of a man from another province later arrested as an enemy of the people. Her youth group forced her to go to five doctors to confirm that she was a virgin, as she claimed. If they had not declared her a virgin, she undoubtedly would have faced expulsion, even arrest.[50] Another young woman who became pregnant after being raped received permission for a legal abortion when health complications ensued. Nonetheless, her district committee expelled her for the abortion, unwilling to believe that she had legitimate medical reasons. In both cases, promiscuity was viewed as a punishable offense for women in the league.[51] Whether the specific allegation was of sexual misconduct or drunkenness, public accusations of degeneracy against female young communists were few. The campaign seems to have targeted men more frequently than women.

The charge of degeneracy became a black mark that would limit the possibility for benefits and social promotion. In the Komsomol organization of the Administration of Military Preparation in April 1939, one member applied for an apartment with a girlfriend, who he claimed was his fiancée. Once he received the apartment, though, he immediately broke off the relationship. He later said that he had not lied to his girlfriend, but that they had applied because she said she was pregnant. When it turned out she was not, his "relationship with the girl

48. For example, among the thousands of victims executed at the Butovo firing range near Moscow, only 3.6 percent were women. McLoughlin, "Vernichtung des Fremden," 78. Political leaders' belief that women were fundamentally apolitical also made them particularly successful protesters during collectivization. See Viola, "Bab'i bunty," 23.

49. Smolensk Archive, WKP 416, 34–198.

50. RGASPI, f. 1m, op. 2, d. 136, l. 87.

51. Ibid., l. 184.

changed." In Bulgakov's novel about the 1930s, *Master and Margarita*, the devil in the guise of a foreign professor named Woland visits Moscow to punish Soviet literary elites for their materialism—perhaps most of all for their pursuit of luxurious apartments. Muscovites were like everyone else, he said, "only the housing problem has corrupted them."[52] Unsurprisingly, after his real estate machinations, the activist's Komsomol group of five members refused to recommend him to the party. When the unhappy bachelor appealed the decision to a party committee that oversaw the group, the party instructor found that "the refusal was correct."[53] Unable to join the party, he remained in the youth league but was noticeably absent from meetings. His detachment was possibly a sign that the now-impossible party membership had been a major reason for his continuing affiliation with the Komsomol.

Drinking was not always grounds for discipline but could have an impact on youth organizers' professional lives in other ways. A meeting of Komsomol activists in Kestenga district (Karelia) met in December 1938 to elect delegates to the province's youth conference. Each candidate's strengths and faults came under discussion. Comrade B., a twenty-five-year-old activist, had to answer for his drinking. He claimed to be controlling his habit, that he drank 200 grams of vodka with lunch "and no more." As his peers looked askance, he said, "That is my own affair. Who of you doesn't drink? Everyone drinks." A friend jumped to Comrade B.'s defense, saying, "No one has ever seen him drunk." The majority of voices countered that the activist had not understood the lessons of the August 1937 purge plenum, continuing to believe that "drinking is his personal affair." One shouted, "That is the old way of doing things."[54]

The association of the activist's drinking with "the old way" was not an isolated incident. When Kosarev denounced Trotskyist degeneracy, he characterized it not only as an issue of degenerate and sober youth but of old and new people. He contrasted older, amoral activists with good, cultured youth. "We have a number of young, healthy people, brought up by Soviet power," Kosarev said, "people whose heads spin after a single shot when they fall into the wrong company. But there are also those old men [activists] whom you couldn't satisfy with a whole barrel."[55] The Komsomol increasingly was devoted to shaping adolescents into refined young adults. However, its ranks were still filled with older activists unable to join the party. As overage members waited impatiently for their

52. Bulgakov, *Master and Margarita*, 138.
53. RGVA, f. 9, op. 30, d. 178, ll. 69–74, 83–85; d. 248, l. 223.
54. NARK, f. 779, op. 21, d. 33, ll. 19, 27.
55. RGASPI, f. 1m, op. 2, d. 133, ll. 55–56.

turn for political promotion, their presence created a clash of cohorts in activist culture. Comrade B. offended not only with his drinking but by being the old type of Komsomol activist. He had joined in 1931 and developed in an atmosphere where socialization was often dependent on drinking. For activists like him, drinking may not have been a mere private affair but an important means of cementing collegial bonds. Official youth culture, armed with the implied threat of the purge, made drinking bouts no longer acceptable.

This cultural divide extended beyond debauchery. The new people that Kosarev envisioned had little in common with the senior organizers in the youth league. Instead of attending institutions of cultured behavior—clubs, theaters, sporting facilities—he claimed that many older activists had become distant from the ordinary youth. Tying into themes of resentment against established bureaucrats, he described the wives of older activists as *sanovniki*, a term for ranking imperial bureaucrats: "If they deign to make an appearance, then they are grandes dames."[56] Accusations of degeneracy as a political offense merged with charges against senior activists who had failed to provide cultured upbringing in schools and in the daily lives of youth.

Trotskyist degeneracy as a public allegation politicized what was before undesirable but apolitical behavior in private life. It was more than a trumped-up accusation among dozens of others. The charge of degeneracy, especially of excessive drinking, was a key element of how youth understood the purge at the local level. The panic over degeneracy reflected the changing dynamics of work among youth, intensified by the desperate search for enemies during the terror. Supposedly degenerate youth leaders had a real basis in the broader disconnect between the previous generation's culture of Komsomol activism and the idealized youth league of communist upbringing.[57] This conflict was not just a symbolic question of old and new culture but coincided with the actual aging of organizers, the so-called pererostki.

Age Has a Political Meaning

By January 1938, 1,390 activists in the league had been removed as enemies of the people or for their connections with enemies.[58] Fifty of ninety-three members of the Komsomol's Central Committee and twelve of its thirty-five candidate

---

56. Ibid., l. 53.
57. Guillory, "We Shall Refashion Life on Earth!," 24.
58. Grekhov, "Rasprava s rukovodstvom Komsomola," 139.

members were arrested.[59] The expulsions and arrests created a vacuum in the league, and hundreds of new organizers would take up positions in youth committees. At a meeting where he instructed activists on how to fill these positions, Kosarev commented that experience was important to finding cadres: "Age has a political meaning." At the same time, he asserted that older Komsomol members were remaining in their positions too long and preventing the younger generation from gaining experience: "We need to promote new and young people more boldly. . . . We must uncork the stoppage."[60] Kosarev's statement reflected a broad tension in Soviet youth culture. He still believed that older organizers were valuable assets. They had gone through the testing grounds of the Stalin Revolution. Nonetheless, their age had a political meaning, and it was not positive. As pererostki grew as a cohort, their presence in the youth league became more noticeable, more out of place with the current culture of youth activism, and more problematic for Kosarev and other youth leaders.

Since 1933, the Komsomol had steadily aged. In youth organizations, like any age-defined association, the average age of members should stay relatively stable as new cohorts join and the oldest cohorts leave. In a hypothetical organization where no members left and no new members joined, after a year the average age would increase by one year through natural means. Something similar to this hypothetical situation happened in the Komsomol after 1933. Throughout the interwar years, the composition of the youth league's membership was related to the possibility of joining the party. Party recruiting was cyclical. At times it occurred in torrents, but at other times it slowed or even stopped altogether.[61] The periods of reduced party recruiting in the 1920s created cohorts of young communists cut off from political promotion. Even more than previous droughts, though, the 1933 moratorium on party membership made it virtually impossible for veteran young communists to move into the party.[62]

With little hope for political advancement, youth activists retained their presence in Soviet political culture by remaining in the Komsomol. As pererostki grew older, the average age of youth league members rose steadily. From 1933 to 1935, the mean age of members had advanced from twenty years old to more than twenty-one (see Table 4 in appendix). At the Tenth Komsomol Congress in 1936, only 14.5 percent of attendees with voting rights were younger than twenty-three, as opposed to 42.7 percent of the voting delegates at the Ninth Komsomol

59. Artizov et al., *Reabilitatsiia*, 2:639.
60. RGASPI, f. 1m, op. 5, d. 41, l. 26.
61. Rigby, *Communist Party Membership*, 50–51, 110–214.
62. Ibid., 200–214.

Congress in 1931.[63] It is possible that when Komsomol leaders increased the maximum age for new members to twenty-six in 1936, they did so to reflect the reality that many members were well over the previous age limit of twenty-three.

Although some older members may have stayed in the league because they enjoyed the sense of community, the decision to remain had not been a happy one for others. Those who wanted to leave the organization often felt they had nowhere else to go. In October 1934, *Komsomol'skaia pravda* printed a letter from Petr Meleshko, a Komsomol organizer who wrote that he was too old to be in the Komsomol but had too little experience and too few connections to do anything else. To make matters worse, regional party and Komsomol officials had pigeonholed him as an organizer to whom they could assign only youth-related work. He complained that at thirty the life of an activist was "very, very difficult."[64] Meleshko's problem was not only a lack of opportunity but his unwillingness to do the tasks the Komsomol required. A picture accompanying Meleshko's letter was an "old man" in the Komsomol—a caricature of a radical activist as the biblical Moses, carrying the commandments "do not stroll; do not play; do not dance."

The commandments stereotyped the radical activism of the 1920s as austere and joyless versus the wholesome entertainment that emerged as the Komsomol's focus in the 1930s. Moreover, the depiction of the older activist as a biblical Jew implied that pererostki were too set in their ways to reform.[65] In the newspaper's discussion that followed the article in the succeeding weeks, young people wrote "to confirm that those like Petr Meleshko are more than a few." Others wrote that age was not a problem, but that older Komsomol workers needed to be willing to work toward the league's new goals.[66] Now that they were asked to mold cultured Soviet citizens, many radical activists were ready to move out of the Komsomol.

The growing presence of pererostki became a concern for Komsomol and party leaders. At a meeting of Ukrainian Komsomol secretaries in higher education in April 1935, the leader of the Odessa Medical Institute expressed concern about the growing disillusionment among older members. Because they could not join the party, he claimed that the ninety or more members at the

---

63. Fisher, *A Pattern for Soviet Youth*, 412.

64. "'Nedorazumenie istorii,'" *Komsomol'skaia pravda*, October 3, 1934, 3.

65. See Weinberg, "Demonizing Judaism," 149.

66. "'Komsomol'skie starichki' ili starye komsomol'tsy," *Komsomol'skaia pravda*, October 15, 1934, 5.

FIGURE 4.1. Petr Meleshko as an "old man in the Komsomol" carrying his commandments. Illustration by Veniamin Briskin, *Komsomol'skaia pravda*, October 3, 1934.

institute were "literally without prospects."[67] Pressure from below was enough that Nikolai Ezhov, then chair of the Party Control Commission, had been forced to address the issue in a December 1935 speech, calling it "incorrect when some party and Komsomol organizations raise the question of mass admission to the party" for pererostki. For many activists, party membership became the unattainable next step in their development as Soviet citizens and in their political lives.[68]

By 1937, leaders in the Komsomol Central Committee faced a pressing and embarrassing problem. The average member's age had advanced to roughly twenty-two years old (see Table 4 in appendix). For provincial youth leaders, the divide between pererostki and adolescent members had begun to present practical issues for youth work. At the April–May 1937 Komsomol Central Committee plenum, a provincial youth secretary named Legorenko claimed that nearly a third of his organization was older than twenty-six and adolescents were skeptical about joining. "There are some cases where the divide in the organization is from fifteen to thirty-three years old," he said, "no less a divide than between a mother and daughter."[69] Legorenko's hypothetical situation exemplified fears of a cultural divide in the membership. Would young people want to join a Komsomol group if its oldest members were the contemporaries of their parents? Iosif Vaishlia, the head of the Leningrad Komsomol, raised other concerns. In many of the local groups in his province, the entire membership was above the age limit. Vaishlia implied that these cells intimidated or prevented younger members from joining, raising the concern that the groups would simply cease to exist once the pererostki finally left.[70]

When the NKVD arrested Komsomol chiefs in provincial committees, their alleged ability to recruit conspirators among disaffected, aging cadres played a role in accusations against them. In Ukraine Sergei Andreev had led the Komsomol for nearly half a decade and planted deep roots among the republic's youth organizers. After the NKVD arrested Andreev, his deputies fell with him. On August 23, 1937, the NKVD interrogated Denis Shovkovyi, the recently deposed second secretary of Dnepropetrovsk province's youth committee. Under psychological and possible physical pressure, he stated that he had recruited his peers and subordinates for the Trotskyist conspiracy of Andreev and his chief lieutenant, Iakov Geiro, the head of Dnepropetrovsk's Komsomol committee. Shovkovyi

67. TsDAHO, f. 7, op. 1, spr. 1247, ark. 131.
68. "Itogi proverki partiinykh dokumentov," *Pravda*, December 26, 1935, 3.
69. RGASPI, f. 1m, op. 2, d. 130, l. 24.
70. RGASPI, f. 1m, op. 2, d. 126, l. 162.

claimed that he had used pererostki activists' dissatisfaction with their inability to join or advance in the party to convince local youth leaders to join him in the anti-Soviet organization. Among the litany of charges against him, he and his co-conspirators were supposed to ruin Komsomol work by filling the organization with Trotskyist degenerate elements.[71]

Kosarev, too, worried about the aging of the Komsomol and believed that entrenched older organizers in mid-level positions presented a particular problem. But unlike his predecessor Nikolai Chaplin, who had endorsed the removal of pererostki in the late 1920s, Kosarev defended the aging rank and file's place in the league. This position drove a wedge between him and provincial leaders, who sought a more active solution to remove ordinary pererostki. Komsomol leaders met just after the April–May 1937 plenum to discuss upcoming elections in the youth league. There provincial secretaries demanded a definitive policy on older members, but Kosarev refused to issue a resolution. When the Leningrad youth leader, Vaishlia, continued to pursue Kosarev on the matter of pererostki, the general secretary snapped: "Why don't they leave? It is hard to get into the party, and many of them will not be admitted. . . . The Komsomol gives them the opportunity to live a political life, a party life."[72] At a later meeting, when provincial youth leaders hinted at the forced removal of overage members, Kosarev responded: "I have to warn you that the desire to get rid of pererostki exists primarily among the leading activists and secretaries in the districts. But we are not talking about individuals but rather about 876,000 people."[73]

Although Kosarev and provincial youth leaders developed divergent views on rank-and-file pererostki, the entire league leadership viewed them as a demographic problem. Provincial leaders directly oversaw local organizations where two or three generations might be members. In contrast, Kosarev's policy on overage Komsomol members was ambiguous, reflecting the unclear position of pererostki in the league. Pererostki were old for the Komsomol, but they were still young in Soviet political culture. Older Komsomol members represented excellent candidates to become the junior cohort in the party whenever joining would become possible. Moreover, the group of the late 1920s and early 1930s was Kosarev's own cohort. They had been with Kosarev throughout his rise to power in the Komsomol, enacting Stalin's revolution beside him. Now in his mid-thirties, Kosarev himself was technically one of the pererostki. The older

71. HDA SBU, f. 16, op. 1, spr. 111, ark. 2–28.
72. RGASPI, f. 1m, op. 5, d. 38, l. 55.
73. RGASPI, f. 1m, op. 2, d. 147, ll. 32, 33, 36.

cohort was a major pillar of support for Kosarev—both now and perhaps later as it graduated into the party. If pererostki could have a political life outside the Komsomol, they would probably stop participating actively in the league or even leave its ranks.

Pererostki became the disproportionate victims of the Komsomol's purges in 1937–38, although there was no premeditated, centralized campaign against them. Members who were twenty-four and older made up roughly 30 percent of the Komsomol in those years, but they accounted for nearly half of all expulsions (see Table 5 in appendix). The age and experience of pererostki meant that they were likely to hold significant positions and become targets, or to have more ties to adults who became caught up in the mass operations. Age itself was not an official pretext for removal from the Komsomol. Nonetheless, pererostki increasingly found themselves in a mass youth culture dedicated to the goals of a cultured upbringing that they did not recognize as their own. Anxiety over the place of old activists in the new youth culture of socialism made pererostki targets for removal as they struggled to enter the political world of adults.

The search for enemies in the ranks of the Komsomol led to large numbers of expulsions from the league. Of the thousands of organizers removed, it is unknown how many went to forced labor camps or were executed. As in the purge more generally, higher-ranking cadres were more likely to face arrest or execution, and female youth leaders seem to have received more lenient treatment than men.[74] Even among high-ranking Komsomol administrators who were removed, though, not all faced execution or even arrest. A Komsomol Central Committee worker named N. Ia. Il'in was removed from the league in October 1938 for his alleged "bureaucratism and callousness in work." A year later, working as a personnel inspector in the state bureaucracy and having apparently not been arrested, Il'in successfully petitioned the Komsomol's Central Committee to revise its verdict on him.[75]

In addition to central youth leaders, suspicion fell on local activists and the rank and file. In 1937 alone, the NKVD arrested 7,639 Komsomol members—far more than the 1,390 leading activists expelled in the same period. This figure

---

74. On the increased likelihood of elites to be arrested, see Fitzpatrick, "The Impact of the Great Purges on Soviet Elites," in *Stalinist Terror*, ed. Getty and Manning, 247–60.

75. RGASPI, f. 1m, op. 3, d. 223, ll. 1, 7–8.

surely encompassed ordinary members.[76] In the second half of 1937, nearly a hundred thousand young people of some four million members were expelled from the Komsomol. In the previous six months, expulsions were just thirty-five thousand. The majority of youth expelled was accused of being hostile elements or of maintaining connections with such people. An arrested relative, co-worker, or friend was likely to draw the scrutiny of the Komsomol, or even arrest by the NKVD. The second largest group of expellees, however, was accused of degeneracy, and this category grew considerably after the August 1937 purge plenum (see Table 6 in appendix). How many non-Komsomol youth were arrested during the terror is impossible to learn. The best estimate may come from the size of different age groups among Gulag prisoners after the terror. Of the nearly 1.7 million labor camp prisoners in 1940, people aged twenty-five to thirty made up roughly 35 percent of the population—about three times their proportion in society. Youth between the ages of nineteen and twenty-four were almost 10 percent, a proportion slightly less than in the population at large. Among adolescents, some 155,506 spent time in NKVD labor colonies during the period from 1935 to 1940.[77]

The unprecedented wave of arrests and executions had an effect on society. When the police arrested hooligans as hostile elements and fallen Komsomol leaders as Trotskyist degenerates, the public treatment of repression demonstrated what might happen to those who strayed too far from official norms of social behavior. The Stalinist moral panic had a message that was not powerful because it was novel but because it transformed disorderly behavior into political deviancy opposed to the new norms of socialist youth culture. While youth organizers at the local level anxiously searched for enemies, they also looked to save youth on the path from drunkenness to degeneracy. Many activists faced arrest and execution, and disorderly behavior carried increasingly harsh penalties. However, the vast majority of youth seem to have watched during the terror, experiencing it as a moment of fear and disciplining.

In the feverish search for enemies in 1937, Komsomol organizers had begun to violate key dictates of their mission to shape the young generation. Instead of disciplining youth into cultured citizens, they were excising large numbers of members from the league's ranks. During the last months of 1937, Komsomol committees expelled members at a rate that had been matched only during the massive postcollectivization membership purge in 1932–33 (see Table 7 in

---

76. Danilov, Manning, and Viola, *Tragediia sovetskoi derevni*, 5, pt. 2:159 (citing TsA FSB RF, f. 3, op. 5, d. 572, ll. 36–43, 46–48, 55, 69).

77. Getty, Rittersporn, and Zemskov, "Victims of the Soviet Penal System," 1025–26.

appendix). The terror had broken the bonds between party members, creating an insurmountable wall of fear that prevented party committees from admitting pererostki, even after the suspension on new party admissions ended. While Komsomol and party leaders continued to call for merciless repression of supposed enemies, at the beginning of 1938 they asserted that mistakes were being made in the expulsion of ordinary members. The dilemma of distinguishing the enemy from wayward youth confronted Komsomol leaders as they embarked on a program of mass rehabilitation in 1938.

THE REHABILITATION OF YOUNG COMMUNISTS

At the end of 1937, reports of mass, uncontrolled expulsions from the ranks of the party reached the country's leaders. At the lower levels of the party and Komsomol, organizers and rank-and-file members were denouncing anyone who might conceivably be unmasked as an enemy later, fearing that they would otherwise be accused of collaboration in anti-Soviet conspiracies. Suspicion was tearing Soviet political society apart. The party's Central Committee convened a meeting in January 1938 where its leaders upbraided provincial chiefs and local organizers for their "mistakes" of hypervigilance in the purge.[1] Nonetheless, these same leaders unremittingly called for vigilance against enemies and, in secret, NKVD operatives continued the mass operations to arrest or execute hundreds of thousands of supposed enemies.[2] What distinguished masked infiltrators from valuable cadres? And after the purge had cast doubt on the legitimacy of so many communists, how would the party repair itself?

The Komsomol played a crucial role in the party's recovery from the terror. The Great Purge had not only discredited individuals but had undermined the system of party membership, including the recruiting of youth from the Komsomol into the party. The moratorium on party membership ended at the close of 1936, and youth leaders had tried to push pererostki from the league into the

1. Khlevniuk, Politbiuro, 225–27.
2. Getty and Naumov, Road to Terror, 520–22; Shearer, Policing Stalin's Socialism, 367.

party. In an atmosphere of mistrust, though, few young communists could join the party. Only in 1938, as political leaders attempted partially to reverse the purge, could the party and Komsomol begin to rebuild Soviet political culture. The admission of mistakes in the campaign of expulsions was a way of stopping the bleeding, and the Komsomol offered a transfusion of new party members.

The party was not the only organization that had made so-called mistakes. While Komsomol leaders attempted to refill the party with new members, they also began the process of rehabilitating the league's own membership. As in the party, youth leaders asserted that the atmosphere of fear had encouraged so-called overinsuring—preemptive denunciations of fundamentally good young communists. In the spring of 1938, Komsomol organizers encouraged youth to appeal their expulsions and pressured activists to show leniency toward appellants. At the core of the appeals campaign was an understanding of youth as political minors. Young communists could not be held to the same standards as adult party members but instead needed the Komsomol's discipline to become exemplary Soviet citizens.

As the purge wound down, Komsomol leaders put a disproportionate emphasis on forgiveness for its members. Nonetheless, they still asserted that enemies lurked—especially at the highest levels of the youth organization. The final act of the purge in the Komsomol spelled the end not only of the Great Terror but of Aleksandr Kosarev's tenure as youth leader. His arrest and execution marked the close of an era in the Komsomol, when the league finished its turn from radical activism to communist upbringing.

Party Recruiting of Youth, 1937

In the autumn of 1936, party Central Committee Secretary Andrei Zhdanov announced that on November 1, party membership would reopen for the first time since January 1933. In previous recruiting phases of the 1920s and 1930s, new party members had come in rapid waves of hundreds of thousands from the ranks of social groups party leaders considered reliable—especially the urban proletariat.[3] After Zhdanov's announcement, though, the reliability of new members was not based primarily on their worker backgrounds. For the first generation that had grown up under Soviet power, loyalty often depended on affiliation with the Komsomol. Pererostki, the long-serving group of league members, would finally have the opportunity to graduate into the party.

---

3. Rigby, *Communist Party Membership*, 110–31.

Admission to the party was a multistep process. All people younger than twenty had to receive a recommendation through their district youth organization to join. Even league members older than twenty effectively had to receive this recommendation. The party's regulations from 1934 demanded as many as five recommendations from existing party members, but the district Komsomol's reference could count as two. When new members joined the party, they entered as candidates and later could petition for promotion to full members. Komsomol organizers were eager to join. One example was an up-and-coming organizer named Shafarenko, the head of the Komsomol in the TsDKA, the Red Army's cultural outreach arm. At twenty-four years old, he applied for his Komsomol group's recommendation for candidate party membership immediately after the moratorium ended. By April 1937, he was already gathering recommendations for full membership in the party. For those already connected to party circles like Shafarenko, joining the party as a candidate and soon a full member had become a possibility.[4]

An important difference distinguished this new phase of party recruiting from previous campaigns, though. As hundreds of thousands of pererostki waited to join the party, the caustic atmosphere of the Great Purge slowed recruiting to a snail's pace. In the Komsomol and the party, the removal of supposed political enemies was proving messier than the regime had intended, creating panic among many party members. When they failed to unmask an enemy, party members often found themselves under suspicion for hiding hostile elements. After the Komsomol's 1937 purge, Kosarev had to castigate himself for his failure to recognize his former colleagues as enemies. From the upper reaches of political society to ordinary factory committees, party members denounced their peers preemptively as a defensive tactic meant to show their own vigilance.[5] The same impetus to denounce colleagues, friends, and sometimes even family broke down existing patronage links and prevented the construction of new political ties. For those youth whose connections to party members were not strong, the purge placed intractable obstacles in the way of political advancement.

When many Komsomol members asked for recommendations, fear of aiding a potential enemy made party members question the benefit of vouching for colleagues and acquaintances. For this reason, an activist in the Commissariat of Defense named Voronov found his candidacy blocked. He arrived in an agitated state at a large meeting of the Komsomol in the commissariat in June 1937. Toward the end of the meeting, Voronov demanded the floor for an impromptu

---

4. RGVA, f. 9, op. 30, d. 80, l. 70.
5. Goldman, *Terror and Democracy*, 205.

speech. Although the meeting agenda had no relationship to party member-ship, he intentionally chose the venue so that his grievance would appear on the record. Voronov, an engineer in the Red Army's General Staff, was an excellent candidate for party membership. He was young, party-loyal, and educated. He also knew a party member—a longtime friend, schoolmate, and fellow engineer at the General Staff. They not only shared an office but an apartment as room-mates. When Voronov brought up the recommendation, his comrade demurred, "Well, you see, I don't really know you." Members of the presidium interjected, "That's dangerous overinsuring." Voronov agreed that his friend was "afraid that if something happens with me, he'll have to answer."[6] The absurd conflict may have been as personal as it was political. Or perhaps Voronov's friend did know something damaging but thought it best not to raise the issue. The presidium's reaction and Voronov's urgency, however, suggest that trust was becoming a broader problem during the purge, stopping some Komsomol members from making or using connections to join the party.

The problem of trust went both ways. Some Komsomol members refused party membership based on their own apprehensions about connecting themselves with potential enemies. At a November 1937 meeting of provincial organizers with Komsomol leaders in Moscow, L. V. Kurkin from Ivanovo discussed the rea-sons that fewer members were joining the Communist Party than the leadership desired. Some communists were refusing to give recommendations, but Komso-mol members were also refusing to take them, opting to "wait a little." Kosarev was taken aback and asked why they had refused. Kurkin explained that the young people feared that "the recommender will turn out to be an enemy of the people." Several Komsomol members from Kurkin's province had joined the party only to have their recommender be unmasked. Kurkin asserted that these cases had cre-ated a "serious problem" and "an absolutely incorrect, dangerous mood."[7]

Current and potential party members were right to worry. When party mem-bers gave recommendations and Komsomol members received them, they cre-ated a bond that had rewards and hazards. The experience of Stalinist repression taught Soviet citizens that personal and professional connections were fodder for censure and arrest. The party and Komsomol demanded members denounce friends and family who were arrested.[8] In the NKVD, operatives used the fam-ily method to fill quotas for arrests in the secret mass operations, transform-ing existing interpersonal links into supposed anti-Soviet conspiracies. If one

---

6. RGVA, f. 9, op. 30, d. 82, ll. 161–62.

7. RGASPI, f. 1m, op. 5, d. 50, l. 55.

8. Goldman, *Inventing the Enemy*.

member of a work collective faced arrest, it cast doubt on their whole web of social interactions. It was just as easy for NKVD investigators to imagine that enemies of the people had undermined the party by filling its ranks with more enemies.[9] For many it was less risky not to recommend or join than to make a connection with a potential enemy during the terror.

By mid-1937, it had become clear to Komsomol leaders that few members were entering the party. Kosarev wrote a resolution in June blaming lower-level organizations for not recommending members, especially pererostki. He demanded that 100,000 Komsomol members enter the party by the beginning of 1938.[10] The head of Gorkii province's youth organization complained in August 1937 that just seventy Komsomol members had joined the party from his province and nearly all were leading members of district committees rather than from the rank and file.[11] Exhortations to increase the number of members joining the party were partially successful, and the amount of applicants for recommendations increased in the second half of the year. Local youth committees seldom turned down recommendation requests for would-be party candidates, most of whom were approaching or past the limits of Komsomol age.[12] Some district youth committees, in the rush to recommend as many youth as possible, even gave support to young people who did not have the requisite number of party references.[13] Despite these efforts, when the Komsomol Central Committee collected data on members who had entered the party in late 1937, the results were still unsatisfactory. Just 46,207 members were recommended. Of those, the party had admitted only 13,051 by November 1937.[14] The Great Purge was creating an environment of wild and indiscriminate repression that affected not only current members but also potential recruits. Increasingly, party and youth leaders became convinced that the purge in political organs had to be reined in.

Correcting "Mistakes"

Amid the corrosive environment of Soviet political society in the fall of 1937, Kosarev and two other youth leaders left Moscow for a tour of youth groups in

---

9. On the NKVD's use of political connections in arrests, see Vatlin, *Agents of Terror*, 39–46. On the broader idea of kinship, see Alexopoulos, "Stalin and the Politics of Kinship."

10. RGASPI, f. 1m, op. 23, d. 1211, ll. 42–43.

11. RGASPI, f. 1m, op. 5, d. 41, l. 33.

12. RGVA, f. 9, op. 30, d. 80.

13. RGASPI, f. 1m, op. 23, d. 1285, ll. 1–2.

14. RGASPI, f. 1m, op. 23, d. 1215, l. 72.

the Donbas and eastern Ukraine. One companion, who later recorded his memories of the trip, described Kosarev's mood as dour after the August 1937 purge
plenum. When they arrived in Donetsk, the province's youth leader took Kosarev
aside and confessed that he feared imminent arrest. As the general secretary vis-
ited youth groups at the mines near Donetsk, he noticed that an extraordinary
number of members were facing expulsion from the league. Arriving a few days
later in Kharkov, a man waited for Kosarev in the lobby of the hotel and followed
him around the city. As the visitors found out, the Kharkov provincial party committee sent the man to guard, or perhaps watch, Kosarev. Enraged, Kosarev dismissed the bodyguard, demanding that he tell the province's leaders that their
behavior was outrageous.[15]

The Moscow group's main task in Kharkov was to attend the city's Komsomol
congress. When they arrived at the meeting, Kosarev sensed that something was
amiss as organizers gave their subdued speeches. An hour into the conference,
an NKVD officer took the floor to announce the arrest of a prominent local
party leader and demanded the expulsion of Kharkov province's current youth
leader, Aleksandra Dunasheva, a former colleague of the arrestee. Kosarev called
for the conference to take an impromptu break and consulted with local party
leaders about Dunasheva's political loyalties. Concluding that Dunasheva was
no enemy, he chastised the delegates, "Look around at what is happening here.
You are afraid to look one another in the eye." Alarmed by what he had seen, he
phoned Moscow to arrange a meeting of provincial youth secretaries in charge
of expulsions and appeals.[16]

In December 1937, the heads of a dozen or more provincial appeals commissions arrived in Moscow to report on expulsions from the Komsomol in their
regions. From Leningrad, an appeals commissioner named Konopleva described
a confused and fear-ridden situation. Members received mixed signals from local
organizers: "They tell youth to be open, honest, and act in good faith, and then
they expel them all the same." District leaders should have overturned unmer-
ited expulsions, but Konopleva claimed that they were hopelessly overstretched.
Organizers were holding meetings from "morning until night," where they saw
seventy to ninety supplicants per session. It was no wonder that they could not
give appellants a fair hearing.[17]

Despite Kosarev's own experiences in Ukraine, the reports surprised him and
his colleagues. He had trouble believing that a youth committee in Stalingrad

15. Sorokin, "Nezabyvaemoe vremia," in *Aleksandr Kosarev*, ed. Mikhailova, 59, 60.
16. Ibid., 60–62.
17. RGASPI, f. 1m, op 5, d. 53, ll. 32, 35.

had expelled a young person because his grandmother, who died in 1906, had been a member of the gentry. In spite of Kosarev's apparent rejection of needless expulsions, some of the provincial appeals commissioners continued to assert the necessity for extraordinary vigilance. The representative from Smolensk boasted about his commission's strong ties with the NKVD and how this helped him catch enemies. Kosarev said the provincial organizer was too intent on catching enemies: "You have your functions and the NKVD has its own." Moderating himself, he added, "You need to keep up the connection with them."[18]

Far from discouraging all expulsions, Kosarev encouraged an increase in repression in some regions. As Kosarev must have known, the NKVD was engaged in several mass operations against national groups. These were primarily diasporas like Germans and Poles, who party leaders feared would turn against Soviet power in a war with their national homelands. Ukraine and Belorussia had particularly large populations of these groups, and Kosarev was insistent on the need for vigilance among youth there. After the Ukrainian appeals commissioner stated that his commission was not doing enough to encourage appeals, Kosarev broke in, "I don't like your speech." The Ukrainian Komsomol organization was "infested with various bastards" whom Ukraine's youth leaders needed to expel before they could think about appeals.[19] At a meeting the previous month, Belorussia's Komsomol leader had claimed that his organization was filled with "Polish contrabandists." In response, Kosarev advised, "Nothing terrible will happen if one or two people are temporarily removed incorrectly."[20]

Although the NKVD's campaign of repression continued in full force, the tide was turning against hypervigilance in the party and Komsomol at the end of 1937. After the January 1938 party plenum announced that mistakes had occurred in the expulsion of party members, Kosarev petitioned Stalin to hold a similar plenum in the Komsomol, convened a month later on February 19. The Komsomol's secretary in charge of appeals, Valentina Pikina, concluded in her report on expulsions that the number of accused enemies in the league was unacceptable, "a slander on a large portion of youth." She framed the problem of expulsion not only as a question of equity and truth but also as a real problem for Soviet labor. In cases where young communists were not arrested, their expulsion led to dismissal from work, even for those whose job was outside the youth organization. Many had been out of work for several months at this time. With nearly 100,000 youth expelled from the youth organization in the past

---

18. Ibid., ll. 44, 50, 94.
19. Ibid., ll. 128–29.
20. RGASPI, f. 1m, op 5, d. 50, ll. 113–15.

half-year, the number of young, well-educated workers who were unemployable was considerable.[21]

Much of Pikina's speech and the subsequent commentaries of provincial youth leaders cataloged unjust and strange expulsions. One youth group expelled a young man whose grandfather had supposedly owned serfs in 1868 (apparently the committee was unaware that serfdom had already been abolished by that year), but on investigation it turned out that the grandfather had himself been a serf. Other cases could have come straight from the pages of the Soviet satire journal *Krokodil*. In Belorussia, a district youth committee expelled a deaf young man because, in response to accusations against him, "he could not make himself clear and said nothing in his defense."[22] Almost all the examples involved bureaucratic bungling of information, suggesting that youth leaders believed the accusations themselves were plausible grounds for expulsion. Even as the momentum of the terror seemed to be reversing, provincial leaders feared forgiving a real offense and revealing themselves as enemies. Although Pikina also did not give many examples of pardonable offenses, she urged provincial leaders to take the appeals process seriously. According to her data, expelled Komsomol members had appealed in just a third of all eligible cases—far too few in her opinion.[23]

At the local level, the party and Komsomol's admission of mistakes triggered a flood of appeals and reinstatements. After the party's January plenum, Smolensk's provincial youth committee reinstated the overwhelming majority of young communists who appealed for readmission to the youth organization. According to the documents in the Smolensk Archive, the province's appeals commission reversed all but 4 expulsions of the 204 appeals it received. The four cases where Smolensk's committee supported the decision to expel all involved young people whose parents were under arrest as enemies of the people. A fifth youth, whose appeal the commission rejected the first time, later appealed successfully after her father was released from NKVD custody.

Despite the large percentage of members who returned to the Komsomol, youth organizers did not believe they were correcting purposeless expulsions. The mistake of lower-level committees was in the degree of punishment but not in identifying the need for disciplinary action. A representative case involved G. I. Novinov, a nineteen-year-old administrator at a school in Roslavl district of Smolensk province. In 1937, Novinov's fellow young communists charged him with being the child of kulaks and having gone on drinking binges. These factors

21. RGASPI, f. 1m, op. 2, d. 136, l. 22.
22. Ibid., ll. 38, 190.
23. Ibid., ll. 24, 25–26, 27–28, 35, 42.

had supposedly led him to undermine the work of the school, and his peers expelled him from their group. The district level organization then heard his case and confirmed the expulsion. Novinov applied for reinstatement with the Smolensk province Komsomol committee in 1938. Provincial youth leaders still found that Novinov's offenses were real and damning to his character. Nonetheless, they reinstated him—but with conditions. Giving him a public reprimand, they demanded he atone for his kulak background and his drinking by becoming an ideal young citizen. Smolensk youth organizers did not forgive Novinov, because he had truly transgressed, in their minds. However, they believed it was important to keep him within the bounds of Soviet political culture where they could reform him.[24]

Reinstatement in the Komsomol mirrored the appeals process in the party. According to an editorial in *Pravda*, the party had received 53,700 appeals at various levels by the time of the January 1938 plenum on mistakes and another 101,233 appeals between that meeting and June 1. Of the total, party committees had reviewed 85,273 cases and readmitted 54 percent of the appealing members.[25] The figures of total appeals for the party were high—improbably high. They were greater than Georgii Malenkov's claim of 100,000 party members expelled for all of 1937.[26] If both the *Pravda* article and Malenkov's statistics were accurate, at least some of the appellants must have petitioned repeatedly. In a case cited in *Pravda*, a former party member named A. Kaminskii attempted to have his case heard for eight months. He sent five petitions to different investigators before he got a hearing with the city's party committee. It is likely that each petition counted as a separate appeal and perhaps that all five were counted as successful appeals.[27] Even accepting the unlikely assertion that all the appeals and readmissions were unique, the number of reinstatements was only 46 percent of the expulsions from the party in 1937.[28]

Compared to the party, chances for readmission to the Komsomol in 1938 were favorable. A very large number of members took advantage of the opportunity

---

24. Smolensk Archive, WKP 416, 34–198.

25. "Po-bol'shevistski vypolnit' postanovlenie ianvarskogo Plenuma TsK VKP(b)," *Pravda*, August 7, 1938, 1.

26. Artizov, *Reabilitatsiia*, 2:623.

27. I. Riabov, "O beznakazannykh klevetnikakh i bespechnykh rukovoditeliakh," *Pravda*, March 29, 1938, 2.

28. Party reinstatement also occurred in the Red Army's political administration. In 1939, Lev Mekhlis, the head of the Red Army's political administration, called for half of all those officers expelled by party commissions to be reinstated. In the end, 30 percent of those army officers discharged in 1937–38 were reinstated. A smaller number of dismissed air force officers returned by the end of 1939, just 16 percent. Reese, *Stalin's Reluctant Soldiers*, 143, 146.

to appeal their expulsions. According to a report with incomplete data (missing figures from several significant provinces, including Moscow), the number of appeals to province-level youth committees in 1938 was 66,600. Of the 54,500 appeals that committees had processed at the time the report was compiled, in 42,200 cases (77 percent) the decision was overturned and the appellant was let back into the youth league.[29] Appellants probably attempted reinstatement within a year of expulsion, meaning that the pool of young people who might appeal in 1938 was about the same as the number of those expelled in 1937, roughly 130,000. Assuming the success rate was the same for those cases that had not yet been opened, appeals at the provincial level in these territories alone reversed about 40 percent of all expulsions from 1937. The figure may not have included those youth who appealed at the district level successfully and did not include the 4,770 who appealed directly to the Komsomol Central Committee. Although the available data will never give a completely accurate total of all expulsions and reinstatements, the number of reversals was probably half or more of the total number of youth expelled in 1937.

Far from all young communists who failed to appeal their expulsions were arrested. NKVD reports calculated that police arrested 15,088 former Komsomol members from January 1936 to July 1938, roughly 6 percent of those expelled in the same period.[30] Many former Komsomol members did not rehabilitate themselves politically but nonetheless remained free. They were too old, too apathetic, or too disillusioned to return to the league. Others may have been frightened of appealing and exposing themselves again to scrutiny. They had remained free even though they lost their membership in the Komsomol. Was regaining it worth potential arrest?

Despite this justifiable fear, young communists enjoyed a remarkable, even puzzling level of security from arrest. Youth outside the Komsomol were not spared repression. People between the ages of eighteen and thirty-five made up a proportion of Gulag prisoners at least as large as their proportion in the population at large. Indeed, the older half of that group was overrepresented in the Soviet penal system.[31] NKVD investigators sprinted to fulfill quotas for arrests in the mass operations, hunting for victims wherever possible. They used torture, threats, and deception to pad the arrest rolls. Investigators even compiled lists

29. RGASPI, f. 1m, op. 23, d. 1385, l. 76, 100.

30. Danilov, Manning, and Viola, *Tragediia sovetskoi derevni*, 5, pt. 2:159 (citing TsA FSB RF, f. 3, op. 5, d. 572, ll. 36–43, 46–48, 55, 69).

31. Getty, Ritterporn, and Zemskov, "Victims of the Soviet Penal System," 1025. It seems possible that the large group of under-thirty adults in the Gulag coincided with the cohort of collectivization. Those dekulakized peasants young enough to survive and even escape exile were prime targets for arrest in the mass operations.

of factory workers with foreign-sounding names, whom they then arrested as spies.[32] In effect, local Komsomol committees who expelled members had begun the investigatory process for the police. Each expulsion rested on an accusation that could have been incorporated into a broader conspiracy. Among former party members, the NKVD arrested 99,188 people from January 1936 to July 1938, a number almost as large as the total number of expulsions from the party in 1937.[33] In contrast, 94 percent of Komsomol members expelled from 1936 to 1938 were not arrested. Why did NKVD officers avoid arresting these politically compromised young communists?

There are only clues to why the NKVD arrested comparatively few Komsomol members. In cases where NKVD operatives had no leads on league members, they may not have thought to seek them out as potential enemies. In Tomsk territory, the NKVD chief, I. V. Ovchinnikov, learned about the removal of the city's Komsomol leader, R. Ia. Springis, only from an article in the local newspaper. Ovchinnikov was embarrassed: "Just think about the situation this put me and the city's NKVD in. The territory's newspaper finds out that Springis is an enemy of the people, he is in charge of 7,000 Komsomol members, and the city NKVD has no materials on him."[34] Soon after, Ovchinnikov's NKVD connected unmasked party administrators to Springis, who had allegedly created a youth terrorist group with at least five other Komsomol members. Springis was executed as an enemy of the people.[35] Although the NKVD caught this supposed enemy after his expulsion from the Komsomol, the lack of preemptive surveillance of the league—even of local leaders—suggests that NKVD operatives may not have been particularly vigilant in monitoring ordinary members. After all, it was alleged kulaks, hostile nationalities, and other anti-Soviet elements that were the targets of the mass operations, not youth.[36]

For rank-and-file members, the newness of their political career also provided protection. Just as the lack of strong party connections made it difficult for youth league members to join the party, their immature social and political connections may have insulated them from repression. One of the areas where Komsomol members sometimes had strong ties was in the NKVD, which relied on the league

32. Vatlin, *Agents of Terror*, 46–49.

33. Danilov, Manning, and Viola, *Tragediia sovetskoi derevni*, 5, pt. 2:159 (citing TsA FSB RF, f. 3, op. 5, d. 572, ll. 36–43, 46–48, 55, 69).

34. Cited in Tepliakov, *Mashina terrora*, 449.

35. Arkhiv UFSB Tomskoi oblasti, d. p-1239, t. 3, ll. 456–60. (Cited in Iakov Krotov, "1936–1937 gg.: Konveier NKVD. Iz khroniki 'bol'shogo terrora' na Tomskoi zemle," available at http://krotov.info/libr_min/11_k/on/veyer_8.htm.)

36. Vatlin, *Agents of Terror*, 85–93.

to mobilize youth to become agents.[37] This connection had contradictory effects. Mikhail Rotfort's acquaintance, a Komsomol worker turned NKVD officer, did not spare his former youth league peers. Indeed, he may have targeted them.[38] At the upper reaches of the Komsomol and party, though, Kosarev had personal connections to Nikolai Ezhov and his well-connected wife, Evgeniia. When the future NKVD commissar took the lead in the inquiry into Sergei Kirov's assassination in 1934–35, Kosarev joined the investigation in Leningrad. The Komsomol chief attended the Ezhovs' lavish parties alongside personages like the *Pravda* correspondent Mikhail Kol'tsov and the writer Isaac Babel.[39] It is possible that through his connections, Kosarev himself may have stopped the arrest of Komsomol members, as his colleagues claimed during the Khrushchev period.[40]

The central reason that youth were not arrested, though, seems to be that party leaders genuinely hoped to discipline politically active youth, molding them for a life as good Soviet citizens. At the April–May 1937 Komsomol plenum, Party Secretary Andrei Andreev chastised the league's leaders for expelling too many ordinary young people instead of hunting true enemies. "Things are, I think, very bad with expulsions," he said, urging the use of lesser punishments to make youth work to redeem themselves.[41]

NKVD reports to the party after 1938 listed some arrestees as Komsomol members but did not specifically target politically active young people. "Youth cases" had been a category for arrest until the beginning of 1937. For example, Ukrainian NKVD agents in 1936 reported that 4 of 141 multiperson investigations were youth cases.[42] By the start of 1938, though, NKVD investigations of young people rarely centered on the Komsomol itself. Instead, arrests of youth coincided with fears about social disorder or targeted suspect groups in the mass operations, such as diaspora nationalities. In Ukraine, police reported on youth conspiracies of broader Ukrainian or Polish nationalist organizations. For instance, NKVD operatives in July 1938 arrested an alleged group of Ukrainian nationalists called the Young Generation. Supposedly existing in all major Ukrainian cities, the group's leaders were accused of recruiting Komsomol members to conduct terrorist acts on behalf of the Ukrainian national cause.[43]

---

37. See, for example, orders for a Komsomol mobilization to the NKVD in RGASPI, f. 1m, op. 3, d. 208, ll. 5, 53.

38. Rotfort, *Kolyma—krugi ada*, 8–9, 18.

39. Jansen and Petrov, *Stalin's Loyal Executioner*, 185.

40. See essays in Mikhailova, *Aleksandr Kosarev*.

41. RGASPI, f. 73, op. 2, d. 40, ll. 32–34.

42. HDA SBU, f. 16, op. 1, spr. 91, ark. 48.

43. HDA SBU, f. 16, op. 1, spr. 297, ark. 69–76, 100–107.

The NKVD became less active in seeking enemies among young radicals. An illustrative case is that of a group called the New SRs, arrested in July 1938 in Chuguevskii district of Kharkov province. The group, named after the socialist party that had enjoyed considerable popularity before and during the revolution, was supposed to have read Thomas More's *Utopia* and wrote stories with anti-Soviet morals. Tellingly, though, NKVD officers had not initiated the investigation of the group. Instead, one of its members appeared at the doors of the local police, ready to denounce his peers.[44] NKVD officers would not hesitate to arrest Komsomol members if they received evidence that youth belonged to supposed counterrevolutionary organizations or to other targeted groups. It seems that politically active youth were not a specific object of suspicion as they had been in the past, however.

The relative indulgence youth activists enjoyed during the Great Terror reflected a shift in young people's place in Soviet political culture. By the late 1930s, youth had become political minors. Although some may have made mistakes, Komsomol activists made even worse mistakes by banishing misguided members rather than teaching them the wrong of their ways. For this reason, Komsomol leaders in 1938 directed provincial youth leaders to review all expulsions they received in the future.[45] This order undoubtedly contributed to the subsequent fall in expulsions from the league. At the same time, it also signified that ordinary young communists were politically immature. The placement of the final responsibility for expulsions with provincial youth leaders—who were effectively young party officials—decreased the agency of ordinary members and lower-level activists to supervise their own members. In contrast to young communists, the purge was a starker affair for party members. While a handful of articles in *Pravda* in 1939 spoke of the party's role in cultivating members through discipline, most suggested that party members either deserved to be in the party or they did not.[46] For Komsomol youth, there was a greater gray area of miscreant behavior that league leaders and activists believed could be corrected.

The acknowledgment of mistakes in the party and Komsomol not only resulted in large quantities of appeals but allowed increased numbers of young

---

44. HDA SBU, f. 16, op. 1, spr. 275, ark. 242–44, 254–56.

45. "Postanovlenie V plenuma TsK VLKSM ob oshibkakh, dopushchennykh komsomol'skimi organizatsiiami pri iskliuchenii iz Komsomola, o formal'no-biurokraticheskom otnoshenii k apelliatsiiam iskliuchennykh iz VLKSM i o merakh po ustraneniiu etikh nedostatkov," *Izvestiia TsK Komsomola*, no. 6 (1938): 7–12.

46. See, for example, "O partiinykh vzyskaniiakh i poriadke iskliucheniia iz partii," *Pravda*, February 13, 1939, 3; "O partiinykh vzyskaniiakh i 'nepolnotsennykh' kommunistakh," *Pravda*, March 9, 1939, 5.

people to join the party. After the January 1938 party plenum, admissions of new members to the party from the Komsomol took off. Youth committees recommended members roughly twice as fast after the plenum as before. After March 1938, party committees accepted more than half of the applicants from the Komsomol, while before they had accepted around 30 percent. From February to September 1938, the party admitted more than 130,000 youth as candidates or full members (see Table 8 in appendix). In spite of the increase in party admissions, Kosarev called even this figure lackluster and continued to decry the failure of local organizations to shepherd young communists into the party. Nonetheless, a large number of older Komsomol members had graduated into the ranks of the party in 1938 and would continue to do so. From 1937 to 1941, roughly two-thirds of party recruiting came directly from the Komsomol, accounting for some 1,200,000 new members and candidates.[47]

These new admissions seem to have come disproportionately from the ranks of pererostki. While their age and association with the old style of radical activism had made them unwanted in the Komsomol, their combination of youth and political loyalty made them desirable as new party members. Party admissions effectively resolved the problem of their cohort in the Komsomol. As pererostki joined the party, they left the Komsomol by choice or necessity. The Eighteenth Party Congress in 1939 prohibited party members and candidates from being in the league unless they held elected activist positions. As pererostki departed, they declined as a proportion of the Komsomol. From January 1938 to January 1939, the average age of members fell by roughly a year, from roughly twenty-two to twenty-one (see Table 4 in appendix). The proportion of members twenty-six or older declined from 16 percent in January 1938 to 10 percent in January 1940.[48] But most telling was that Komsomol leaders ceased to fret over or even mention pererostki. One of the last references to pererostki was in an article in April 1939 announcing the reversal of the policy giving preference to old Komsomol activists over more junior members for party recommendations.[49]

Public attempts to end the cannibalizing recriminations in the party reopened the road to Soviet political culture. Aleksandr Kosarev's cohort was leaving the

---

47. Apresian and Sulemov, "Komsomol kak rezerv partii," in *Pozyvnye istorii*, 1:126, 127, 129. A directive in the Red Army demanded that 80 percent of party recruits come from the Komsomol. Kariaeva and Smorigo, *Partiino-politicheskaia rabota v Krasnoi Armii. Dokumenty*, 446.

48. RGASPI, f. 1m, op. 126, d. 344, ll. 14, 16, 17; d. 372, ll. 40–41.

49. "Voprosy i otvety," *Izvestiia TsK Komsomola*, no. 9 (1939): 24–26. An annual report from the youth committee of Lopasne district (Moscow province) in January 1939 criticized itself for promoting only pererostki: "There was an improper understanding that we needed to recruit pererostki in the Komsomol for the party and this could not but reflect on [our poor] work." OKhDOPIM, f. 648p, op. 1, d. 14, l. 52.

Komsomol and by the summer of 1938, it seemed that the youth leader himself had successfully navigated the contradictory perils of excessive vigilance and political negligence. However, the final act of the Great Terror in the Komsomol would be among the most violent, bringing the end of Kosarev's long reign as general secretary.

Fall of the House of Kosarev

On November 9, 1938, Kosarev wrote an anxious letter to Stalin: "Comrade Stalin! I beg an audience with you to discuss Komsomol issues."[50] Kosarev, in his ninth year as Komsomol chief, did not get his audience. He was correct to worry, although in public he seemed to be at the height of his authority. In October 1938, the Komsomol had commemorated the twentieth anniversary of its founding, and at the celebratory parade, Kosarev gave the main speech to roaring applause. He was a great friend of star athletes and the patron—or more—of up-and-coming movie starlets like Valentina Serova.[51] By the end of the year, though, he and dozens of other youth leaders found themselves deposed and arrested.

The seeds of Kosarev's arrest were planted more than a year before his purge in November 1938. In July 1937, as large numbers of his subordinates in the Komsomol were arrested, Kosarev attempted to gain an audience with Stalin about the arrests, only to reach the head of the Party Special Section, Aleksandr Poskrebyshev. Stalin's chief assistant rebuffed Kosarev, "If you are needed, he will call you."[52] Kosarev was not blameless, though. After the initial arrests, Kosarev sent Ezhov and Stalin a list of eleven supposed enemies among high-ranking Komsomol central and provincial workers on July 17.[53] Apparently the list was too short. Twenty-five years later, Pikina recalled that Stalin summoned the three remaining secretaries and the newly appointed Osoaviakhim head, Pavel Gorshenin, to discuss the search for enemies on July 21. Kosarev claimed that he had no materials to show that other youth leaders were enemies of the people. Stalin countered that Kosarev was simply unwilling to denounce underlings and insisted that the Komsomol leadership unmask more enemies. Pikina described Kosarev's bleak reaction to the meeting: "He told us that he could hardly understand how such a number of enemies had suddenly appeared in our country."[54] Nonetheless,

---

50. RGASPI, f. 558, op. 11, d. 756, l. 120.
51. Edelman, *Spartak Moscow*, 129; Figes, *Whisperers*, 376.
52. Trushchenko, *Kosarev*, 369.
53. RGASPI, f. 1m, op. 23, d. 1211, ll. 70–71.
54. Pikina, "Gody sovmestnoi raboty," in *Aleksandr Kosarev*, ed. Mikhailova, 121–22.

FIGURE 5.1. Kosarev in 1936. RGASPI, f. 1m, op. 18, d. 2472, l. 17.

Kosarev suppressed whatever doubts he held and called for an intensification of vigilance in the Komsomol.

Despite Kosarev's compliance with Stalin's wishes, NKVD investigators opened a file on him in September 1937, just after the Komsomol's first purge plenum in August 1937.[55] Kosarev had been aware of what was at stake during the plenum. At the end of the meeting, Kosarev had responded to comments and criticism about his own conduct in his closing address. He divided criticism into categories of "fair" and "slander"—with the loudest slander coming from Elena Knopova, acting head of Soviet sports. Knopova, a graduate of Moscow's prominent Industrial Academy, had come up through the ranks of the Komsomol. She received Kosarev's recommendation in 1936 to move to the sports administration with its newly appointed chief, Ivan Kharchenko. Knopova then became its head after Kharchenko was removed as an enemy of the people just weeks before the plenum. Among her allegations against Kosarev, the most damaging was that he had protected enemies like Kharchenko, whom she had unmasked. Kosarev turned Knopova's accusations around on her: "Could this not be an attempt to paralyze my activity in the struggle to unmask enemies—in particular, the person of Knopova?"[56]

Although Knopova and Kosarev would snipe at one another for the next year, the youth leader's key detractor became a former Komsomol instructor named Ol'ga Mishakova.[57] In the wake of the Komsomol's summer 1937 purge, its Central Committee had sent Mishakova to monitor the Chuvash republic's youth congress, where delegates would search for local enemies. Mishakova attempted to persuade activists at the congress to remove the first and second secretaries of the republic's Komsomol for their alleged connections with enemies of the people. When the delegates refused, she appealed to Kosarev who removed the Chuvash youth leaders himself.[58] Mishakova then continued to denounce Chuvash politicians, persuading Georgii Malenkov, the head of the administration of party personnel, to remove the first party secretary of the republic from his post. In January 1938, the mood turned against "slanderers," and the Chuvash party organization denounced Mishakova for her denunciations. The Komsomol Central Committee removed her from her position in March as someone who

55. Artizov, Reabilitatsiia, 2:640.

56. RGASPI, f. 1m, op. 2, d. 133, l. 93.

57. Knopova denounced Kosarev for his role in the infamous soccer match between the Basque national team and Spartak Moscow. Komsomol leaders allegedly ordered local officials to offer girls and booze to the visitors so that they would not be in top form and even ordered Spartak players to injure players from the opposing side to ensure victory. See Edelman, Spartak Moscow, 106; RGASPI, f. 82, op. 2, d. 970, ll. 46, 48–49. Kosarev responded by settling new Komsomol administrators in Knopova's apartment (a property she had received as a league worker) and by demanding her removal from her position by Molotov. GARF, f. 7576, op. 1, d. 345, l. 70; RGASPI, f. 1m, op. 23, d. 1321, ll. 35–39, 47. Knopova was later arrested by Stalin's order and sentenced to a labor camp term in January 1940, APRF, op. 24, d. 377, l. 133 (cited in Memorial, "Stalinskie spiski," available at http://stalin.memo.ru/spiski/pg12133.htm).

58. RGASPI, f. 1m, op. 23, d. 1212, ll. 41–48.

had overinsured in her accusations against innocent cadres. Even after losing her position, though, Mishakova continued to make allegations against various party and youth leaders—including Kosarev in a letter to Stalin in October 1938. Based on Mishakova's letter, Stalin directed Matvei Shkiriatov, a member of the Party Control Commission, its internal inspectorate, to investigate the matter.[59]

Even before the Mishakova affair, though, Stalin and his subordinates were gathering evidence against Kosarev. In September 1938, Party Secretary Andrei Andreev solicited a denunciation from a former youth worker who had been close with Kosarev. The worker placed the Komsomol leader in the apartments of various officials who were later revealed to be enemies of the people. Her letter also alleged that Kosarev in the mid-1930s had come to classes on Marxist-Leninism with wine in hand. On the eve of Kosarev's removal, no fewer than eight Komsomol administrators sent denunciations about him to party secretaries Andreev and Zhdanov.[60] Meanwhile, Kosarev had lost his allies in the sports administration and his longtime lieutenants from the Komsomol itself. Other subordinates had been purged or moved to new work. The most important loss was Gorshenin, arrested in early November 1938 on the eve of Kosarev's own trial.

According to an apocryphal story, Stalin saw Kosarev at a ball shortly before the purge plenum in November. As the two clinked glasses, Stalin said, "Traitor! I'll kill you!"[61] Based on Kosarev's rather measured behavior at the plenum and in the weeks before, this account seems unlikely. Kosarev still knew that something was afoot. He had attempted to get an audience with Stalin following Gorshenin's removal. Additionally, he admitted at the plenum that he had learned about Shkiriatov's investigation into the Mishakova case.[62] Nonetheless, it seems that Kosarev believed well into the proceedings that he could remain leader of the Komsomol.

At the insistence of party leaders, on November 11 the Komsomol's Central Committee reinstated Mishakova and hastily organized a plenum to begin on November 19. The meeting lasted four days and its agenda had just one item: the Mishakova affair. Kosarev, who technically convened the plenum, gave the floor immediately to Shkiriatov to discuss his investigation. Shkiriatov portrayed Mishakova as a vigilant young official fighting against a hostile leadership in the

59. See Shkiriatov's report from the November Komsomol plenum, RGASPI, f. 17, op. 120, d. 351, ll. 65–102; Grekhov, "Rasprava s rukovodstvom Komsomola," 140–42; and Pikina, "Gody sovmestnoi raboty," 124.

60. RGASPI, f. 17, op. 120, d. 351, ll. 6–8, 9–60. Whether party secretaries solicited these letters or the Komsomol workers sent them in response to rumors circulating is unknown.

61. For the apocryphal story, see Vaksburg, The Prosecutor and the Prey, 168.

62. RGASPI, f. 17, op. 120, d. 353, l. 129.

Komsomol. After Shkiriatov's report, Kosarev was allowed to speak but was constantly interrupted. After Mishakova cried, "You lie, Kosarev!" the youth leader blurted out, "I'm still in the party."[63]

Kosarev's defense was that Petr Vershkov, formerly in charge of the Komsomol's internal organization, and other subordinates had instigated Mishakova's removal. As general secretary, he was guilty of negligence but not antiparty activity. Hearing Kosarev's speech, Vershkov (now party secretary of Saratov province) became desperate, saying to his former boss, "Look now at what they are accusing me of." Kosarev replied coldly, "Listen, Comrade Vershkov, I'll answer for my mistakes, you'll answer for yours."[64] Kosarev's attempts to distance himself from the Mishakova affair fell on deaf ears, though. He portrayed himself as a boy leader, a naïve but well-meaning youth organizer. This approach only earned him the reproach of Party Secretary Andreev. The Politburo member accused the thirty-five-year-old Kosarev of intentionally infantilizing himself: "Don't try to paint yourself as some kind of nursing child. . . . You've run the Komsomol for ten years."[65]

The crucial moment in the plenum was Stalin's intervention. On the morning of the plenum's second day, a Komsomol worker criticized Kosarev mildly for misunderstanding the meaning of the August 1937 purge plenum. Stalin, who attended only that session, asked whether Kosarev had misunderstood the August 1937 plenum's exhortation to remove enemies or had intentionally concealed hostile workers in the youth organization. "Perhaps he understood, but did not admit it," Stalin began and then suggested, "or maybe this is a system and not a mistake?"[66]

Stalin's question bolstered attacks against Kosarev, and it hinted at degeneracy by referencing the August 1937 purge. Kosarev at first denied any postpurge drinking bouts. On the fourth and final day of the plenum, though, Zhdanov dropped a bombshell regarding Kosarev and Gorshenin, the purged civil defense leader. Just days before, a fisherman named Andreenko had read a *Komsomol'skaia pravda* editorial criticizing Kosarev and realized he had crucial evidence against the Komsomol leader. The fisherman wrote Zhdanov that he had at least twice witnessed Kosarev on debauched fishing trips with Gorshenin on the Istra River just outside Moscow: "Once they got so drunk that they almost overturned the boat and drowned. Gorshenin was so drunk he burned his boots in the campfire,

63. RGASPI, f. 17, op. 120, d. 351, ll. 65–120, 103–24.
64. RGASPI, f. 17, op. 120, d. 353, l. 129.
65. Ibid., l. 135.
66. RGASPI, f. 17, op. 120, d. 352, l. 134.

and he had to find new shoes to get back to Moscow." The two kept up the inhabitants of the village Pokhlebaiki all night with their loud, drunken swearing.[67]

Here was proof positive that Kosarev had engaged in degenerate activity and, even worse, had attempted to hide his drinking with an enemy of the people. The evidence led Zhdanov to remark, "After the arrest [of Gorshenin] we have to ask the question, were Gorshenin and Kosarev just catching fish?"[68] Vershkov, too, was implicated in the fishing plots. He had claimed that he was not a close friend of the other youth leaders. When Komsomol workers in the audience pressed him about his presence at the outings, however, he admitted that he had joined Kosarev and Gorshenin. "Oh, a bunch of fishermen!" a Komsomol worker exclaimed from the crowd.[69] The trips linked Kosarev with both Gorshenin and Vershkov under suspicious circumstances. Moreover, they showed that Kosarev did not understand the meaning of the August plenum. He had, after all, engaged in drinking despite his denunciation of degeneracy. Stalin's suggestion that Kosarev had intentionally disregarded the August 1937 plenum appeared to be true.

Kosarev denied his guilt until the last. After Zhdanov and Andrei Andreev spoke, he exclaimed, "This is an absolute fabrication, an absolute slander." Vershkov gave a more moderate defense, calmly claiming his own innocence and that of Kosarev. Shortly after, though, the Komsomol Central Committee voted to remove Kosarev and the other youth league secretaries, including Pikina, from their positions. Vershkov lost his position as party secretary in Saratov province. The NKVD arrested and executed almost all of them. Only Pikina survived to spend a decade in the labor camps and then years in exile. Nearly twenty years later, under Khrushchev, she would receive rehabilitation and become one of the party workers responsible for reinstating purge victims. After dispatching the old leadership, the plenum elected new youth secretaries headed by Nikolai Mikhailov, the thirty-two-year-old editor of *Komsomol'skaia pravda*. Mishakova became secretary for student affairs.[70]

On the surface, Kosarev's mishandling of the Mishakova affair and his relationship with an enemy, Gorshenin, spelled his doom. Although these factors provided the ammunition for his removal, Kosarev's demise was probably linked to a factor that did not come up at the plenum—his connection with the NKVD chief Nikolai Ezhov. In July 1937, Ezhov had fulfilled Stalin's orders and directed the NKVD to undertake the mass operations. After the campaign of mass terror

67. RGASPI, f. 77, op. 3, d. 19, l. 57.
68. RGASPI, f. 17, op. 120, d. 353, l. 153.
69. Ibid., l. 188.
70. Ibid., ll. 230–32, 236.

ended, though, Stalin needed scapegoats for the "excesses" of repression. When Lavrentii Beria, a longtime member of Stalin's political family, became deputy commissar of the NKVD, Ezhov must have noticed a pattern. He himself had replaced the disgraced Genrikh Iagoda after working as Stalin's unofficial liaison in the NKVD. Ezhov effectively lost control over the commissariat and began to drink heavily.[71] Other NKVD officials saw the pattern, too, and some went into hiding. Apologizing for his failure to recognize these enemies, Ezhov resigned in November 1938, just days after his wife committed suicide. Beria was named commissar soon after and lost no time arresting the former commissar and his appointees.[72] For Kosarev, this connection, too, seems to have been deadly. In his April 1939 interrogation, Ezhov's nephew A. N. Babulin would link Kosarev to a host of arrested figures who had been in the social circle of Ezhov and his wife.[73]

Kosarev's purge was one of several endings at the close of 1938. Although Mikhailov and the new leadership would remove Kosarev's loyalists from the Komsomol, the purge in the youth league was effectively over.[74] Throughout the country, the period of mass repression ended, allowing new political bonds to form and giving pererostki the ability to join the party. In joining the Communist Party, they helped recreate an apparatus that repression had torn apart. Their exit from the youth league and Kosarev's arrest marked the final chapter in the transition of youth culture from the radicalism of the 1920s and early 1930s to the Komsomol's new emphasis on discipline and cultivation.

The story of the purge was about more than destruction. The Komsomol's attempt to rehabilitate youth in 1938 reinforced key aspects of Soviet youth culture that had emerged under socialism. Youth had become political minors whose rehabilitation as young communists was often more important than their expulsion for misdeeds. Through good work and good behavior, Komsomol leaders hoped to redeem wayward young people and turn them into worthwhile citizens. As millions of young people joined the Komsomol, organizers would undertake this mission as part of a mass organization during a time of increasing international tensions.

---

71. Khlevniuk, *Politbiuro*, 214–15.

72. On the "purge of the purgers," see Vatlin, *Agents of Terror*, 62–73; Shearer, *Policing Stalin's Socialism*, 368; and Getty and Naumov, *Road to Terror*, 531.

73. Khaustov et al, *Lubianka*, 74–78 (citing APRF, f. 3, op. 24, d. 375, ll. 61–70).

74. RGASPI, f. 1m, op. 3, d. 201, ll. 96–100.

A MASS YOUTH ORGANIZATION

On September 1, 1939, Germany invaded Poland, marking the start of World War II in Europe. Just a week earlier, German and Soviet leaders had sealed their non-aggression pact with secret protocols for the division of Eastern Europe. Soon the Soviet Union annexed large parts of Poland, Romania, and the Baltic states and went to war with Finland that winter. Despite the pact, Soviet leaders continued to fear a major war would break out with Germany or Japan. The limited military ventures in Eastern Europe and the fear of a broader conflict spurred Soviet leaders to enact increasingly drastic policies at home. The most extreme of these policies, the mass operations of 1937–38, had attempted to remove potential fifth columnists from vulnerable areas of the country or from society as a whole.[1] After the period of mass terror ended, the regime instituted laws and policing practices to discipline society for war. In 1940, the Supreme Soviet (the legislature of the USSR) introduced a severe law against labor shirking that created harsh penalties for seemingly minor on-the-job offenses like tardiness. That same year, police mounted a renewed campaign against hooliganism.[2] Even as the threat of war fueled various forms of repression, it also encouraged regime leaders to

---

1. A number of recent works have been published about NKVD Order no. 00447 and the other mass operations. For the operations as policy see Hagenloh, *Stalin's Police*, chapter 6; and Shearer, *Policing Stalin's Socialism*, 320–70. On borderland deportations in this period, see Polian, *Ne po svoei voli*, 115–23.
2. Solomon, *Soviet Criminal Justice under Stalin*, 299–322.

expand their base of support through the inclusion of more youth in political society. In the Komsomol alone, roughly six million young people joined the league from 1938 to 1940.

The huge wave of new members sealed the Komsomol's transformation from an exclusive league of activists to a mass organization for socialization and social promotion. It had become an organization to make youth Soviet. The change in the Komsomol's purpose reflected a reconfiguration of what it meant to be a good Soviet citizen. Youth leaders de-emphasized class-based ideological aspects of Marxist-Leninist political education in favor of broad attempts to generate populist support for the regime through Soviet patriotism.[3]

The rewards for Komsomol membership were increasingly tangible. During the Great Terror, young party leaders experienced rapid social mobility as veteran cadres fell victim to arrest. Future grandees like Leonid Brezhnev formed the "new class" of Soviet authorities that would be the backbone of the party-state until the 1980s.[4] At the lower levels, large numbers of ordinary young people in the Komsomol experienced the terror and its aftermath as a period of immense opportunity. Increasingly, they came to expect that a function of the youth league was to coordinate their social and professional promotion. One scholar of the postwar period characterized advancement under Stalin as a "big deal"—a crass and grudging exchange of obedience for material rewards.[5] In contrast to this view, though, neither regime leaders nor ordinary youth viewed social mobility as being inconsistent with socialism. Instead, youth leaders believed that promotion would create a new cohort of young people whose experience would allow them to build and defend the USSR. The status and material benefits youth gained simultaneously rewarded and strengthened their ability to contribute to socialism.

The main beneficiaries of Stalinist community building were well-educated promotees. However, party and youth leaders made a claim on youth broadly through regime-sponsored entertainment. During the Great Terror, the youth press had emphasized that hooligans and Trotskyist degenerates used drinking and other forms of bad behavior to undermine the state. As the scale of repression declined in 1939, though, Komsomol leaders increasingly understood boredom as a major factor driving young people to behave in anti-Soviet ways. Cultured entertainment, officials asserted, would occupy youth while involving them

---

3. On Russian nationalism as part of this campaign, see Brandenberger, *National Bolshevism*, 95–114.

4. Fitzpatrick, *Education and Social Mobility*, 234–54.

5. Dunham, *In Stalin's Time*, 3–23.

in a community that could monitor and reform supposedly anti-Soviet behavior. Belief, benefits, and belonging were core components of Soviet youth culture in the late 1930s. These elements were not just a means of ensuring stability, however, but created a foundation for mobilization in the anticipated future of war.

A Shorter Course for Recruiting

The year 1938 marked a turning point for the Komsomol in mass recruiting and political education. Since 1933, the party and Komsomol had limited admissions of new members. After the purge of the league's membership at the end of collectivization, leaders feared that enemies would penetrate political society through the organization. Even in 1935, when Kosarev announced that the social makeup of the Komsomol would change under socialism, he did not signal a significant increase in the scale of recruitment.

Entrance to political society began to reopen in late 1936, when Soviet leaders lifted the moratorium on admission to the party. Related to the expansion of membership in the party and Komsomol, party leaders simplified requirements for political knowledge prior to admission. In 1938, party leaders released the long-awaited *History of the All-Union Communist Party (Bolshevik): Short Course*, better known as *The Short Course*. Commissioned in 1935 and edited by Stalin himself, it provided a simple and unified version of the party's history. The Bolsheviks had been mired in theoretical debates from the inception of the party to the oppositions of the 1920s. Party leaders claimed that the new textbook would end these debates and provide a definitive narrative.[6] *The Short Course* not only codified Stalinist mythology, though, but also significantly lowered the standard for political education.

At the same time that *The Short Course* was entering its final edits, the doors to admission in the Komsomol opened wide. To join the league, a young person had to obtain two recommendations from existing members before passing an admissions interview at both the local and district levels. At the district level, the interview functioned as a nerve-racking political examination. By 1938, however, youth leaders had begun to question the relevance of this interview. At a meeting of Komsomol leaders in February 1938, the then organizational secretary, Petr Vershkov, remarked that the league was a "nonparty organization" that could not reasonably expect applicants to wield the same knowledge as would-be party

---

6. For information on the composition of *The Short Course*, see Zelenov and Brandenberger, "*Kratkii kurs istorii VKP(b),*" 1:169–420.

FIGURE 6.1. Admissions to the Komsomol at a department store in Sverdlovsk, 1937. RGAKFD, 2-86405.

members. He cited a case where district activists asked an applicant to name the enemy of the Spanish Republic. The applicant could remember that the enemy in Spain was a Fascist party but was rejected because he could not remember its proper name, the Falange.[7] Party Central Committee Secretary Andrei Andreev added to Vershkov's comments, suggesting that obstruction of admission was the fault of mid-level activists who had closed the Komsomol "willingly or unwillingly."[8] At a time of ongoing mass arrests, Andreev's hint that stifled admission was a form of sabotage probably motivated many activists to broaden access to membership.

Although huge numbers of youth applied for membership, the district interview remained as a political check into 1939. The new influx of members soon made the interview an impossibility in many places. In April 1939, at the first Central Committee meeting after Kosarev's purge, Nikolai Mikhailov pushed to eliminate the political examination altogether. Nikolai Romanov, the future leader of postwar Soviet sport and then an up-and-coming Komsomol worker,

7. RGASPI, f. 1m, op. 2, d. 137, l. 131.
8. RGASPI, f. 73, op. 2, d. 41, l. 12.

asserted that some district committees held as many as two hundred meetings per year and saw 150 to 200 applicants per meeting. Many of the applicants were disappointed because their interview was a mere formality. Under these circumstances, Romanov said it was understandable that some committees had taken the initiative and stopped conducting interviews without authorization from Moscow.[9]

Lower-level youth organizers believed that the issue of the district admissions interview placed the political legitimacy of the Komsomol at stake. The leader of Moscow city's Taganskii municipal district responded to Romanov: "What would be the significance of admitting someone to the Komsomol without [the admissions interview]? It would mean rubber stamping the decision of local Komsomol committees."[10] Delegating admissions to local groups would undermine the exclusivity of the league as a reserve of the party. Despite these protests, Mikhailov soon after gave all district youth leaders the right to admit youth by correspondence.[11] District-level organizers could still interview new members if they believed it necessary, but it is likely many activists welcomed the reprieve from this time-consuming duty. The decision to lessen restrictions on admission reflected the aspirations and limitations of youth culture. Mikhailov wanted to enroll large numbers of youth in the league and the district committee interview was a bottleneck. Worse, it was often a formality. Unlike many district youth leaders, local activists were typically not party members and were less authoritative than their superior in the district. However, entrance into a nonparty organization did not require the new cohort of young people to pass through the same political examination that their activist older siblings had.

Central signals to expand admission in the Komsomol encouraged large-scale, sometimes coercive methods of recruiting youth at the local level. In Lopasne district (Moscow province), the youth committee admitted dozens of new members at almost every meeting between 1938 and 1940. The people who recommended the new members were just a handful of activists—often local youth secretaries or senior activists who were already in the orbit of the district committee.[12] The presence of just a few recommenders suggests that local organizers were not only endorsing self-motivated applicants but recruiting or even intimidating youth to join the league. Coercion in admissions became the source of an argument

---

9. RGASPI, f. 1m, op. 2, d. 169, ll. 139, 147. On Romanov's role in Soviet sport in the postwar period, see Parks, "Red Sport, Red Tape."

10. RGASPI, f. 1m, op. 2, d. 170, l. 92.

11. RGASPI, f. 1m, op. 2, d. 171, ll. 154, 155; "Konsul'tatsiia," *Izvestiia TsK Komsomola*, no. 10 (1939): 26–27.

12. OKhDOPIM, f. 648p, op. 1, d. 11.

between two organizers at a meeting of Kiev province's youth leaders in February 1940. When one raised the accusation that the other had recruited too few new members, the other asked: "Are we conscripting youth into the Komsomol or admitting them? I believe we rejected conscription." Provincial Youth Secretary Nikolai Sizonenko interrupted to moderate: Conscription was excessive but attraction was necessary.[13] The line between coercion and persuasion was a thin one, and elements of both were often present simultaneously.

The case of Nikolai Melnikov, a young man who later told his story as an émigré, illustrates the pressures and rewards for new recruits. In 1938, Melnikov was a sixteen-year-old apprentice at Leningrad's Vyborg machine plant. He and a group of boys fell under the influence of Mikhail Sheikin, the deputy political director of the school at the plant. Sheikin plied them with passes to sanatoriums and theater tickets while telling them about the Komsomol. Nikolai became more involved in the group and a minor celebrity at the factory after he published poems in the local newspaper. His writing led to acquaintanceships with Leningrad's movie stars and other benefits. "I gradually realized that the Komsomol opened the door to a life that was worth having," he said. All the same, Melnikov was not yet a member and worried the committee would reject him if he applied.

One day in January 1938, Sheikin summoned him to his office. Smiling widely, the political director commended Melnikov's hard work, discipline, and the active role he played in the factory's social life. He said, "It's youngsters like you that are needed by the Leninist Komsomol, many millions of boys and girls." Melnikov demurred that he was not sure about joining, but that day he and Sheikin reviewed the Komsomol's program and regulations together. Sheikin then asked Melnikov to continue studying both documents and make a decision after a few days. Nikolai was not alone: "The very same day I heard that Sheikin was tackling all my friends in the course in the same way. We all agreed to join."

Sheikin prepared Melnikov and his friends for their entrance—in 1938, it still involved a political examination. Melnikov had to learn "the names of the members of the Politburo . . . study the constitution, and thoroughly grasp the main principles of the statutes and program of the Komsomol." This training was overkill, although Melnikov's audience at the district committee was intimidating: dressed in military-style clothing, they regarded the new members with condescension. "The committee members looked like budding Party functionaries," he remembered. One asked Melnikov whether the Komsomol was "a party or non-party organization." Nikolai answered that it was not a party organization

---

13. DAKO, f. 9, op. 3, spr. 28, ark. 30–31.

FIGURE 6.2. Political education at a factory Komsomol. RGAKFD, 0-41574.

but could not articulate why. Nonetheless, his answer was enough to pass the test, and he became a member.[14]

Melnikov's story involved all the main factors in Komsomol recruiting: loyalty to the regime; material rewards; coercion from above; and peer pressure. When he wrote his memoirs while living abroad, Melnikov tried to camouflage his adolescent activism as naivety. Nonetheless, Melnikov seemed to have enjoyed his work as an organizer, even though he claimed later that he had been ignorant that he had supported Stalin's regime through his activism. Material perks—his movie passes and local fame—made him realize that membership would make his life more comfortable. Prodding from Sheikin, a trusted mentor, prompted Melnikov to consider joining the Komsomol. Although he remained uncertain about applying, social pressure from his friends helped him agree in the end. Each young person joined the Komsomol for his or her own reasons, but these factors were at work to varying degrees in every instance. As Melnikov's case shows, they were not mutually exclusive.

As a cohort, the new members of 1938–39 bore many similarities to Melnikov. Three million new Komsomol youth—approximately half of all admissions—were also under eighteen years old or students. Besides adolescents, young women made up an increasingly large number of admissions after 1937. The biggest change was the sheer magnitude of expansion in the Komsomol, though. Its ranks more than doubled in two years. By 1940, it included roughly 30 percent of all age-eligible youth (see Table 1 in appendix).

---

14. N. Melnikov, "Road to Life" in *Soviet Youth*, ed. Novak-Decker, 216–18.

These new Komsomol members not only had to do less to join the league, but their political education as members was less intensive than that of previous cohorts. After the purge of Kosarev's circle, Ol'ga Mishakova oversaw the Komsomol's education programs and made consistent efforts to simplify them. Speaking in May 1939 about a retraining program for propaganda workers, Mishakova proposed nearly exclusive training in *The Short Course*, forgoing more extensive immersion in the Marxist-Leninist oeuvre. Traditional education was also overtaking political training as a requirement among propagandists. Mishakova insisted that trainees have a minimum of ten years of schooling—a relatively high level of education in the Soviet Union at the time.[15] Not only was extensive political education unnecessary for most cadres, but Mishakova in a speech in Karelia claimed that activists of "middle levels of development" were incapable of grappling with "all sources of party history." The rank and file needed lectures and small-group conversations because the "masses in the Komsomol are not ready to study party history."[16] Mishakova's handling of political education was characteristic of the treatment of party history in the Komsomol. The league's main goal in political education was to give large numbers of youth a homogeneous and pragmatic understanding of history that would allow them to interpret current events in line with the regime's wishes.

In most groups, youth organizers' political education coincided with Mishakova's wishes. Virtually all instruction focused on *The Short Course*. A basic familiarity with the book became a requirement for youth who wanted to enter the party. Applicants who read three of its twelve chapters were qualified as would-be party members.[17] Those who undertook no political education might face the charge that they had "not worked on themselves" and be denied a recommendation to the party.[18] For more active youth, another form of political education was participation in a so-called theoretical conference, where a presentation was another way of preparing for party membership. Often these presentations were quite topical. One member received his group's recommendation to the party on August 19, 1939, after he mentioned that he would be participating in an upcoming conference with the topic "Just and Unjust Wars." He summarized his presentation: "When a war is fought for independence or liberation—that is a just war. When a war is fought to take colonies, to suppress other nations—unjust."[19]

---

15. RGASPI, f. 1m, op. 3, d. 120, l. 68.
16. NARK, f. 1229, op. 3, d. 41, ll. 112, 114.
17. RGVA, f. 9, op. 30, d. 177, l. 124; d. 179.
18. OKhDOPIM, f. 648, op. 1, d. 17, l. 133.
19. RGVA, f. 9, op. 30, d. 180, l. 101.

The soon-to-be party member's topic was prescient, or perhaps he simply echoed editorials from the Soviet press on the eve of annexations in the west. Soon the Red Army would be fighting a "just war" against Finland and conducting "liberations" of the Baltic states and territories annexed from Poland and Romania. On August 23, Soviet and German leaders signed the nonaggression pact that would divide Eastern Europe between their countries. The pact represented a shift in Soviet foreign policy. Stalin had previously hoped that the threat of Franco-British intervention would deter Germany from invading its eastern neighbors. After French and British leaders acquiesced to Hitler's invasion of Czechoslovakia in the Munich Agreement of 1938, Stalin lost faith that the Western states would guarantee the independence of the Eastern European countries that stood between the USSR and Germany.[20] With its nonaggression pact with Germany, the Soviet Union not only seemed to buy several years to prepare for a major conflict with the capitalist world, it also offered Stalin the ability to carve out a defensive buffer zone from newly annexed territories. As Soviet and German armies mobilized to implement the division of Eastern Europe, Soviet newspapers gave little attention to German aggression—previously the subject of loud denunciation. Instead, they used print space to laud Soviet territorial expansion as "national unifications."[21] Before the onset of war and after its outbreak, political education took on a more pragmatic role, emphasizing the righteousness of the USSR and the unity of its people rather than a more esoteric, class-based study of Marxist-Leninism.

The threat of war and its arrival affected youth culture in other ways, too. Even before conflict broke out in Europe, Komsomol leaders had linked preparation for war broadly to training in the Komsomol. Stalin himself had signaled the need for more military training among members in the youth press in 1938. In a letter to Stalin on January 18, 1938, a district-level propagandist named Ivan Ivanov wrote about a dispute over the "victory of socialism." Did socialism's triumph over internal class enemies make the military overthrow of Soviet power impossible? Ivanov said that even under socialism, intervention from abroad was still possible. His superior, the youth secretary of Kursk province Vasilii Urozhenko, argued that overthrow was not possible. Stalin responded personally that Ivanov was correct and that "it would be silly and stupid to close one's eyes" in the current environment of capitalist encirclement. He continued, "We must keep the entire people in a state of mobilized preparedness before the danger of military attack so that no 'accident' or trick of our external enemies catches us

---

20. Gorodetsky, *Grand Delusion*, 5–6.
21. Brooks, *Thank You, Comrade Stalin*, 152–58.

unawares."[22] At the February 1938 Komsomol Central Committee plenum, Aleksandr Kosarev had echoed Stalin and denounced Urozhenko, linking admissions and political upbringing to success in future battles with the capitalist world. After calling for an expansion of the Komsomol's ranks, Kosarev condemned Urozhenko's "demobilized mood" and said: "You won't sit a sixty-year-old in an airplane, nor on a tank, you won't teach him how to wield difficult modern military technology in just a short period of time. In the looming war—and there will be one—our young people will play a big role."[23]

When war arrived, it changed the face of Komsomol groups and placed an increasing burden on the league to mobilize youth into the army. On September 1, 1939, in advance of the occupation of western territories, the Supreme Soviet passed a law that lowered the call-up age from twenty-one to nineteen, creating a double cohort in the military. The concentration of youth subsequently conscripted from the Komsomol meant that entire district committees left for the army. In Orel province, six district youth committees lost every member. The effect was so disruptive that the month the law was introduced, Mikhailov entreated Politburo members to contain the number of conscriptions from the Komsomol, especially of provincial youth leaders.[24]

As experienced organizers went to the army, more women and younger activists joined the league's administration. The average age of youth leaders at the provincial and city level fell by roughly a year from 1939 to 1940. The percentage of women in mid-level leadership positions, between 20 and 25 percent, drew closer to the overall percentage of women among membership, nearly 40 percent in 1940.[25] The same tendencies occurred among lower-level activists. Half of the organizers who attended district and city youth conferences in 1940 were twenty or younger, while only 40 percent had been that age in 1938.[26] Although external conditions rather than policy had forced these changes in the composition of the Komsomol, youth leaders celebrated the changing population of activists as the realization of long-held goals for the league.[27]

The new organizers were more often unpaid than their predecessors had been. In the spring of 1940, the league's Central Committee decreased the number of professional Komsomol organizers by 59 percent—eliminating positions predominately at the local and district levels. By the end of the process, the number

22. "Pis'mo t. Ivanova i otvet t. Stalina," *Molodaia gvardiia*, no. 2 (1938): 8–9, 10–11.
23. RGASPI, f. 1m, op. 2, d. 138, ll. 179–81.
24. RGASPI, f. 1m, op. 23, d. 1328, l. 48.
25. RGASPI, f. 1m, op. 23, d. 1395, ll. 4; op. 126, d. 359, ll. 26–27.
26. RGASPI, f. 1m, op. 126, d. 359, ll. 23, 24.
27. Ibid., ll. 28–33.

of members per paid organizer rose from two hundred to five hundred.[28] Komsomol leaders claimed that increasing volunteerism was the motivation and payoff of the cuts. According to press accounts, organizational work that was formerly the preserve of paid activists would create discipline among the rank and file.[29] However, it seems that budgetary concerns were the major factor behind the cuts. At the June 1940 Komsomol Central Committee plenum where the cuts were announced, one organizer claimed the reductions were in line with an article he had seen in *Pravda* "about cutting staffs, cutting administrative and other costs to a minimum." Mishakova shouted him down quickly.[30] When factories began to pay activists from their own budgets rather than lose them, though, youth leaders quietly gave their approval.[31]

To organizers who had joined the league earlier, the Komsomol of 1940 was difficult to recognize. During the league's elections in September 1940, a Komsomol Central Committee instructor named Voronin supervised the group from Moscow's School no. 478. The assistant Komsomol secretary at the school was named Adzhubei, apparently the future editor of *Komsomol'skaia pravda* and *Izvestiia*, and son-in-law of Nikita Khrushchev, Aleksei.[32] To Voronin's disapproval, Adzhubei asserted that the newest members were "not bad but they don't want to work in the Komsomol." The new members had joined "for their own personal reasons," because membership was a path to success in school and their future careers. He wondered aloud if the seriousness of the group would decline with the graduation of senior members. In his mind, the cohort that had recently joined was different from those that had come before. Instead of leading a small group of fervent activists, he now headed a large organization of those he believed were well-meaning but indifferent careerists.[33]

Voronin chastised Adzhubei because he disparaged the motivations of Komsomol youth—a political faux pas. Yet Adzhubei was almost certainly correct in his assessment. The beginning of World War II in Europe was crucial to the changing nature of Komsomol activism. The threat of war convinced party leaders to seek greater social stability through the expansion of a formerly exclusive

28. RGASPI, f. 1m, op. 2, d. 234, ll. 90, 91–92; d. 235, l. 43.

29. A. Rybkin, "Vovlechenie komsomol'tsev v obshchestvennuiu zhizn'—moguchee sredstvo ukrepleniia ditsipliny," *Komsomol'skii rabotnik*, no. 23 (1940): 10–11.

30. RGASPI, f. 1m, op. 2, d. 204, ll. 105–7.

31. "Otvety na voprosy aktiva," *Komsomol'skii rabotnik*, no. 17 (1940): 29.

32. Adzhubei, born in 1924, noted in his memoirs that he attended School no. 478. Adzhubei mentioned that he went on a geological expedition in "the summer and fall of 1940 and 1941," making it possible but unclear that he was in Moscow at the time. It seems likely that this Adzhubei was Aleksei or a relative. Adzhubei, *Te desiat' let*, 193–96.

33. RGASPI, f. 1m, op. 23, d. 1386, ll. 91–94.

organization of activists. At the same time, the exodus of youth into the army in the autumn of 1939 meant that new organizers came from the ranks of those who were less experienced, younger, and more often female than in the past. In this environment, leaders placed an emphasis on forging a broad political community and took up pragmatic policies to mobilize youth as capable and loyal cadres. These same goals motivated Komsomol leaders as they backed a campaign of mass promotion for youth.

Social Promotion for Youth

The durability of Stalin's regime was due in part to the opportunities it provided supporters for social advancement. The party recruited hundreds of thousands of factory workers in the early 1930s for education in factory schools, creating a privileged group in Soviet society.[34] Huge numbers of industrial workers catapulted into positions of responsibility as Soviet leaders attempted to resolve seemingly endless shortages of cadres and to replace victims of the purges.[35] These new employees became the backbone of the Soviet elite and included people who would become figures of national prominence.[36] Stalin himself placed a special emphasis on promoting cadres—particularly from the ranks of the young. At the Eighteenth Party Congress in 1939, he asserted that old cadres, with all their experience, were too few and often too stuck in their ways. Because of youth's openness to new methods and because young people made up the majority of the educated cadres in the country, Stalin proclaimed, "It is necessary to promote the young boldly and quickly."[37]

In the Komsomol, access to social promotion had long been an advantage of membership.[38] During the Great Terror, thousands of youth had become the beneficiaries of the purge of party and Komsomol elites. A prominent example was Yuri Andropov, the general secretary of the Communist Party in the early 1980s. Andropov began his career as the youth secretary of a factory in Rybinsk in Iaroslavl province in 1937. In the course of a little more than a year, he passed through several intermediate postings to become the head of that province's Komsomol

---

34. Fitzpatrick, *Education and Social Mobility*, 239–49.

35. Lewin, "Society, State, and Ideology During the First Five Year Plan," in *Making of the Soviet System*, 221; Kotkin, *Magnetic Mountain*, 86–94; Reese, *Stalin's Reluctant Soldiers*, 108.

36. On promotion at the highest levels, see Hough, *Soviet Prefects*, 38–55.

37. "Otchetnyi doklad t. Stalina na XVIII s"ezde partii o rabote TsK VKP(b)," *Pravda*, March 11, 1939.

38. Guillory, "We Shall Refashion Life on Earth!," 201.

in 1938. His rise occurred so quickly that he did not become a full party member until 1939. In 1940, Mikhailov tagged him as the new leader of the Komsomol in the recently formed Karelian republic—an important position because the territory bordered a hostile state.[39] During the terror, Kosarev had characterized timely promotion of youth like Andropov as a necessity for the future of war. At a November 1937 meeting of provincial youth secretaries, he demanded faster promotion of younger cadres, saying "they will be the ones leading youth during wartime in the most dangerous areas on behalf of the party."[40] Despite the importance Kosarev had assigned to cadre management, the league's efforts under his leadership had been ad hoc mobilizations or involved promoting youth within the ranks of the Komsomol.

Under Mikhailov the Komsomol's role in promotion in the country grew. Soon after he became secretary of the youth league, its Central Committee formed a department for cadres. Unlike its predecessor, the department for leading Komsomol organs, the new department's mission was not just to manage cadres within the youth league but also to facilitate advancement for young people throughout the Soviet Union. In the Kirgiz SSR in April 1940, the local cadres department counted 2,902 promotions it had facilitated. Only 392 promotees went to positions within the Komsomol, while most went to positions in state institutions or enterprises.[41] Youth leaders did not just want to move young people into new positions outside the Komsomol but into significantly more important positions. The head of the Central Committee's cadres department, Ivan Grishin, referred to these vertical moves as bold promotion, echoing Stalin's phrase at the Eighteenth Party Congress. At the April 1939 plenum of the Komsomol Central Committee, Grishin presented a hypothetical case where the head of a collective farm took over the more important position of secretary in a district youth organization: "That would be bold promotion. That person would have big things ahead of him in his life."[42] Komsomol leaders believed that rapid promotion was essential for giving young cadres the experience they would need to construct and defend socialism.

Promotion into significant appointments was the best-case scenario, yet Soviet publications also profiled cases of advancement that were less prominent. From late 1938 to 1941, the youth press published regular accounts of ordinary promotion. In Olonets district of Karelia, Tonia Niuchalina went from an accountant to

39. RGASPI, f. 1m, op. 18, d. 164a, l. 1.
40. RGASPI, f. 1m, op. 5, d. 51, l. 150.
41. RGASPI, f. 1m, op. 3, d. 234, l. 64.
42. RGASPI, f. 1m, op. 2, d. 169, l. 181.

running a bank. Chauffer Vasia Volkov became the boss of a garage. At the upper end of the scale, Komsomol member Pavel Prokop'ev, the former chair of the district executive committee, had recently become the deputy head of the Karelian Council of People's Commissars (SNK).[43]

An April 1939 article in the journal *Komsomol'skii rabotnik* profiled the work of a department store in Moscow. The article began by presenting a young worker, E. Eremushkina, who recently received promotions both at work and from candidate to full member of the party. The author spared no detail, quoting her new salary as up to an enviable 1,700 rubles per month—comparable to the official salaries of soccer stars.[44] What characterized this kind of promotion was its relatively small scale and, though it was not connected to Komsomol or party work, the explicit link to membership in the Komsomol or party organizations. In effect, the youth press was advertising the ways that official culture was improving young people's positions in the world.

Outside of the press, rank-and-file members asserted that the league was a vehicle for their personal success. Leaders in the Commissariat of Defense's Komsomol organization made promotion of local youth an official point of discussion in meetings during the summer of 1938. The Komsomol group among garage workers in the commissariat gave its assessment of local promotion, "Many Komsomol members have been promoted recently to important work: two people as chauffeurs to the assistant commissar." Others had made a move from clunkers to "good, big cars."[45] At a meeting of the military publishing house in April 1939, one member exhorted his fellows to accelerate the country's progress to communism. Then, modestly, he hinted that one means of building communism faster would be to find him and a colleague better-paying jobs in their area of specialization.[46] In the group of the Red Army's newspaper, *Krasnaia zvezda* (Red Star), a member named Iaskovich complained that the youth organization did not do enough to promote cadres, especially because "I don't like my work." A colleague responded that disliking one's job was not reason alone for promotion, yet no one asserted that the meeting was the wrong forum for talking about advancement.[47]

43. A. Malyi, "Komsomol'tsy na rukovodiashchei rabote," *Komsomolets Karelii*, August 12, 1938, 3. See also M. Romanov, "Vospitanniki Komsomola," *Komsomolets Karelii*, May 8, 1939, 3; and A. Tiagunin, "Molodye vydvizhentsy," *Komsomolets Karelii*, July 26, 1939, 3.

44. I. Fedosov, "Bol'shoi raikom i nebol'shaia organizatsiia," *Komsomol'skii rabotnik*, no. 7 (1940): 20–22. Robert Edelman points out that soccer players also found ways of supplementing their nominal stipend. Edelman, *Spartak Moscow*, 89–93.

45. RGVA, f. 9, op. 30, d. 150, 23ob.

46. RGVA, f. 9, op. 30, d. 177, l. 265.

47. RGVA, f. 9, op. 30, d. 181, l. 44.

The annexation of new territories in 1939 and 1940 was another opportunity for promotion that Komsomol members seized upon.[48] In 1940, seeking positions that would open in the new districts, hundreds of members sent applications to Karelia's youth league for placement in various posts. The interest in working in annexed Vyborg was so great in Vologda that the town's youth secretary inquired on behalf of the entire city's youth for information on how to apply for jobs. From distant Kabardino-Balkaria, a Pioneer organizer named Semen Bitenskii offered his services because "my work does not please me."[49] Most often the republican youth committee responded by urging applicants to correspond with a special commission in Karelia's government, set up for vetting new workers in the still securitized zone. Tellingly, many young people nonetheless went to the Komsomol first, believing that it was the starting place and best hope in their search for promotion.

Observers who later left the USSR remembered the Komsomol of the late 1930s as a place of opportunity and careerism. In the early 1950s, Harvard social scientists conducted hundreds of interviews with people who had left the Soviet Union about various aspects of their life in the USSR, including as Komsomol members. One former league member spoke dourly of his time in the league, initially saying that membership had just burdened good students like him with organizational work. After reflecting, he moderated his opinion and admitted there were advantages for students, such as better food and living conditions.[50] Wolfgang Leonhard came to the Soviet Union in 1935 with his German communist mother. As a young adult in the postwar period, he would become a leading member of Germany's pro-Soviet ruling party, the Socialist Unity Party of Germany. His life under Stalinism, though, particularly the arrest of his mother, had made him disillusioned with Soviet socialism, and he fled Soviet-occupied Germany in 1948. His memoirs detailed his experiences in the Komsomol before the war, dividing members into four types: naive enthusiasts, realistic enthusiasts (his category), those who used the Komsomol for socializing, and careerists. He elaborated on the careerists: "They wanted to make something of their lives and often said so quite frankly. They saw in the Komsomol nothing but a springboard to enable them to advance their careers more quickly."[51] Although Leonhard accused these members of being opportunists, he still recognized they were correct in seeing the league as a vehicle for advancement.

---

48. The opportunities these new lands presented resembled the earlier Khetagurovite campaign for young women to settle the Far East. Shulman, *Stalinism on the Frontier of Empire*, 119–48.

49. NARK, f. 1229, op. 3, d. 23, ll. 8, 12.

50. Harvard Project on the Soviet Social System. Schedule A, Vol. 14, Case 189, sequence 30.

51. Leonhard, *Child of the Revolution*, 81–82.

These glimpses of ordinary promotion suggest that rank-and-file members gave social mobility a meaning that party and youth leaders were aware of and appealed to. The Komsomol was well known as a path to advancement, particularly for ambitious would-be leaders. For ordinary members, though, promotion could have simpler advantages like extra comforts at work or the adventure of going to a new city in an exotic location. Nina Kosterina even wrote that her school's director found money to buy Komsomol members breakfast: "We destroyed rolls and kielbasa with greed, like hungry wolflings."[52] When Komsomol members protested that their group had neglected their promotion, they demonstrated an understanding of career advancement as a function of the youth organization. By the late 1930s, social mobility for youth was no longer to be a haphazard affair. It had become one of the major administrative functions that the Komsomol's leadership and members expected youth groups to provide.

Differentiating the pragmatic and ideological aspects of Stalinist social promotion is difficult. When young people demanded advancement and suggested it would aid the construction of socialism, were they behaving out of self-interest or did they believe their promotion would contribute to society? Available evidence among Komsomol records suggests that simultaneous dedication to socialism and to one's own advancement often went hand-in-hand. For their part, youth leaders stressed the ways that promotion would fortify the Soviet state by creating a cohort of experienced and trustworthy young cadres. They did not present social mobility as a bribe for loyalty but instead as a core part of a well-functioning socialist society. Alongside career advancement, youth leaders employed entertainment and other means of community building as safeguards against instability among young people.

Community as Prophylaxis

Social volatility was a cost of Soviet efforts to modernize and motivated repression by the state. Throughout the 1930s, labor turnover presented an enormous problem for Soviet leaders as the expansion of industry and the collectivization of the agriculture both forced citizens to seek new opportunities and presented access to work.[53] Labor hunger made it relatively easy to move anonymously from construction site to construction site, and the prospect of unverified, perhaps anti-Soviet populations roaming the country terrified Stalin and other party

---

52. Kosterina, *Diaries*, December 2, 1937.
53. Kotkin, *Magnetic Mountain*, 86–94.

leaders. They pushed for the introduction of internal passports, sweeps of marginal populations from the cities, and mass terror in 1937–38.[54]

The onset of war in 1939 became the impetus for new campaigns intended to discipline society. On June 26, 1940, the Supreme Soviet issued a law that established harsh penalties for workplace malfeasances, including violations as minor as tardiness. Within the first month of the campaign, more than 100,000 violations had been reported, and prosecutions under the law only increased.[55] At Stalin's insistence, a new edict raised the minimum sentence for hooliganism to one year, signaling a new campaign against the crime. The number of arrests for hooliganism doubled from 1939 to 1940, based mostly on a huge campaign in the final four months of 1940.[56] Although the measures of 1939–40 were severe, they represented only one half of the regime's fight against social disorder. The other half included policies meant to prevent at-risk groups, especially youth, from falling into trouble from the start.

Komsomol and party leaders envisioned educators as the center of discipline in Soviet upbringing. Over the course of the 1930s, a large number of teachers had joined the Komsomol. At the end of the decade, at least a quarter of all teachers were in the league, including half of teachers with less than five years of experience.[57] At the urging of the party leaders Andrei Andreev and Georgii Malenkov, Nikolai Mikhailov convened a Komsomol Central Committee plenum dedicated to the problem of discipline in schools in December 1939. In his speech, he asserted that student activism had sometimes taken the form of hooliganism against teachers.[58] In the past, youth groups in schools had included both teachers and students, inviting situations where students could impose reprimands on teachers or contravene their orders. In one case, a Moscow tenth-grade class delivered its collective refusal to take an examination in a formal note to the teacher: "To chemistry teacher A. S. Panovaia. We the students of Grade Ten at School no. 75 considered the proposal that you introduced on October 10 and came to the conclusion that we categorically refuse to write a test because we were not in class on November 5."[59] Now young teachers were given their

54. Shearer, *Policing Stalin's Socialism*, 246–53.

55. Solomon, *Soviet Criminal Justice under Stalin*, 317.

56. Part of the reason that arrests rose so dramatically from 1939 to 1940 was that in 1939 the USSR Supreme Court ruled that personal attacks were not hooliganism. This change resulted in a drop in prosecutions for hooliganism in 1939. In 1940, though, political pressure caused police and judges to ignore this ruling and prosecute cases of personal attacks as hooliganism. Solomon, *Soviet Criminal Justice under Stalin*, 328–32.

57. Ewing, *Teachers of Stalinism*, 139–40.

58. RGASPI, f. 1m, op. 2, d. 188, l. 51.

59. Ibid., l. 58.

own organizations that participated in monitoring student youth groups. The teacher-pupil relationship was not only a means of imparting knowledge but of shaping behavior. While young radicals of the 1920s had challenged generational hierarchies, youth organizers a decade later emphasized obedience to elders. Mikhailov stressed that youth would take this attitude into their future careers as "government employees, soldiers, Red Army commanders, Stakhanovites, and commanders of industry."[60]

Although traditional education and teachers formed an increasingly important part of the Komsomol's vision of a disciplined adolescence, anxieties also arose over teachers who gave up on unruly pupils. Their lack of determination had supposedly allowed high numbers of youth to drop out of school. At the same December 1939 plenum, a youth leader from Moscow claimed that forty-five hundred schoolchildren had already left schools in the province in the 1939–40 school year. Leningrad's youth leader reported dropouts in the city numbered nearly twenty-four thousand, adding that teachers were often to blame for these cases. Teachers themselves received assessments based on their students' grades. One who feared the black mark of a failed student was alleged to have told a pupil, "Kolia, you're not making very much of yourself—go get a job."[61] Secretary Nikolai Romanov maintained that these dropouts would not just suffer from a lack of learning. Away from the disciplinary force of teachers, they would "fall under the influence of criminals, felons, and sometimes even class-alien elements."[62]

The tension between negligence and discipline among teachers appeared in the Komsomol-sponsored 1940 film *Spring Thaw* (Vesennyi potok). The film opens as a young teacher and former orphan, Nadezhda Kulagina (Valentina Serova), returns to her hometown to teach in the local primary school. She runs into trouble immediately when she finds that the class contains several boys whose behavior borders on hooliganism. The school's senior teacher, Grushin (Mikhail Astangov), demands the expulsion of the main troublemaker, Dimka. Kulagina defends Dimka, who she believes is a good but misguided boy with a heartfelt interest in zoology. Despite her good work with the children, the group's best pupil, distraught over family problems, falsely accuses Kulagina of physical abuse. Based on these accusations, the school suspends the young teacher. Kulagina does not despair, though. With the help of her romantic interest, the Pioneer counselor who doubles as the physical education instructor, she turns Dimka into an excellent student by appealing to his love of animals. Then Dimka,

---

60. Ibid., l. 65.
61. RGASPI, f. 1m, op. 2, d. 189, l. 12.
62. Ibid., l. 149.

a natural leader in his class group, rallies his peers to convince the star pupil to retract her denunciation. The young teacher's efforts succeed in restoring peace and order to the group. Kulagina represented the Komsomol's ideal instructor: a disciplinarian who was willing to involve herself personally in the lives of her students to ensure their academic and personal well-being. Grushin represented the old way of teaching: the distant instructor who punished redeemable pupils for the sake of convenience.

In the Komsomol in schools, discipline meant intervening in students' coursework or pulling them back to the classroom if they had dropped out. An article by M. Kropacheva, a teacher from a Leningrad school, demonstrated the ideal disciplinary scenario. When one of her students received several bad grades in the first quarter, she mobilized his group mates, who spoke to the student about raising his marks. These talks had little impact, so she moved to stronger measures, giving him an official reprimand from the Komsomol. Not only did the reprimand succeed with the struggling student, it served as an example for other students not to fall behind.[63] Beyond the pages of the youth press, too, this form of discipline seems to have worked. In 1940 and 1941, Kiev province's Komsomol reinstated several students, expelled previously for failing grades that had since improved.[64]

Keeping young people in the schoolhouse was one form of ensuring their development as proper citizens. The community of the Komsomol was another. A major concern among youth leaders, though, was that the league was too boring to attract members and keep them involved. As Ol'ga Mishakova complained to a group of organizers in Karelia in 1940, the lack of official evening activities had driven youth toward "card games, drinking, and a whole range of behavioral perversions." Without the Komsomol to organize entertainment, she worried that youth would engage in "deviations in behavior, like drinking or youth marrying multiple times or card games."[65] The alternative was sports, dances, hobby circles (e.g., sewing), and other community activities. These occupations had an instrumental value. Entertainment in the Soviet Union was purposeful— a means of improving the population and teaching practical skills.[66] Yet another purpose of recreation and participation in the Komsomol was to fight boredom and, by doing so, to beat hooliganism before it took root.

Local activists also asserted that the lack of community activities was a cause of inappropriate behavior. The youth group of *Krasnaia zvezda* in October 1939

---

63. "Kak my provodim obshchie sobraniia," *Komsomol'skii rabotnik*, no. 2 (1940): 24–25.
64. DAKO, f. 7p, op. 3, spr. 35, ark. 143; spr. 36, ark. 221.
65. NARK, f. 1229, op. 3, d. 4, l. 117.
66. Edelman, *Serious Fun*; Grant, *Physical Culture and Sport*, 49–71.

brought disciplinary proceedings against a member who lost his Komsomol card at a restaurant after drinking 150 grams of vodka. Apparently, he had been with at least one stranger. Many of his peers wanted to know who these mystery men were, and most important, if he had revealed military secrets to potential spies. Other members of the group, particularly its leaders, wanted to know why he was drinking in the first place. They placed the blame on a lack of activities that would allow members "to spend their time in a way that is more interesting and meaningful."[67] A youth conference in the town of Lopasne in Moscow province in 1940 revealed similar concerns about the lack of cultured outlets for youth. The secretary of Lopasne's school youth group pleaded with district youth leaders for more and better community spaces. Lacking infrastructure, young people met on the highway for nighttime strolls while in the pitch-black park, people could "do whatever to whomever."[68]

In the Komsomol's goal to reform and restrict youth, law enforcement played a central role in establishing the boundary between forgivable malfeasances and unforgivable crimes. Once arrested, young people were irrevocably outside Soviet official culture. In October 1940, the police arrested a large number of Kiev's students for hooliganism. Meanwhile, in the past year, 1,116 children had dropped out of Kiev schools. Komsomol leaders linked these two trends. Outside schoolhouse walls, they said, "weak-willed sections of youth" fell into the world of crime. A report to the Komsomol Central Committee claimed, "[The groups had] their own rules and chiefs—déclassé, socially dangerous elements— and used hostile methods, drinking bouts and degeneracy, to recruit youth into criminal activity." Nikolai Mikhailov chided Kiev city youth leaders for forgetting the lesson of the August 1937 purge plenum, that degeneracy was "one of the methods of enemy work." The incident, he said, was not an ordinary crime but had "a political meaning."[69]

Mikhailov reached similar conclusions about a case of hooliganism at Moscow State University. The students of the Soviet Union's leading university should have been exemplary—especially when more than three-quarters were Komsomol members. When league administrators investigated the university in April 1941, though, they uncovered a seedy underbelly of "card games, drinking bouts, hooliganism, and violations of the dormitory code of conduct." Even local activists from the university were quoted as saying that it was acceptable to go on drinking binges to mark "extraordinary" occasions like birthdays, the end of the

67. RGVA, f. 9, op. 30, d. 181, l. 47.
68. OKhDOPIM, f. 648p, op. 1, d. 18, l. 13.
69. RGASPI, f. 1m, op. 3, d. 246, ll. 35–47, 48; d. 249, l. 52.

semester, and new acquaintanceships. Although the university had well-behaved Komsomol members, they were too occupied with studies to notice and act on the alleged degeneracy of their peers.

Investigators' findings confirmed youth leaders' fears: Degeneracy unchecked would lead to hooliganism and political deviation. In groups in the history department, degeneracy had given way to candid discussions of current politics. In a seminar on revolutionary leaders, one student said: "It's impossible to compare Stalin with Lenin, as you might compare Marx with Engels, because Stalin is vain. He loves applause." Youth leaders characterized the discussion as the worst of a "system" rather than an isolated incident. Apparently, some fourth-year students treated seminars as "a place where they can raise pointed questions, even if these questions have a counterrevolutionary character." The university had immediately expelled the implicated students before the investigators prepared the report. Additionally, Mikhailov ordered the removal of the assistant head of Moscow State's youth committee in connection with the affair.[70]

Youthful romanticism was another target Mikhailov and other Komsomol leaders hoped to suppress. Radical young poets of the "new school" movement gathered at Moscow's Institute of Philosophy, Literature, and History. Lauding the activists of the 1920s, they urged Stalin to continue the revolution—to overturn existing generational hierarchies and cultural norms. Mikhail Kul'chitskii wrote "A Conversation with Comrade Stalin," where he demanded the Soviet government ban "venal poems about our motherland":

> Do the numbers blush on your watch, Stalin,
> When you look over the new journal at leisure,
> And see how the literary prostitutes,
> Sell your name on its pages?

Like their activist counterparts of the 1920s, these poets classified themselves not only as pro-Soviet but as even bigger supporters of the Marxist-Leninist mission to construct socialism than many authorities. Their romanticism was counter to the disciplinary demands of Stalinist youth culture, though. During Khrushchev's de-Stalinization campaign in the 1950s and 1960s, cultural leaders would rediscover the "new poets" (many of whom died in the war) and credit them as a form of anti-Stalinism.[71]

---

70. RGASPI, f. 1m, op. 3, d. 370, ll. 3–4, 53.

71. Ilya Kukulin, "Expansion as Revolution Renewed: An Approach to Soviet Poetry of 1939–1941," paper presented at Occupations and Liberations in World War II: New Research on the Soviet Experience, Georgetown University, October 31, 2014.

Youth like the "new poets" came under the watch of the NKVD, whose agents sought out groups that supposedly threatened the Soviet sociopolitical order. In Ukraine, investigators uncovered anti-Soviet organizations at schools where tenth-graders did not appear at the celebratory march of the twenty-first anniversary of the October Revolution.[72] In January 1939, officers unmasked the blandly named Illegal Party in the village of Dunino, Kharkov province. The supposed party included seven nineteen- and twenty-year-olds, led by a Komsomol member named Sokol. The conspiratorial party's main activities were to "steal kolkhoz property, beat passersby, and organize drinking bouts." Sokol and his rowdy friends were the causes of social disorder, not unlike other young men. The police turned Sokol and his peers into an anti-Soviet organization and arrested the alleged leader.[73] In a similar case, investigators reported to the NKVD head Lavrentii Beria about a group of alleged anarchists in Kiev city's School no. 40. A secret informant in the school told operatives that its three leaders were "conducting work to recruit new members into their counterrevolutionary group, predisposing them to degeneracy and criminality." Their activities up to May 1939 included attacking Komsomol members and other students, ripping up wall newspapers, scaring teachers, and engaging in sexual activities with girls. In the context of a North American high school, these young people would have been teenage bullies. In Stalin's Soviet Union, their harassment of peers and teachers turned into a conspiracy reported to the head of the secret police.[74]

In the NKVD, any organized meeting outside the framework of Soviet official culture had the potential to become a conspiracy. When police arrested youth on charges like these, local youth groups banished the violators as unredeemable. The criminal justice system and the NKVD were the ultimate arbiters of who was unfit to join proper Soviet society. In cases when courts had already sentenced members, youth committees invariably decided to expel the miscreants.[75]

When the NKVD or the courts were not involved, Komsomol organizers sought to save youth who had strayed through minor disciplinary offenses or by dropping out of school. Indeed, after the end of the mass operations, even limited numbers of youth from supposed class-enemy backgrounds could join and stay in the league. The danger that young people might commit future transgressions motivated organizers to recruit even more members and to prevent the expulsion of existing young communists. Instead of allowing them to fall into the grasp

72. HDA SBU, f. 16, op. 1, spr. 336, ark. 5–8, 11–17.
73. Ibid., ark. 1–4.
74. Ibid., ark. 35–58.
75. RGVA, f. 9, op. 30, d. 260, ll. 286–89, 323–24, 365, 382; DAKO, f. 7, op. 3, spr. 32, ark. 111–51.

of the penal system, Komsomol groups were supposed to keep young people in Soviet disciplinary institutions like schools or the league itself.

The role of the Komsomol as a mass youth organization was to monitor young people, ensure they adhered to norms of behavior, and corral them if they strayed beyond acceptable limits. As it gained more members, the ideological content of the Komsomol became less demanding, although it did not disappear entirely. What youth leaders hoped to impart to members was loyalty, social discipline, and adherence to cultured behavior. Even material rewards went hand-in-hand with the transformation of youth into good Soviet citizens and future leaders. Activity in the Komsomol was not only meant to forge good citizens. It was also supposed to rescue young people whom officials believed could pose a danger to themselves and to the regime. Through activism and recreation, youth leaders hoped to save and redeem youth from the perils of bad grades, hooliganism, and worse. In their mission to construct a Soviet generation, they also hoped to constrict the populace, heading off potential dissent or anti-Soviet behavior before it reached the critical point that would demand the intervention of the courts or the NKVD.

As it gained a mass membership, the Komsomol took on characteristics of youth leagues in other states, particularly of its would-be enemies in Germany and Italy. Even after the Komsomol's expansion in the late 1930s, its age saturation, about a third of Soviet youth, still did not approach that of the Hitler Youth in Germany.[76] Nonetheless, youth leaders in each of these authoritarian states came to an understanding that the regime should enjoy a total claim over the nation's youth. In the Soviet Union, the Komsomol was to include the best of a community of youth that opposed anti-Soviet forces. The effort to expand the league was meant to grow the population of youth who would support the USSR in a war and limit those that could become fifth columnists. As the apparent likelihood of such a war increased, Komsomol membership took on another purpose: the paramilitary training of Soviet youth.

---

76. Kater, *Hitler Youth*, 23; Andreev et al., *Naselenie Sovetskogo Soiuza*, 121–26; RGASPI, f. 1m, op. 126, d. 393, ll. 5–6, 11, 20.

PARAMILITARY TRAINING ON THE EVE OF WAR

The period between August 1939 and June 1941 appeared to be a time of peace for the Soviet Union. Through its nonaggression pact with Germany, the country seemingly avoided a major military conflict for several years. The Soviet-Finnish War of 1939–40 was a devastating blow to the Red Army, proving its ineffectiveness in the face of a smaller but determined enemy. Nonetheless, the annexation of its new western territories came with a cost of relatively little bloodshed. The 1938 film *If Tomorrow War Comes* (Esli zavtra voina) had promised that the Soviet Union would be prepared for a war that had seemed inevitable. Now the theaters were filled with comedies and historical films like *Bogdan Khmelnitskii* (1941), about the friendship of Ukraine and Russia. Even works about the Finnish war, for example the film *Girlfriends on the Front* (Frontovye podrugy, 1941), characteristically explored none of that conflict's devastating implications for Soviet military preparedness. Beneath the surface of Soviet culture, though, political leaders and activists continued and accelerated efforts to militarize society—above all, through programs for the young, the source of combatants in a war.

Earlier in the 1930s, cultured behavior for young men in the Komsomol had taken on aspects of military-style discipline. Youth leaders had increasingly considered paramilitary training a duty for the league's men. The preparation of youth in the late 1930s and early 1940s marked an intensification of this militarization. From 1939 onward, Red Army planners directly collaborated with civilian Komsomol leaders to implement paramilitary programs for large numbers of youth. The Komsomol-Red Army programs aspired not only to supplement but to replace parts of basic training. The immediate catalyst for this collaboration was the Soviet-Finnish War, from which Soviet leaders sought to draw lessons more broadly for future conflicts.[1] Soon after the Finnish war, though, Germany's victory over France in the summer of 1940 gave the Soviet leadership even more reason for alarm.[2] Stalin and others had expected that the war in Western Europe would occupy Germany for years, as World War I had. Germany's victory increased the possibility that it could open up another front against its ally, the Soviet Union.

Another factor that informed the militarization of the USSR's youth programs was youth leaders' study of foreign organizations. In spite of its reputation as an isolated dictatorship, administrators in Stalin's regime were absorbed by developments in other European countries—and particularly in its authoritarian states.[3] Information about the youth associations of the USSR's hostile neighbors, above all those in Germany, was a source of anxiety and inspiration. As they denounced Fascist militarization of youth, they also took on an understanding of physical and military training as a pillar of modern youth programs.[4] By 1941, Komsomol organizers envisioned the league itself as a parallel military structure, capable of being converted for war in an instant.

Learning from the Enemy

The Bolshevik Revolution placed Soviet leaders in a paradoxical relationship with the broader world. As Marxists, they believed in the inevitability of world revolution and the righteousness of their own political system. The ultimate goal of the Soviet-dominated Communist International (Comintern) was to overthrow existing political structures in foreign countries, although Soviet foreign policy often took precedence in its immediate aims. For much of the interwar period, the Soviet Union was a pariah state, isolated from traditional diplomatic channels. Soviet leaders nonetheless recognized the need for contact with the broader world and fostered cultural ties with creative and scientific elites abroad,

---

1. The records of party Central Committee meetings about the lessons to be learned from the war have been published in the document collection "*Zimniaia voina.*"

2. Gorodetsky, *Grand Delusion*, 25, 33.

3. Weiner, "Nature, Nurture, and Memory," 1122.

4. Research on Italian and German youth organizations suggests that Soviet youth leaders were largely correct in their assessment that these programs intended to prepare youth for army service. See Koon, *Believe, Obey, Fight*; and Kater, *Hitler Youth.*

particularly among leftists.[5] Moreover, Soviet intellectuals participated in global artistic and scholarly communities, keenly following and often contributing to the developments in international science and culture.[6]

In the late 1930s, Stalinist leaders proclaimed the superiority of their country's political system and culture. The USSR had achieved socialism—making it the most highly developed polity in the world—while the bourgeois world was mired in decadent capitalism.[7] Although Stalinists were scornful of Western achievements, they were also fearful of capitalist influences. During the Great Terror, NKVD officials turned connections with foreign experts into signs of supposed spying.[8] Despite this antipathy toward the outside world, awareness and interest in developments outside the Soviet Union continued even in the darkest days of the terror.

In the sphere of sports and youth programs, Soviet administrators also studied the practices of their foreign counterparts. Experts frequently justified the study of foreign sport as a scientific endeavor that would allow Soviet athletes "to catch up and overtake" their foreign counterparts, as slogans of the time proclaimed.[9] Although Soviet sports authorities examined information from various countries, the models they analyzed most often were from other authoritarian states. A meeting of Ukrainian physical culture workers convened in November 1935 to discuss plans for specialized ten-year sports schools. In his comments, the head of the Ukrainian Institute of Physical Education, V.A. Bliakh, argued that any sports school needed to encourage discipline and be militarized "to some degree." As an example, he brought up an eight-year school for physical training in Japan. A colleague tentatively raised the possibility of using Mussolini's Italy as a potential model.[10] Experts like Bliakh had to qualify their interest in these programs. After all, they understood these regimes as enemies of the Soviet Union. However, these models were attractive for sports leaders because they appeared to be accomplishing desirable goals like military and disciplinary training.

Komsomol leaders were aware of developments in foreign physical culture as well as in foreign youth programs. Youth leaders received intelligence about organizations in other countries from Red Army attachés and intelligence officers. Usually the reports had to do with defense-related aspects of these organizations.[11]

---

5. David-Fox, *Showcasing the Great Experiment*, 40–46.

6. Hoffmann, *Cultivating the Masses*, 101–10; Clark, *Moscow, the Fourth Rome*, 31.

7. David-Fox, *Showcasing the Great Experiment*, 285–311.

8. For example, chess theorists were purged in 1937 for their publications in a "German-Fascist" journal. Bernstein, "Valedictorians of the Soviet School," 405.

9. TsDAHO, f. 7, op. 1, spr. 1329, ark. 3; Edelman, *Spartak Moscow*, 80–84.

10. TsDAHO, f. 7, op. 1, spr. 1326, ark. 6–7, 9.

11. The Komsomol archive contains many files with such reports. See RGASPI, f. 1m, op. 23, d. 1152; d. 1207; d. 1287; d. 1447.

On the 1936 report called "About Military-Fascist Youth Organizations Abroad" the reader, almost certainly the then Komsomol leader Aleksandr Kosarev, underlined the sections about the militarization of German youth extensively. His markings suggest that he found Germany's use of compulsory military training in schools and in the Hitler Youth especially interesting, if only to denounce.[12] Kosarev's report at the Tenth Komsomol Congress in 1936 included sections that were nearly identical to "About Military-Fascist Youth Organizations Abroad."[13] His main point in the speech, and that of all public information about foreign youth organizations before 1939, was to contrast the peace-loving but defense-ready nature of Soviet youth with the warlike nature of Fascist countries—Germany, Italy, Japan, and Poland in particular. The 1937 article called "Fascism Prepares a New War" made a similar point. Reprinted widely in the youth press, it claimed that Fascist organizations trained youth from childhood to young adulthood "in the spirit of chauvinism and militarism."[14]

Behind closed doors, original materials about Fascism were privileged documents. In a strange but revealing episode from early 1937, Mikhail Chernov, son of the commissar of agriculture (also Mikhail) and a worker at the TsDKA, found his father's NKVD-translated copy of *Mein Kampf* at their home. His friend, another Komsomol organizer at TsDKA, learned about the book and asked to borrow it. Initially the organizer asked local party members informally whether it was acceptable to read the book, apparently to their indifference. He also naively asked the younger Chernov if he could read the book on the tram and showed it to members of his local Komsomol committee. The organizer later claimed that he had only been interested in the book to learn about the enemy. Moreover, he said, the book was such drivel that he was unable to finish it.[15]

After several weeks, party members reconsidered the political threat of the organizer's reading materials, and the party committee intervened. The case was particularly dangerous because, as one Komsomol leader in the commissariat asserted, it would reflect poorly on the country if the public learned "that in the Soviet Union Hitler's book is being read." A commission removed the youth organizer from the party and Komsomol, and he was probably arrested. Chernov was expelled from the Komsomol and later arrested, although it seems likely that his detention was in conjunction with his father's arrest. The older Chernov was arrested and then executed in 1938 after being tried in the third Moscow show

---

12. RGASPI, f. 1m, op. 23, d. 1207, ll. 3, 4.
13. RGASPI, f. 6m, op. 10, d. 1, l. 55.
14. *Komsomolets Karelii*, August 2, 1937, 3.
15. RGVA, f. 9, op. 30, d. 82, ll. 142–46, 166–70.

trial. Besides the two leading culprits in the *Mein Kampf* incident, the party committee rounded up all those who had been exposed to the book, giving many of the activists official reprimands that cost them their positions in the Komsomol organization. In all likelihood, the case of *Mein Kampf* was really about a young man who wanted to impress his peers with his access to secret knowledge. At the same time, the affair also revealed youth organizers' curiosity about Fascism and, on the part of authorities, a fear of the spread of information outside officially mandated channels.[16]

In state administrations that depended on the study of materials from abroad, workers were conscious that these sources posed a danger. One of the main tasks of the Moscow Physical Culture Institute was to analyze and translate foreign methodological works about sport and physical fitness. Because of the perceived danger of bourgeois and Fascist ideas, though, censors limited the materials available to the institute. At a meeting of institute researchers in 1937, a translator named Nepomiashchii complained that censors were confiscating too many foreign journals that he needed for work. Referring to a German publication, he said, "This magazine has a Fascist spirit and a strong one, but we have enough immunity that we aren't scared of it."[17] Soviet officials believed Fascist information was infectious, capable of turning the unsuspecting and weak into Fascist sympathizers. At the same time, the researchers also believed that it was necessary to translate and study these sources in spite of the danger. They needed to understand their enemies—and perhaps even to learn from them.

The urgency behind the study of Fascist youth programs was a product of both the broad tensions between the USSR and its potential enemies and the specific outcome of the Spanish Civil War. In that conflict, Soviet leaders found a proxy for the future war that they envisioned between socialism and Fascism. Soviet advisers with the Spanish Republican Army faced off against German and Italian forces who aided the nationalist Falange indirectly with training and directly in combat. Besides advisers from the USSR, though, Trotskyists and other leftists had come to the republic's aid, leading to political conflicts and schisms between the various socialist groups.[18] When Franco's forces emerged victorious, Stalinist leaders came to believe that non-Soviet aligned socialists had sabotaged the republic's defenses. For Stalin the chief lesson of Spain was that internal discord would generate a fifth column during a war with the capitalist world. Fear of

---

16. RGVA, f. 9, op. 30, d. 81, ll. 312, 315–18, 319–22. In another case, a Komsomol member expelled for carrying a picture of Hitler claimed, "I was studying his face so that if I ever met him I'd be able to give him one [hit him]." RGASPI, f. 1m, op. 2, d. 136, l. 102.

17. GARF, f. 7576, op. 1, d. 325, l. 10.

18. Chase, *Enemies Within the Gates?*, 196–97.

potential anti-Soviet internal dissent was a major factor motivating the Great Terror.[19] It is likely that the Spanish Civil War taught Soviet leaders other lessons as well. It is not difficult to imagine that the victory of the Falange validated Fascist methods of paramilitary training in the eyes of Soviet leaders.

When sports administrators and physical education experts met in October 1937 in Moscow to discuss changes to the GTO program, the specter of war loomed. Elena Knopova, acting head of the sports committee, explained why the sports experts had gathered in her opening address: "The world is on the brink of war. This isn't some kind of outlook on the future. The world is really on the edge of war. War has essentially begun." The new program reflected Knopova's stark proclamation about the wartime situation. The architect of the new GTO norms was A. D. Novikov, a researcher at the Moscow Physical Culture Institute. Novikov explained that his revised program had come from a variety of sources "not only our domestic experience but the experiences of state physical preparation programs around the world." As Novikov continued to speak, he made clear that these worldwide practices were primarily those of Fascist states.[20]

Novikov took two main ideas he saw in the programs of the USSR's would-be enemies and adapted them to the Soviet context. The first was the need to keep reserve soldiers physically prepared for the duration of their potential army service. Novikov hoped the new GTO program would achieve this goal by placing expirations on the program's certification, forcing young people to retake the exam after several years if they wanted to maintain their GTO qualification.[21] The second was to increase the focus on physical activities with military applications like shooting, grenade throwing, and swimming in clothes. In some cases, these militarized activities were carryovers from the previous GTO program (e.g., grenade throwing) but with more stringent requirements. For the revised version of GTO, Novikov and his colleagues made military goals the essence of the program rather than just one of its goals.

Of course, Novikov also emphasized that the goals of the GTO program were different from those of its foreign counterparts. Soviet physical education militarized youth for defense rather than for aggression. Yet the purposes of Soviet and foreign programs were fundamentally similar. According to Novikov, foreign

---

19. Khlevniuk, "Reasons for the Great Terror."

20. GARF, f. 7576, op. 9, d. 7, ll. 1–2, 9–10.

21. Having a GTO badge was more than just a matter of pride. A stated benefit of the program was that participants would gain priority access to sports facilities. Implied benefits included better access to promotion in the Komsomol and the party as an active member of Soviet society. On the GTO program and its relationship to the new Soviet person, see Grant, *Physical Culture and Sport*, 37–41.

sports programs did not "just exist for their own sake" but functioned to prepare youth for the military, just as the GTO program was to prepare youth for the Red Army. Without Novikov's research notes, it cannot be certain what foreign practices he wrote directly into the GTO. It is clear, though, that he accepted the guiding principle of these organizations: Militarized youth fitness programs were essential for a strong army.[22]

Germany's victories in Europe in 1939–40 impressed Soviet youth leaders. After signing the nonaggression pact with Germany, Stalin and other Soviet leaders were shocked when the Wehrmacht stormed through France in a matter of weeks. This success further impressed on youth leaders the apparent achievements of German programs. Soviet studies of sports and youth paramilitary activity among its new allies presented analysis in neutral or favorable tones. They ceased to call these countries "Fascist," for example, favoring the proper name of the state. Grigorii Gromov, a Komsomol Central Committee secretary, said in a meeting about the children's book publisher Detizdat: "The Germans have put out engaging military games. Is it really impossible for us to give those kinds of things to children—to create interesting military games and channel their creativity in that direction?"[23]

In July 1940, the head of the sports administration, Vasilii Snegov, sent Stalin, Molotov, and Voroshilov a report on the state of physical culture and sport in the USSR. The report focused heavily on the comparison of Soviet and German sport, and included a long appendix about German programs. Snegov opened, "Recent events have shown that physical preparation . . . is by far not the least important factor in victory [in war]." He linked the outcome in France to Germany's "intensive work in the physical upbringing of its population, particularly of youth." Among other suggestions, Snegov implied that the Soviet Union could replicate the German system by including more hours for physical education in the school program and one day per week of war games, as he said the Germans used.[24]

Sports authorities' praise of German youth programs became so effusive that it drew criticism from Komsomol leaders. In 1941, the Moscow Institute of Physical Culture published a journal called *Sports Abroad* whose coverage of Germany

---

22. GARF, f. 7576, op. 9, d. 7, ll. 9–10, 15. Novikov also modified the program to allow for the wide range of ecosystems and sports cultures in the USSR. For example, exam takers could substitute extra marches for skiing in areas where the climate would not permit skiing. It is also worth noting that, perhaps due to the chaos and turnover the purges of sports personnel caused, the GTO revisions were not finalized until 1939. RGASPI, f. 1m, op. 3, d. 213, ll. 28–35. Novikov came under intense scrutiny in 1937–38 for his connections to purged cadres in physical culture. GARF, f. 7576, op. 1, d. 325.

23. RGASPI, f. 1m, op. 3, d. 238, l. 95.

24. RGASPI, f. 1m, op. 23, d. 1433, ll. 1–19, 28–39.

struck Mikhailov as so laudatory that he denounced the publication to Politburo Candidate Member Aleksandr Shcherbakov, a central figure in propaganda
work. Mikhailov complained that the journal gave voice to "the Germanophile
idea" and cited one passage as particularly offensive: "When undertaking a game
on the field, in the forest and so on, [German] youth learn from the tactics of
their army. This allows youth to enter the army already having certain military
skills. . . . Learning from this material will bring major benefits to our organizations of physical culture."[25] Written in May 1941, Mikhailov's letter may have
represented a shifting view of Germany as an imminent threat once again. More
likely, though, is that Mikhailov believed the praise of Germany in the journal
was too public. Overall, Mikhailov and other Komsomol leaders continued to
express interest in understanding how German and other foreign youth programs operated.

Paramilitary training for youth grew out of the militarized atmosphere of the
1930s and 1940s in authoritarian states. Soviet youth and sports officials readily
studied their neighbors for programs they could adapt to the USSR. The desire
to replicate paramilitary practices reflected an understanding common across
authoritarian regimes that youth was a resource to be cultivated for war. As
Europe entered World War II, youth leaders not only intensified defense training
but sought the wholesale conversion of Komsomol groups into military units.

"If Tomorrow War Comes"

In August 1939, as Soviet and German leaders were finalizing their nonaggression
pact, the Komsomol's Central Committee met to discuss paramilitary training.
L. O. Shteinbakh, the head of the league's office of military and physical culture cast
shame on those members who could not fight: "We often say 'if tomorrow war
comes' but does every Komsomol leader really understand what he will do and
what each Komsomol member will do . . . in the event of war in our country?"[26]
Soon after, on September 1, 1939, the Supreme Soviet lowered the call-up age
in the USSR from twenty-one to nineteen. The double conscription cohort, the
continuing threat of war, and the Soviet military's disastrous performance in the
war with Finland all made defense training a central issue in the youth league.
As they intensified training, Komsomol leaders increasingly engaged Red Army
planners in their attempts to raise a generation of soldiers.

---

25. RGASPI, f. 1m, op. 23, d. 1453, l. 16; d. 1454, ll. 151–54.
26. RGASPI, f. 1m, op. 2, d. 178, ll. 184, 188.

During the Soviet-Finnish War of 1939–40, party and military leaders called on the Komsomol to furnish military units directly for the first time since the civil war. The Winter War was a result of the nonaggression pact's placement of Finland into the Soviet sphere of influence. Soviet leaders made an ultimatum to the Finnish government—first privately in 1938 and then publicly in the fall of 1939—to cede territories around Leningrad, believing the region could be a launching point for an invasion of the USSR. Unwilling to accede to these demands, Finland began to mobilize its military for war with the Soviet Union. In the conflict that began in November 1939, the Red Army endured humiliating losses to an enemy that was numerically weaker but better trained for winter conditions. Desperately needing militarized skiers for the Red Army, party leaders commanded Nikolai Mikhailov to recruit ski brigades from the ranks of Komsomol members in January 1940.

Mikhailov considered the orders critically important and acted with urgency. On January 10, he telegraphed youth leaders in cold-weather territories, giving quotas for recruiting in each province, the total figure coming to about fifteen hundred young men for five battalions. In the end, local Komsomol organizations would send enough members to fill seven units. The recruits were to be "politically capable, decisive, brave, and physically fit."[27] The majority of youth committees jumped at the chance to influence the outcome of the war and set about recruiting youth with urgency. An internal report made a special note of Yuri Andropov, the future Soviet leader who was then secretary of the Iaroslavl provincial youth committee. Besides rapidly fulfilling the recruitment quotas, Andropov volunteered himself for conscription. Although he ultimately did not participate directly in the conflict, his organization and others were able to fulfill and exceed the control figures in a matter of days.[28]

The recruiting phase occurred faster than the army could handle the new soldiers. On January 14, Mikhailov updated the party secretaries Andreev and Malenkov that the youth league would be able to recruit more than a sufficient number of soldiers and would commandeer skis from sports associations.[29] In a memo to Stalin, Mikhailov claimed that these battalions were ready to fight. Army reports and remembrances tell a different story, though. Military and Komsomol

---

27. RGASPI, f. 1m, op. 23, d. 1439, ll. 4–6, 9–11, 12–14; d. 1454, ll. 41–44.

28. RGASPI, f. 1m, op. 23, d. 1439, ll. 62–66, 69–71.

29. The issue of skis was no small matter. The April 1940 party Central Committee meeting of Red Army commanders with Stalin and other political leaders dissected the mistakes of the war. One commander not only lamented the lack of training but the absence of skis: "Things are bad with ski training, but it's an important subject. We don't have the skis we need—short, wide skis—you just can't get them." Chubaryan and Shukman, *Stalin and the Soviet-Finnish War*, 47.

leaders sent home many recruits (almost 18 percent in one battalion) for practical and, to a lesser extent, political reasons. Inspectors from the Commissariat of Defense reported to Mikhailov, "The military preparation of the formed battalions is characterized by an absolute lack of training on skis."[30] In an interview from 2006, the battalion member Georgii Prusakov recalled his recruitment and training for the Leningrad Komsomol battalion. A student at the time, he "knew skiing pretty well," and when his local Komsomol secretary asked him if he would like to join, he agreed. It is unclear whether all recruits volunteered as Prusakov claims he did. For preparation he said his group had roughly five days of ski and firearms training before his battalion left for the front. In the short time that remained in the war, the battalion experienced 628 casualties among its 764 members.[31]

The episode indicated a turn in the Komsomol's relationship with the military. Previously, the youth league had interacted with the Red Army through intermediaries. Its activists had provided political supervision during conscription campaigns, mobilized youth for Osoaviakhim training and military academies, and participated in fundraising for the military. While these activities continued into 1939 and beyond, Komsomol organizers also began to recruit youth directly for combat service. As war spread throughout Europe, youth leaders and Red Army officers increasingly worked together to militarize youth—especially within the Komsomol itself.

The league's participation in the Winter War was the logical continuation of policies that had increasingly intertwined the league with the military. Early in 1939, Nikolai Mikhailov had renewed a program from 1935, a campaign of military training camps for Komsomol workers. Unlike the 1935 camps run by Osoaviakhim, the 1939 camps were organized through the Red Army. Moreover, the ambitious two-month program in the 1939 camps focused primarily on military skills rather than on training that could apply to work in the civilian youth organization as well.[32]

The Komsomol-Red Army collaboration came at the expense of Osoaviakhim. In the two years before the German invasion of the USSR, skepticism about the ability of Osoaviakhim to fulfill its duties surfaced among Komsomol leaders. After the arrest of the civil defense head and former Komsomol secretary Pavel Gorshenin in October 1938, its new chair became Pavel Kobelev. Under Kobelev Osoaviakhim grew considerably—from nine million to thirteen million members over the course of 1939. These numbers rose in part due to the simultaneous expansion of the Komsomol. Three million members belonged to both

30. RGASPI, f. 1m, op. 23, d. 1439, ll. 97, 98, 99–100, 103–112; d. 1440, l. 8; d. 1441, l. 30.

31. "Prusakov Georgii Vasil'evich," *Ia pomniu*. http://iremember.ru/pekhotintsi/prusakov-georgiy-vasilevich.html.

32. RGASPI, f. 1m, op. 3, d. 214, ll. 2, 43–50; d. 208, l. 99; d. 210, l. 45; op. 23, d. 1327, ll. 99–102.

FIGURE 7.1.   Military training in Ordzhonikidze territory, 1937. RGAKFD, 2-82569.

organizations.[33] The increased membership did not make youth leaders confident that preparedness had increased, though. At a Komsomol Central Committee plenum in June 1940, Mikhailov interrupted a speech by Kobelev to assert that only half of Osoaviakhim members actively participated in any form of training.[34]

Various complaints from the Komsomol and elsewhere poured in about the civil defense organization. Local activists claimed that Osoaviakhim cadres, who were spread thin in rural areas, were not providing support.[35] Ranking sports committee leaders accused Osoaviakhim of limiting access to firearms, creating a bottleneck in the shooting section of the GTO program.[36] Another criticism of the civil defense society was that its training was contrived. Osoaviakhim published one book called *Military-Chemical Games*, a collection of gas mask training activities including "three-legged race in gas masks," "chess and checkers tournament in gas masks," and "hammering nails in gas masks."[37]

33. RGASPI, f. 1m, op. 2, d. 188, l. 190.
34. RGASPI, f. 1m, op. 2, d. 204, ll. 70–71.
35. OKhDOPIM, f. 648, op. 1, d. 14, ll. 59–60.
36. RGASPI, f. 1m, op. 23, d. 1432, ll. 101–4.
37. "Khronika," *Izvestiia TsK Komsomola*, no. 14 (1937): 30–31.

A Leningrad youth official in 1940 claimed that even the name Osoaviakhim, an amalgam of several NEP-era chemical and air defense organizations, was no longer appropriate.[38] In the wake of the Soviet-Finnish War, Red Army personnel attacked Osoaviakhim, the sports committee, and, to a lesser extent, the Komsomol for failing to make civilians ready to become soldiers. At the April 1940 meeting of party and Red Army leaders to discuss the Soviet-Finnish War, Khadzhen-Umar Mamsurov, the commander of a special ski detachment in the war, denounced the recreational focus of the sports committee and Osoaviakhim. After calling soccer useless—to the great disapproval of his fellows at the conference—he said that mass fitness tests were much more effective as defense preparation.[39]

Of course, the outcome of the Winter War had much larger repercussions for the army than shifts in paramilitary training. Perhaps the most visible change was that Marshal Semen Timoshenko replaced Kliment Voroshilov, the longtime commissar of defense. The new commissar embarked on a broad set of reforms that aimed to modernize and mechanize the Red Army. At the same time, he also stressed the role of the Komsomol as a direct agent of militarization. On June 3, 1940, Timoshenko wrote a call to arms to youth leaders.[40] He began his letter to the Komsomol's Central Committee by citing Stalin's exhortation from his 1938 exchange with the youth organizer Comrade Ivanov: young people should remain in a state of "mobilized preparedness." This state of readiness was only possible when ordinary youth mastered the Red Army's military technology, which in turn required a high level of physical fitness. According to Timoshenko, the mobilization in September 1939 that followed the Supreme Soviet's law on conscription had been a failure precisely because physical preparation among the new recruits was so poor. He blamed the agencies responsible for training— Osoaviakhim and the sports committee—and their failure to cooperate to create a unified military preparation program. Osoaviakhim only taught shooting, and the sports committee only taught fitness. Timoshenko closed by asking the Komsomol to lead the way, to direct youth to a true hybrid of physical and military training that would prepare them for service in the army.[41]

---

38. RGASPI, f. 1m, op. 23, d. 1444, l. 92.

39. Chubaryan and Shukman, *Stalin and the Soviet-Finnish War*, 237.

40. It is unclear whether the timing of these changes coincided with Germany's conquest of France, but it seems likely. Some might interpret this increased emphasis as a prelude to an offensive war against Germany. The thesis of planned offensive in 1941 is dubious. Although there were plans for an attack, most evidence suggests that Stalin felt the country was not ready for war in 1941 and wanted to avoid it at all costs. At the same time, Soviet leaders clearly ramped up efforts to place the country on a wartime footing in the summer of 1940, evidently concerned about the German victory. Gorodetsky, *Grand Delusion*, 6–7.

41. RGASPI, f. 1m, op. 23, d. 1438, ll. 7–11.

Soon after, on June 7, 1940, Mikhailov convened a plenary meeting of the Komsomol's Central Committee where military training was a central issue. Mikhailov suggested that developing "military instincts" was important as a part of the broader upbringing of youth. In fostering these instincts, though, his main priority was the immediate need for training that would transfer easily into the army.[42] In his search for practical military preparation, Mikhailov singled out training for young women as a counterexample. The Komsomol secretary said that despite the "natural urge" of women to defend the country, readying women for combat service was a waste of resources: "Experience shows that in the conditions of battle, women bring a bigger advantage as nurses."[43] Others continued Mikhailov's criticism. Ivan Vidiukov, the head of the Komsomol in the Red Army, was even more blunt about the role women would play in war: "Mikhailov made the question very clear (laughter from the crowd). People shout 'girls to the planes' or 'girls to the tanks,' but you yourselves know that girls will not go to the army, nor into a plane, nor into a tank."[44]

Others criticized the lack of pragmatism in defense training. Osoaviakhim's head, Kobelev, complained at the same meeting that parachutists jumped for recreation rather than as serious training to become paratroopers.[45] Previously, sports committee members had argued that parachuting was a means of developing intangible qualities like courage necessary for battle. Youth leaders had also asserted that paramilitary training for women had a heartening psychological effect on general preparation.[46] As the threat of war grew, though, youth leaders abandoned these programs in favor of those they believed would bear immediate results in war.

Based on Timoshenko and Mikhailov's appeals for practical training, Komsomol leaders began new paramilitary projects for activists and the rank and file soon after the plenum. On June 17, 1940, the league's Central Committee initiated a certification program among all Komsomol secretaries and department heads at the district and provincial level—some four thousand organizers. Only women and physically unfit men were exempt from the military training test. After passing the certification, these workers were to be sent to training

---

42. RGASPI, f. 1m, op. 2, d. 203, l. 55.

43. Ibid., l. 61.

44. RGASPI, f. 1m, op. 2, d. 204, l. 25.

45. Ibid., l. 63.

46. For example, a leader of the Dinamo sports organization reflected a general opinion when he claimed during a discussion of revisions to the GTO in 1937 that parachute jumping was necessary to engender courage among youth. GARF, f. 7576, op. 9, d. 7, ll. 69–73. On prewar training for women, see also Krylova, *Soviet Women in Combat*, 35–83.

camps or to serve a short traineeship in the military. Outside of paid organizers, the Central Committee ordered youth activists at the lower levels to complete a paramilitary program. The training was 240 hours total, including fitness drills, shooting practice, tactics, topography, and both ski and foot marches. Study groups would meet in the city, district, or territorial center and would include up to thirty people. The same resolution demanded that twenty-four hours a month of free time be devoted to military training for activists. Unlike the GTO program, which claimed to satisfy the desires of youth for recreation while preparing them for service, the Komsomol's military program had no such pretensions. These programs were serious business—a premilitary system for future soldiers.[47]

While activists completed the certification, military and youth leaders drew up a holistic program of military and physical preparation for youth. In addition to planning for more intense training, now youth leaders envisioned the transformation of the league as a whole into a military unit. A November 15 draft resolution by the Komsomol Central Committee, "On the Organization of Military-Physical Training of Members of the Komsomol" turned classroom youth groups into "companies," school youth organizations into "brigades," and district organizations into "battalions." These groupings would allow instructors to conduct large-scale tactical and strategic training in ways that were previously unmanageable. The instruction included 250 to 300 hours, depending on how much training a participant had completed in the past. The Red Army's training manual provided the core material for lessons. According to the memo, women and men would undertake the training separately. Men would train in topography, camouflage, physical preparation, and shooting. Women would practice signaling, first aid, telephony, marching, and fitness preparation. For extra preparation, male trainees between ages twenty-two and twenty-six, prime service age, would carry a training rifle on marches to simulate a real march.[48]

Komsomol leaders forwarded the draft resolution to General A. A. Tarasov, the inspector of physical preparation and sport in the Red Army, who responded with enthusiasm and minor revisions. He asserted that the Red Army had only a limited training capacity and, as matters stood, it wasted effort on training recruits in "elementary skills": "shooting, topography, formation marching, obstacle courses, grenade throwing, bayonet fighting, skiing, swimming, and so on." Tarasov dreamed of a paramilitary program that would be the equivalent of basic training in the Red Army. With a cohort of pretrained soldiers, the Soviet

---

47. RGASPI, f. 1m, op. 23, d. 1430, ll. 1–4.
48. RGASPI, f. 1m, op. 23, d. 1432, ll. 59–66.

military could focus on preparing specialists like tank drivers.[49] With Tarasov's input, the Komsomol leadership released its resolution on defense training in late November 1940. All league members were supposed to begin military and physical training on January 1, 1941. Further emphasizing the militarization of the Komsomol, the resolution promised members who completed the training would receive a special uniform.[50]

The plan was the culmination of a decade of militarization among young communists. The league's official program had long asserted that it was the reserve of the party and even responsible for national security to some degree. Now, unlike before, leaders also suggested that the youth league was a direct reserve of the Red Army. Since the early 1930s, youth leaders increasingly viewed the ideal young person as a cultured soldier. Discussions about paramilitary training even began to focus on young people's bodies. At the Komsomol Central Committee plenum in June 1940, the head of Bashkiria's youth committee said, "Can we really be militant supporters of our party if we are sickly? If we do not have strong muscles?"[51] Youth leaders' plans for military training envisioned the league as a source of recruits, even a potential supplementary army. When youth participated in these programs, though, realities often did not match the hopes of youth leaders and the Red Army.

The Parade Grounds: Paramilitary Training on the Eve of War

From late 1940 to the outbreak of war in June 1941, paramilitary instruction dominated life in the youth league. Even Pioneers and young children took part in defense exercises. During the winter, the Komsomol-affiliated children's newspaper *Pionerskaia pravda* and the military newspaper *Na shturm* organized tactical games for children in multiple cities. The papers enlisted military officials, including General Tarasov, to help in the endeavor. Participants completed exercises in marching, firearm assembly, and topography. During the drills children received modified military titles—essentially the same as in the military but with the word "young" tacked on (e.g., "young private first class"). According to a report on the games, 100,000 children took part in Moscow alone, and throughout the Soviet Union as many as 700,000 children participated. In addition to

49. Ibid., ll. 67–72.
50. Ibid., ll. 50–56.
51. RGASPI, f. 1m, op. 2, d. 203, l. 89.

FIGURE 7.2.   March of Young Pioneers in gas masks, 1935. Photograph by Viktor Bulla. Tsentral'nyi Gosudarstvennyi Arkhiv Kinofotofonodokumentov Sankt-Peterburga (TsGAKFFD SPb).

these events, the Komsomol and Pioneers organized a yearlong competition of military skills for children in 1940 that drew in approximately 1.5 million participants.[52] These competitions attempted to lay the groundwork for future paramilitary work, teaching the basic military skills that children could perfect as they grew into adults. Perhaps more important than the skills they would teach, though, the campaigns created a militarized mentality and an understanding, albeit unrealistic, of what war involved.

Military games among young adults were more intense than the children's activities. In the early morning on October 27, 1940, youth activists from Kiev organized a citywide military game meant to simulate an invasion of Ukraine's capital. At midnight, the military department of the Komsomol received a call: "This is the chief of staff of antiair defense in Kiev—raise the alarm. Airborne forces from an unknown country have landed at the airfield near Darnitsia [a district on the east bank of the Dnieper] and are moving toward the city." Aleshin-Minin, a reserve commander in charge of the Komsomol military subdivision,

52. RGASPI, f. 1m, op. 23, d. 1471, ll. 116–18; op. 3, d. 243, ll. 128–35.

ordered activists to gather members. He assigned each a packet of secret instructions addressed to the homes of youth secretaries from local groups, ordering them to meet at the House of Defense (*Dom oborony*) in the center of town at 4 am. After they received the orders, "district committees . . . turned into mobilization headquarters." As district youth leaders scurried from group to group, the town garrison issued an order: "Move out at 6 am . . . uncover and exterminate the enemy." After ten kilometers of marching in the morning darkness, scouts encountered the enemy (the youth organization of Darnitsia) and the defenders of Kiev took up positions in nearby woods. In spite of a clever feint by the enemy, complete with fake trenches, the Komsomol group from Kiev outmaneuvered its opponent and won the game.[53]

Not every war game was as elaborate as Kiev's, but all attempted to simulate wartime conditions. In November 1940, Moscow's Komsomol organization put on a militarized orienteering race in the city. The press account of the race placed an emphasis on how it had taught participants the marching and topographical skills they would use in a war. A member of one team in the race reportedly complained, "They sure did pick a path for a march." His teammate responded, "Did you want asphalt? In a war there won't always be asphalt." The article concluded that marches were a wonderful tool—but only if participants understood them as a "serious military affair" and not a "lackadaisical stroll."[54] In both the case of this race and military games like those in Kiev, the goal was not just to train skills and discipline but to create realistic scenarios. Nowhere was this truer than in Karelia, the recent theater of the Soviet-Finnish War.

The war had changed Karelia's political structure and significance. After adding territory via annexation in that war, Karelia became a union-level republic (formally equal in status to Ukraine and the other Soviet republics), and its party and Komsomol leadership saw an influx of new faces. In June 1940, the Komsomol's Central Committee nominated Yuri Andropov to head the new republic's youth league. Mikhailov likely chose Andropov because of his successful mobilization of skiers from Iaroslavl province for the Komsomol ski brigades. As youth leader of Karelia, a major aspect of Andropov's work became the preparation of military-ready skiers. The Winter War had exposed the weakness of ski brigades in the Red Army, a failure anomalous in a country where opportunities to practice skiing abounded. As Soviet leaders attempted to rectify this failure, Andropov's republic became the center of a massive skiing campaign, the Komsomol Ski Cross.

---

53. N. Sizonenko and V. Segal, "Sila lichnogo primera," *Komsomol'skii rabotnik*, no. 24 (1940): 9–11.
54. E. Dochkal, "Komsomol'tsy na marshe," *Komsomol'skii rabotnik*, no. 23 (1940): 21–25.

The ski cross expanded from a local competition to a national event. According to internal Komsomol documents, Andropov was inspired by Petrozavodsk's military signaling school, which had challenged a youth group from Arkhangelsk to a ski competition. The winner would be the organization that had more members complete the GTO skiing test. On November 26, Andropov picked up the initiative and expanded it into a broad competition between provinces in the Russian north. Soon after, the Komsomol's Central Committee further expanded the campaign to encompass all areas of the Soviet Union whose climate would permit skiing.[55]

The goals of the campaign were simultaneously specific and broad. Youth leaders developed the ski cross as a reaction to the failure of military preparation in the war with Finland, a decision Marshall Timoshenko lauded.[56] At the same time, Andropov commanded youth activists to organize the ski competition in "battalions, brigades, and units." A month into preparations for the cross, on December 25, Mikhailov emphasized that activists should not consider it an independent campaign but the beginning of a system of "regularized military preparation."[57] The broader goal was to use the ski cross as the first step in developing the training program Komsomol leaders had created with Red Army planners.

Komsomol leaders worked with local sports committees to organize the countrywide examination during the final week of January 1941. Between December and January 31, organizers arranged lessons for all youth—from beginners to expert skiers, and of Komsomol and non-Komsomol youth. In Vedlozersk district, youth groups began preparations by forming groups where five novices would be attached to a strong skier who acted as the commander.[58] The requirements for the test differed by sex, age, and skill, but at all levels participants had to complete two ski marches (one for speed and one for distance) in a set amount of time. In the final days of the campaign, Karelia's leaders went to local organizations to exhort youth to complete the test and to monitor the proceedings. Andropov himself went to Kalevala, a town in the northwest of the republic.[59] The results were impressive: In Karelia alone, roughly a third of all members had passed the test—almost ten thousand young people. According to a newspaper account, 4.85 million youth (both inside and outside the league) completed the norms. The Komsomol Ski Cross, considered a success among youth leaders, continued during the war and became the template for other campaigns. The league conducted a

55. NARK, f. 1229, op. 3, d. 135, ll. 6–7; RGASPI, f. 1m, op. 23, d. 1437, ll. 22–41.
56. RGASPI, f. 1m, op. 23, d. 1430, ll. 29–33; d. 1437, ll. 42–44.
57. RGASPI, f. 1m, op. 3, d. 239, l. 173.
58. NARK, f. 1229, op. 3, d. 135, ll. 14–17.
59. Ibid., l. 13.

gymnastics competition in the spring of 1941 and planned tests in track and field, cycling and swimming that the German invasion disrupted.[60]

In a newspaper account about the results, Andropov both congratulated and warned Komsomol organizers. The ski campaign had begun to prepare youth for service in the Red Army. The problem was not that the ski cross was unsuccessful but that it was just a start. Andropov worried that with the ski cross at an end, youth would soon forget their commitments to defense training. He related a conversation he had with a young woman participant from a factory in Petroza-vodsk. When he asked her if she had plans for future skiing expeditions, she said: "Oy, no, are you kidding. I'm lucky I passed the test."[61]

Andropov shared concerns with other Komsomol leaders, who were anxious about the regularity of military training as well as its strenuousness. At a Komso-mol Central Committee meeting in August 1939, the head of the department of student youth claimed that Osoaviakhim's Voroshilov Shooter program occurred at firing ranges where "they give you a soft feather bed, carpeting, and a trumeau mirror."[62] At the June 1940 Komsomol Central Committee plenum, Mikhailov expressed disappointment that some of the militarized marches resembled par-ties rather than serious defense training. Anatolii Pegov from Moscow's youth committee admitted that it was his organization that Mikhailov had in mind. One event had provided a bus with hot cocoa to follow the marchers.

Vidiukov, the head of the Komsomol in the Red Army, claimed that these "cozy conditions" misled youth about life in the army. Films that depicted the military with group sing-alongs accompanied by an accordionist created a notion that army life would be fun rather than demonstrating "the necessity for being physi-cally tough and strong."[63]

Paramilitary work was possible in bigger cities like Moscow or, for region-specific activities like skiing, in Petrozavodsk. In towns and the countryside, though, these activities were frequently nonexistent. Local Komsomol workers lamented their inability to conduct quality training but were unable to correct these issues. In May 1939, the Novo-Petrovskii district (Moscow province) Komsomol held a meeting dedicated to paramilitary work among youth. One activist characterized the training as "campaign-like." Young people "began to learn the workings of a rifle, went to shoot, but now the work has died out." Characteristically, paramili-tary training suffered from a lack of equipment. Of the forty-four Komsomol

---

60. Ibid., l. 9; RGASPI, f. 1m, op. 23, d. 1454, ll. 53–54; *Komsomolets Karelii*, February 28, 1941, 1.

61. Iu. Andropov, "O zadachakh voenno-fizkul'turnoi raboty v Komsomole," *Komsomolets Karelii*, March 16, 1941, 3.

62. RGASPI, f. 1m, op. 2, d. 179, l. 129.

63. RGASPI, f. 1m, op. 2, d. 203, l. 62; d. 204, ll. 14, 20.

FIGURE 7.3. Militarized march in Gorkii province, 1940. RGAKFD, 0-33801.

groups in the district, only sixteen had access to a rifle, making shooting practice impossible in most organizations.[64]

Another factor that limited the effectiveness of military training was the lack of food in the country. Even though the worst years of hunger had ended in 1933, food was never in abundance. Much of the population, especially in the countryside, suffered from malnutrition.[65] Authorities even had trouble finding participants to take part in holiday parades because young workers complained that they were starving.[66] Medical services also were spread thin in the country, contributing to poor health among the population.[67] Undoubtedly, there were many young people who were too unfit to take part in paramilitary training because they were too hungry or suffered from lack of medical care.

Besides issues of deficient equipment and provisioning, the main obstacle to paramilitary training was apparently a lack of will among local youth organizers. Komsomol leaders used disciplinary tools, even expulsion, to combat political indiscretion, shape social behavior, and enforce membership policy. In promoting paramilitary preparation, central resolutions demanded that youth who failed to do the training face "strict discipline." This discipline did not have the same effect as the Great Terror's moral panic against degeneracy, though. At the local level, youth organizations rarely punished activists who failed to fulfill their training obligations. Any disciplinary action was usually limited to verbal reprimands rather than a more serious written reprimand or expulsion. Moreover, participation in paramilitary activity was rarely a road to promotion like success in the workplace or at school. Some activists were fervent about defense preparation and often attracted a substantial number of youth who did real training. However, the relatively limited use of both carrots and sticks to promote military work constrained the effectiveness of defense preparation in the Komsomol.

Komsomol administrators were not the only ones involved in assessing the effectiveness of paramilitary training for youth. Part of the regular school and higher education program involved military training classes. A department within Narkompros—administered in Moscow by twelve Red Army officers—developed and monitored the implementation of this curriculum. In the spring of 1941, cadres from the department intensified their scrutiny on military instruction in higher education. At Moscow State University, they assessed defense training as being relatively successful, despite somewhat outmoded instruction. In contrast,

64. OKhDOPIM, f. 5358, op. 1, d. 12, ll. 9–10.
65. Osokina, *Our Daily Bread*, 155–77.
66. Grant, *Physical Culture and Sport*, 137–38.
67. Hoffmann, *Cultivating the Masses*, 123–24.

the Moscow Foreign Language Pedagogical Institute did not insist on mandatory attendance and trainees treated instructors with disrespect, addressing them by their last names and not by their ranks.[68] As in the rest of the country, institutions with human and material resources could conduct sophisticated paramilitary training, but these institutions were few.

How did youth themselves experience defense training? Few young people who left behind diaries or wrote accounts later in life suggested that military training was a central part of their lives. At the same time, it appears in most of their accounts to varying degrees. The German émigré Wolfgang Leonhard disparaged his activities in Osoaviakhim and the Komsomol in the 1930s and early 1940s: "In practice . . . our role in this society [Osoaviakhim] was limited to the duty of paying our subscriptions and attending lectures on air-raid defense three or four times a year."[69] Anfisa Dudina, who also later emigrated, disliked the training but said that most Komsomol youth completed the mandatory program.[70] Elena Volkova would serve in the Red Army as a nurse and had considerable preparation for war through her activity at an air club outside Moscow. In the 1990s, she remembered that school lessons taught her "elementary nursing, fieldcraft and the use of the rifle and the machine gun."[71] Veterans who gave interviews in the postwar period attested to the ubiquitous nature of defense training but often cast doubt on its effectiveness. Mikhail Rassadnikov remembered that as an adolescent from the countryside there had been ski training and marches but that sports as entertainment had been more important for him and his friends.[72]

Ultimately, the main effect of paramilitary preparation may have been psychological. Lev Mishchenko, a student of physics in 1941, participated in his university's "part-time military training scheme." Even though he later characterized the program as virtually useless in the war, it allowed him to become a junior commander when he volunteered with other members of his faculty and perhaps persuaded the volunteers that they were well-prepared for combat.[73] In February 1940, Nina Kosterina received a special honor for serving as company commander of her youth group during a militarized march on Red Army Day. Her group had gone from Moscow to Skhodnia, on the outskirts of Moscow's Khimki suburb, and then to Nakhabino, another suburb—a total distance of at

---

68. GARF, f. 2306r, op. 70, d. 6152, ll. 1–3, 22–24.

69. Leonhard, *Child of the Revolution*, 113.

70. A. Dudina, "Lost Years," in *Soviet Youth*, ed. Novak-Deker, 237.

71. Cited in Braithwaite, *Moscow 1941*, 110–11.

72. "Mikhail Ivanovich Rassadnikov," *Ia pomniu*, http://iremember.ru/samokhodchiki/rassadnikov-mikhail-ivanovich.html. For a similar assessment, see "Klavdiya Fedorovna Schastlivaya," *I Remember*, http://iremember.ru/zenitchiki/schastlivaya-klavdiya-fedorovna.html.

73. Cited in Braithwaite, *Moscow 1941*, 120–21.

least thirty kilometers. She characterized her company's actions as "a complete success" and treated the march with great significance. In a diary entry she concluded, "I am ready for war."[74]

From the mid-1930s, Stalinist administrators became increasingly adamant about the need for military readiness among the young people who would fight in what seemed like an imminent war. Their attempts to train youth intensified in 1939 and grew even stronger over the next two years. The Komsomol's aim to cultivate soldiers drew on a common idea in authoritarian Europe—that the purpose of youth organizations was to prepare young people for war. In the goal of imparting defense training, the Komsomol was probably not as successful as its counterparts. One historian asserted that the "hallmark of socialization was militarization" in the Hitler Youth, an organization that had extensive institutional ties with the Wehrmacht.[75] In contrast, Komsomol leaders had connections to party, civil defense, sports, and educational organizations but fewer to the Red Army until 1939. Perhaps because the youth league was an institution of social promotion, monitoring, and indoctrination, its leaders were unable to alter how organizers approached the issue of military preparation. In addition, paramilitary programs could do little to compensate for undernourishment in the population. This factor limited the number of youth who could participate in training and ultimately who would be physically fit for military service. It is impossible to assess the precise impact of the Komsomol's defense programs. It is clear, however, that they did not come close to the goal of replacing Red Army basic training.

Although the preparation youth received before they went to war was horrifically inadequate for combat, it would be incorrect to dismiss the impact of paramilitary activities. It perhaps did not contribute to the capacity of young people to fight, but it did affect their ability and willingness to mobilize. Komsomol paramilitary training had taught them how to organize themselves quickly into semimilitary formations. Most were undertrained for battle—but who could have prepared for the Soviet experience of World War II? Training in the Komsomol, not only in paramilitary exercises but in a broader culture of mobilization, would be a factor that enabled the Red Army to tap the league's ten million members rapidly in the crucial first months of the war. When the Germans attacked, young people could tell themselves that they had known war was coming and, perhaps, even believed they were ready for it.

---

74. Kosterina, *Diaries*, February 24, 1940.

75. Kater, *Hitler Youth*, 28–32. However, attempts of Hitler Youth leaders to organize social and political promotion through special schools (named Adolf Hitler schools) largely failed, in Kater's view. Soviet youth leaders, in contrast, used the youth league to further promotion quite effectively.

YOUTH AT WAR

Germany's invasion of the Soviet Union on June 22, 1941, threw the country into a state of disarray. Soviet people from high-ranking politicians to ordinary citizens had acknowledged the likelihood of war throughout the previous decade. Indeed, in 1931 Stalin had asserted that the USSR would be at war within ten years.[1] Even though Soviet citizens had prepared for conflict, the immediate reality of war was a shock. Moreover, the country had not expected the desperate, defensive struggle that unfolded. Instead of fighting on foreign soil, the Red Army and Soviet partisans found themselves thrown back into the heart of the USSR's European territory. When Soviet leaders attempted to mobilize the full force of the state and its people for the conflict, youth were perhaps those from whom the war demanded the most as combatants, workers, and supporters of Stalin's regime.

The central question in the history of the Soviet Union in World War II was how the country survived and emerged victorious despite its losses. Purges had eliminated both capable military leaders and the willingness among those remaining to challenge the orders of Stalin.[2] Military and police officials who assessed incoming conscripts in the final years before the war were dissatisfied with their

---

1. I. V. Stalin, "O zadachakh khoziaistvennikov," *Socheneniia*, 13:38.
2. Erickson, *Soviet High Command*, 507.

fitness, training, and even basic literacy.[3] Parts of the population, especially in the countryside, welcomed the Germans as Russia's liberation from Soviet power.[4]

Despite these weaknesses, the great strength of the Soviet system was its ability to mobilize society into factories and combat. Although the invasion was a shock in the immediate term, the broader structures of Stalin's regime were made for total war. Youth leaders drew on established modes of mobilizing young people into the army and the economy. At the beginning of the war, the mechanism of paramilitary training that developed in the previous decade provided millions of soldiers for the Red Army. In other ways, wartime mobilization resembled older modes of economic mobilization from the First Five-Year Plan. Young enthusiasts enlisted for the wartime struggle, while the state employed coercion to bring others into arms. The success of Stalin's regime in mobilizing the population behind the war came at a cost. The system that put millions of underprepared youth into combat amplified the losses of Soviet lives.

On the home front, the regime hoped that young people would be its supporters with much of the adult population absent. Adolescents entered factory positions and the Komsomol, where youth leaders wanted to cultivate new activists who would have a broader sense of responsibility for the Soviet home front. The reliance on youth as a wartime constituency, however, revealed the inability of the regime to fight total war while asserting control over society in the rear. As the war came to a close, youth leaders stepped back to assess its consequences. How would the Soviet regime need to raise a cohort that had lived under the Germans? What did it mean to have a generation of young combatants and workers? The horrors, burdens, and unexpected freedom of war made its mark on those who survived. For Soviet leaders, though, the war left the core methods of raising youth unchanged. In militarization, mobilization, and re-Sovietization, the war both strengthened and justified the practices of communist upbringing developed in the 1930s and early 1940s.

Youth into Soldiers

As Soviet tanks rolled through the streets of her city on the way to the front, a young woman with the nickname Chizhik received a call: "Report to the headquarters of the Red Cross immediately." Chizhik arrived with hundreds of other

---

3. Reese, *Stalin's Reluctant Soldiers*, 163–86; RGASPI, f. 17, op. 121, d. 98, ll. 40–51.

4. Budnitskii, "Great Patriotic War and Soviet Society"; Bernstein, "Rural Russia on the Edges of Authority."

girls, all ready to bear the hardships of military life as nurses. Of course, Chizhik was a character played by Ol'ga Fedorina in the film *Girlfriends on the Front*. In that film, the enemy was Finnish, and the war was a regional conflict fought on the border. But mimicking her character in the movie, Fedorina mobilized in June 1941, joining Leningrad's People's Militia along with 2,349 other women.[5] In the first half-year of the war, uncounted numbers of youth went to the army, People's Militias, and partisan brigades. Millions underwent paramilitary training. Mobilization was not just like in the movies, though. The desperation of the war created unexpected means of mobilization into the partisan movement and urban undergrounds of Soviet loyalists. In these irregular forces and in the army, the mass mobilization drew on intensified versions of prewar patriotism, coercion, and convention.

The start of the war saw the regime continue or intensify prewar practices. After the Wehrmacht overran the Red Army in the USSR's western borderlands in a matter of days, Soviet authorities issued calls for the conscription of huge parts of the adult male population. By the end of 1941, the Red Army was 9.5 million strong, nearly double its prewar size. Most young people's experience of mobilization in the summer of 1941 was similar to their experience in paramilitary training or the partial mobilization of 1939–40. Before the war, the local youth leader might have summoned a group of young people and told them that it was their patriotic duty to undertake a training march or accept a nomination for officer training school. In the war, when local youth leaders summoned a group of youth, their patriotic duty was to go to the army, People's Militia or partisans, and then to the front. While prewar defense training had often failed to inculcate military skills, it provided an effective framework for mobilization.

The numbers of youth who went to the army through extramilitary mobilization are astounding. A Soviet-era account counted seventy thousand petitions in Moscow to various institutions to join the Red Army from the first three days of war, including fifty thousand youth who wrote to the Komsomol.[6] On July 3, Stalin gave his first wartime address over the radio and called for the formation of supposedly voluntary People's Militias at the local level. In Moscow militia recruitment began almost immediately after the speech as district-level committees of the party secretary, military council head, and head of the NKVD selected service-capable men between the ages of seventeen and fifty-five. Moscow's party secretary ordered local committees to mobilize two hundred thousand men from

---

5. RGASPI, f. 1m, op. 6, d. 5, l. 12.
6. *Opolchenie na zashchite Moskvy*, 4.

the capital in two days and seventy thousand from the rest of the province in three days.[7]

Although orders in Moscow gave exemptions to men in high-priority jobs, they did not specify how to prepare the would-be militiamen. Evidence from Leningrad's militias suggests that recruiters were less concerned about the ability of these outfits to fight than they were about raw numbers. By July 1, 1941, thirty thousand Komsomol members from the city had gone to militias. Another 27,225 members went to the Red Army.[8] Army officials writing about the readiness of the Second Division of the Leningrad militia on July 16 found that fewer than half of the rank-and-file soldiers were trained. The division had no mortar specialists, and its medical battalion had five doctors but no surgeons. Nonetheless, the need for soldiers exceeded the need for training. The army officer writing the report concluded that the division was fit for "the tasks of defensive battle."[9] Lack of supplies also presented a problem. Early in the war, Ukrainian party Secretary Nikita Khrushchev informed Stalin that Ukraine was ready to send 375,000 people to militias. Despite the presence of would-be soldiers, Khrushchev ended by writing, "There are no weapons for the volunteers."[10]

Memoirs of combatants provide glimpses of what these mobilizations were like. The novelist Ion Degen, then a sixteen-year-old in Vinnitsa province, joined a nonmilitary "volunteer brigade" of ninth and tenth graders organized at a Komsomol meeting ten days into the war. Two days later, the thirty-one-member brigade merged into the regular Red Army. In the rapid mobilization, Degen did not receive Red Army documentation, and his Komsomol card was his only means of identification.[11] In another case, a teenage Komsomol member from Briansk named Viktor Aver'ianov received unexpected orders from a factory party committee to meet with the local NKVD as the Germans neared the city. The police official told the young man that he would stay in the occupied city's underground. He answered, "If I have to, I have to."[12]

Paramilitary training continued to enable quick mobilization throughout the war. A Komsomol Central Committee investigator went to Brusovskii district of Kalinin province in January 1943. During his visit, local organizers decided to check how prepared members were to mobilize in the event that they received

---

7. Ibid., 29–31.

8. RGASPI, f. 1m, op. 6, d. 5, l. 1.

9. TsAMO, f. 217, op. 1221, d. 93.

10. *1941 god*, vol. 2, 453 (Citing APRF, f. 3, op. 50, d. 477, l. 6).

11. "Degen Ion Lazerevich," *I Remember*, http://iremember.ru/tankisti/degen-ion-lazarevich.html.

12. Shtopper and Kukatov, *Nelegal'nyi Briansk*, 74–75.

an order to send "volunteers" to the army. The local youth committee arranged a meeting of 630 youth from a training brigade "under the guise of mobilization to the front." According to the instructor, all the young people showed up and their mood was "buoyant and happy." So realistic was the drill that the parents, in tears, came to send off their children. As the would-be soldiers marched off, local party members ambushed them, pretending to be Germans. "Although some were frightened and began to cry," the investigator wrote, "they were few. It was important that the operation . . . was successful in approximating conditions at the front."[13] While the investigator focused on the success of the training operation in simulating real war, just how well the operation prepared those youth is unknowable—and was largely beside the point. The effect of wildcat training mobilizations before and during the war was to facilitate the introduction of fresh forces, ready or not.

Outside of conscription into conventional forces, young people frequently joined the partisans. The significance of the movement came as a surprise to Soviet leaders who had expected to fight on or near enemy soil, not deep in Soviet territory. Military personnel in the 1930s included some advocates of guerrilla warfare, but these cadres largely disappeared in the purge of the military.[14] Nonetheless, many insurgent brigades formed sporadically at the start of the war. Entire Soviet armies faced virtual destruction as the Germans captured them in huge encirclements. Red Army leaders, on Stalin's orders, refused requests by units to attempt to break out of encirclement, retreat, and regroup. When soldiers that German troops did not kill or capture found themselves unable to reconnect with the main army, many went to the forest and became partisans.

Even as they reconciled themselves to the reality of irregular warfare, carrying out partisan war presented a tension for Soviet leaders. They wanted to use partisans to undermine the German occupation but feared the insubordination of relatively independent irregular forces. At the outset, Soviet leaders attempted to mobilize only insurgents whose party loyalty was impeccable. On July 18, 1941, a Politburo order called for the spread of partisan warfare using party members who were veterans of the civil war, who had proven themselves in the current conflict or who were members of police organs.[15] The desperation of the war caused Stalin to change course in September 1942, calling for a broader people's war that would incorporate more than those people considered absolutely loyal. In spite of attempts to establish central control, partisan warfare as experienced

---

13. RGASPI, f. 1m, op. 47, d. 85, l. 53.
14. Slepyan, *Stalin's Guerrillas*, 20–21.
15. Khaustov et al., *Lubianka*, 298.

by fighting battalions involved the complex negotiation of allegiances. Far from Moscow, guerilla commanders could and did pursue agendas independent of the center from the start of the war.[16]

Youth inside and outside of the Komsomol became central elements of the partisan movement. Young people were more physically able to carry out partisan warfare than the elderly. Adolescents and young adults could also justify their presence in occupied territories, while occupiers might suspect that adult men of military age had been separated from the Red Army. In addition, young people were more likely to have technical skills that made them excellent saboteurs.[17] For these reasons, youth in occupied territories joined the partisans and became targets for brigades to recruit. A young man from Orel region interviewed in emigration recalled that a combination of animus and compulsion forced him into the partisans. The brutality of the local occupying troops in the region motivated some to join the partisans. But despite his being a member of a politically engaged family—both brothers had been local officials and his father had been a party member before being arrested for Trotskyism in 1936—his mother attempted to keep him from joining. Eventually local guerillas compelled him and other adolescent boys to join.[18]

Organizing partisans became a core part of Komsomol activity, a role that youth leaders had not anticipated but took up quickly. At the start of the conflict, Yuri Andropov reported as youth secretary in Karelia to his superiors in the Komsomol Central Committee that circumstances had forced his committee to make an "exceptional"—and probably unexpected—decision to leave behind organizers to direct partisans after the Finnish army occupied the republic.[19] As more territories fell under occupation, other youth committees joined Andropov in going underground to fight. With so many youth working behind enemy lines, either sent by Komsomol committees or caught there in the Red Army's retreat, the league had a stake in increasing their effectiveness. Its leaders even commissioned scientific research on new types of flammable liquids for creating improvised explosives. The result was a guide to making various explosive mixtures, each taking into account the availability of materials on different fronts and the goal of using these explosives to combat German armored superiority.[20]

The most famous partisan of the war, Zoia Kosmodem'ianskaia, joined on a Komsomol assignment a month after she turned eighteen years old in

---

16. Slepyan, *Stalin's Guerrillas*, 16, 135–85.
17. Ibid., 96.
18. Harvard Project on the Soviet Social System, Schedule B, Vol. 11, Case 358, Sequence 1.
19. RGASPI, f. 1m, op. 6, d. 9, l. 34.
20. RGASPI, f. 1m, op. 47, d. 12, ll. 50–52.

October 1941. Fighting behind enemy lines near Moscow, she received orders to set fire to a village where Germans had stopped. Near the village, enemy soldiers caught, tortured, and executed her by hanging. The photograph of her mutilated corpse, published first under the name "Tania," became a rallying symbol for the country during the war and after. In the last years of the Soviet Union, Kosmodem'ianskaia became a controversial figure because of revelations that local peasants or even another partisan may have played a role in her demise.[21] Nonetheless, she became a powerful image during the war because she represented the tens of thousands of young people who participated in irregular forces.

Besides fighting Germans with weapons, young partisans played a critical role in maintaining a sense of Soviet authority under occupation. In 1941, Germans arrested and executed the twenty-three-year-old partisan Liza Chaikina for spreading Soviet propaganda in rural Kalinin province. Early reports claimed that the Germans had caught Chaikina distributing copies of Stalin's landmark, defiant speech on Red Square on the anniversary of the October Revolution in 1941.[22] Her feat made her one of the war's first partisan heroes. The crucial scene in Nikolai Biriukov's Stalin Prize-winning novelization of her story, *Chaika*, has Katia Volgina (the fictionalized version of Chaikina) refute German claims of "Moscow kaput" after the partisans receive leaflets with Stalin's speech. Separating fact from fiction in mythologizing accounts about Chaikina is difficult. Nonetheless, it is not hard to imagine the effect that news from Moscow might have had on the occupied countryside. The thought that Soviet power was still alive and could return must have bolstered partisans and threatened those who had cooperated or might cooperate with the occupiers. Mobilization in the war among youth was as much ideological as it was military.

In the cities, local Soviet loyalists under occupation formed undergrounds to conduct insurgent activity. In larger cities, it seems that police and party activists were the main figures in these organizations.[23] However, young people played an important role, too, especially in smaller towns where the footprint of the party was often smaller than that of the Komsomol. The most famous youth underground was the Young Guard in the town of Krasnodon in Voroshilovgrad province of Ukraine. Aleksandr Fadeev's hit novel about the group and its film adaptation became a touchstone for the youth after the

---

21. Harris, "Lives and Deaths of a Soviet Saint," 277, 279–82.
22. *Komsomol'skaia pravda*, December 30, 1941.
23. Shtopper and Kukatov, *Nelegal'nyi Briansk*.

war, although the story of its activity was a matter of dispute even before the novel appeared.[24] The Young Guard began its work roughly a month after the Germans arrived in July 1942. Popular accounts lionized the group's armed resistance to the occupiers, including the execution of several local police and Germans. Another important aspect of its work was the disruption of the occupiers' attempts to send Ukrainians to Germany as laborers. Like Chaikina, though, the group's most significant activities included those that preserved a sense of Soviet rule under occupation. By distributing leaflets with Soviet propaganda, underground members provided an alternative narrative apart from that of the occupiers.

Although the Soviet state and society mobilized large numbers of youth for war, these young people were often unprepared. In the years before the war, Komsomol organizers in conjunction with the army had created paramilitary training programs out of a series of fitness campaigns. Although these programs aimed to replace basic army preparation, youth leaders frequently accused local groups of turning substantial training plans into Potemkin marches. Despite the new urgency of the wartime period, paramilitary training changed little after the war's start. At a meeting of Moscow organizers in July 1941, Nikolai Pronin, a division commander in Moscow and future head of the military's training program for civilians, continued to urge youth to replicate Red Army structures in the Komsomol.[25] Efforts by the Red Army and Komsomol reinforced existing methods of defense training, urging youth organizers to intensify the way that they prepared youth for war but not to adapt to the new conditions. The outcome remained the same. Particularly in the first months of the war, paramilitary programs organized mobilization rather than training.

Similar to the prewar period, Soviet leaders involved in paramilitary training assessed the USSR's defense preparation in comparison to Germany. When Deputy Commissar of Defense Efim Shchadenko received a Commissariat of Enlightenment proposal that he believed had inadequate provisions for paramilitary training, he responded with a long invective in August 1942. He wrote that accusations of "hooliganism, crudeness and lack of culture" had dampened Russians' natural talent for fighting. In contrast, Germans had cultivated combat abilities among their young people and "weren't afraid that someone would accuse them of supporting vestiges of the Middle Ages." He concluded,

---

24. Fürst, *Stalin's Last Generation*, 137–66. For disputes over the factuality of the Young Guard story throughout the Soviet period, see Ioffe and Petrova, "*Molodaia gvardiia*."

25. RGASPI, f. 1m, op. 5, d. 99, l. 14, 35, 50.

"In Fascist Germany every boy looks like a German soldier. . . . They know how to teach their youth there."[26]

Only as losses grew to disastrous proportions did Stalin and the political leadership of the country reconsider the place of training in their mobilization strategy. Throwing enormous numbers of soldiers into combat was not enough to win the war. By Stalin's order on September 18, 1941, the Red Army reintroduced Universal Military Training (*Vseobshchee voennoe obuchenie*, or Vsevobuch). The training program assumed nearly all responsibility for premilitary preparation, previously under the auspices of Osoaviakhim.[27] Much like the program the Komsomol had introduced in 1940 for its members, Vsevobuch included 110 hours of training that would supplement or even supplant basic training. Unlike the essentially voluntary Komsomol program, which had not achieved its goal of regular paramilitary training in practice, Vsevobuch was mandatory for the service-eligible.[28] General Pronin was also willing to deviate from the program when circumstances demanded. As the German army closed in on Moscow in October 1941, Pronin realized that Vsevobuch would not have enough time to train recruits fully to participate in the battle. On October 14, Pronin ordered recruits near the front to undertake a minimal Vsevobuch program. The four-week, fifty-six-hour program aimed to give soldiers the essentials—training to use "rifle, mortar, grenade, to destroy tanks and to work in a unit."[29]

In a technical sense, mobilization drew on paramilitary programs of the previous several years, but as a broader practice, it bore similarities to mobilization from the Soviet collectivization and industrialization drive. From 1929 to 1933, party and Komsomol committees had recruited hundreds of thousands of activists to organize industrialization and collective agriculture. The parallels between Stalin's revolution and the beginning of the war are striking. Stalin and his leadership circle seem to have believed that through sheer will and extraordinary mobilization, Soviet power would overcome the German enemy as it had overcome the supposed class enemy within the country. The regime sent millions of people to fight in a war they were poorly prepared for and refused to adapt its strategies in ways that would have increased their chances of survival.

Why did young people go to war? The press uniformly lauded youth who volunteered for the front, printing young people's declarations of patriotic devotion to the country. Local archives are full of similar petitions to join the People's Militias

---

26. RGASPI, f. 1m, op. 47, d. 40, l. 15.
27. *Russkii arkhiv: Velikaia Otechestvennaia*, 2:88–89.
28. RGASPI, f. 1m, op. 47, d. 3.
29. RGASPI, f. 82, op. 2, d. 803, ll. 104, 106.

written with unflagging patriotism and cribbing quotes from speeches, films, and normative documents.[30] It is tempting to dismiss these formulaic documents as the mask of voluntarism that hid the essence of compulsion. However, genuine enthusiasm was a major factor that drove mobilization. In part, it seems likely that volunteers may not have imagined what kind of conflict would unfold in its first days of the war. Prewar antifascist propaganda in the Soviet press had created a sense of confidence in the inevitability of Soviet victory.[31] Who would have thought that a raw militia would end up on the front lines in less than a month?

Even after the nature of the war became clear, young people continued to volunteer. Many understood that their country's fate was in the balance and ran to its defense. When Komsomol organizers in Riazan province formed a volunteer brigade in November 1941, a young man attempted to join despite being blind in one eye. He hid his condition from doctors for several days but eventually was refused.[32] Nikolai Melnikov, the future émigré from Leningrad who joined his factory's Komsomol in his teens, spent the first two months of the war at an infantry school before going to the front. He recalled that enthusiastic Komsomol members enlisted by the thousands in the first days of the war and were sent to bolster the army as it retreated: "As [Komsomol members] lacked military training, having been brought up filled with the spirit of easy victories and false Soviet patriotism, they lost their lives to no purpose in the very first actions."[33]

Melnikov's cynical assessment underplayed real expressions of patriotism that made young people fight. A day after the invasion, twenty-year-old organizer Nina Kosterina wrote in her diary, "Well, then, I am ready . . . I want action, I want to go to the front." Her role as an activist in various paramilitary training operations gave her the confidence that she could go into combat. Kosterina had grown up on a diet of Soviet press that told her war was coming and that youth would become soldiers. She and most other young people from towns had some level of paramilitary training. For some it may have seemed that the war against Germany was the next stage of revolutionary struggle. It was their generation's October Revolution or Great Turn. Soon after the start of the war, Kosterina joined a partisan brigade, dying before the year's end.[34]

---

30. See, for example, the petition of a young man that borrows from the Komsomol's official program in *Opolchenie na zashchite Moskvy*, 26. For the Komsomol program, see *Tovarishch Komsomol*, 1:534–35. On proclamations of selfless devotion to wartime cause, see Berkhoff, *Motherland in Danger*, 67–95.

31. Berkhoff, *Motherland in Danger*, 8–9.

32. GARO, f. P-3, op. 2, d. 67, l. 1.

33. Melnikov, "Road to Life," in *Soviet Youth*, ed. Novak-Deker, 226.

34. Kosterina, *Diaries*, June 23, 1941.

For young women, the war also offered the opportunity to forge new gender roles. Kosterina seems to have wanted to go to the front not only out of Soviet patriotism but also because of a desire to experience combat. Figures vary on the number of women who participated in the war. Official figures cited some eight hundred thousand women in the armed forces while a recent study claimed the correct figure was over one million women.[35] Like other recruits, women encountered the same mechanisms of mobilization as their male counterparts. However, many of these women may have wanted to escape the strictures of traditional gender identities by becoming combat fighters. Before the war, women had written letters to Komsomol and Red Army leaders asking for placement in military schools or in the army. In response, they generally received suggestions that they should train for noncombat roles in nursing or pilot training.[36] In the media and in films like *Girlfriends on the Front*, women had gone to war, but their place was typically limited to specializations like signaling, nursing, and civil defense. Even in the desperate first period of the war, authorities envisioned women in these auxiliary roles. As the conflict continued, however, Soviet women joined the effort in significant combat roles, most famously as snipers and pilots. Despite their introduction into the traditionally masculine sphere of combat forces, many women did not reject femininity but attempted to combine it with new experiences.[37]

Other people in the USSR saw the war as an opportunity for advancement and reward. Like the soldiers of virtually every army, Red Army soldiers used their conquests as an opportunity to loot, often with official approval.[38] Combat rewards also came from the state. Within a year of the German invasion, the Soviet military organized payments to soldiers as prizes for destroying armored vehicles and aircraft. The state also expanded its medals program, creating a system of compensation that was more important than simple remuneration.[39] In the postwar period, these honors became a source of symbolic capital that veterans could draw on to settle grievances and gain social advancement.[40] Although most soldiers and partisans focused on survival, some envisioned the role the war

---

35. Markwick and Cardona, *Soviet Women on the Frontline*, 150.

36. RGVA, f. 9, op. 34, d. 28, ll. 5–8; TsDAHO, f. 7, op. 1, d. 1263, l. 184.

37. Anna Krylova tends to emphasize the way that the war offered women a different "gender scenario" by allowing them to be fighters in addition to maternal figures. In contrast, Markwick and Cardona are more skeptical than Krylova about the role of women during the war, emphasizing the role of coercion. Krylova, *Soviet Women in Combat*, 18; Markwick and Cardona, *Soviet Women on the Frontline*, 150.

38. Edele, *Stalin's Veterans*, 30–34.

39. Reese, *Why Stalin's Soldiers Fought*, 206–12.

40. Edele, *Stalin's Veterans*, 44–46.

would play in Soviet mythology after it ended and recognized the opportunity to construct their wartime biography. Children of kulaks, for example, exculpated their parents' guilt by fighting on the front lines after the state grew desperate enough to allow supposed class aliens to fight.[41] The exigencies of war shifted the needs of the state in other ways, privileging different abilities than in the 1930s, when Stalin cultivated white-collar workers above all. In the partisans in particular, peasants were often better survivalists than people from other backgrounds. Guerrilla activity offered them advancement that they had not known in peacetime.[42]

Although patriotism, personal motivations, and even material reward drove many, compulsion also played an important role in filling the ranks of the Red Army. Every modern state punished the service-obliged who refused to fight or who deserted, although Stalinist measures were undoubtedly more severe than those of other countries.[43] One of the USSR's first wartime laws established penalties for the families of deserters. Through October 1941, police stopped 657,364 soldiers as suspected violators of the July 1940 law on desertion, punishable by death during war.[44] Of these, 25,878 faced arrest and 10,201 execution. The largest contingent of the arrestees (8,772) was charged with desertion.[45] Cases from the military tribunal stationed in Riazan in October 1941 almost exclusively involved soldiers who deserted multiple times. A typical case was of a twenty-one-year-old Russian peasant from Gorkii province. Charged twice before with desertion and subsequently sent back to the army, the third charge resulted in his execution.[46] The historian Roger Reese argues that the preponderance of detentions without formal charges meant that police picked up many soldiers who were lost, fell behind their units, or avoided combat. Soldiers who missed taking part in battles were probably less often the targets of judicial repression than those who refused to serve outright.[47]

The relative leniency in the implementation of the law on desertion belied a broader culture of repression that aimed to put men in uniform. Police mood reports recorded volunteers' patriotic petitions to join militias but also alerted party leaders to instances when youth refused to go to the front. In June 1941, at

---

41. Lovchenko, "Spetstrudposelentsy Severnogo kraia," 140; Viola, *Unknown Gulag*, 178.

42. Slepyan, *Stalin's Guerrillas*, 258.

43. On conscription and resistance in the context of the United Kingdom, France, and the United States, see Flynn, *Conscription and Democracy*, 248–59. Reese, *Why Stalin's Soldiers Fought*, 171–72, addresses Soviet desertion in a comparative context.

44. *Voenno-istoricheskii zhurnal*, no. 9 (1988): 26–28 (citing RGVA, f. 4, op. 12, d. 98, ll. 617–22).

45. Khaustov et al., *Lubianka*, 2, no. 1:114–15.

46. GARO, f. P-3, op. 2, d. 17, l. 19.

47. Reese, *Why Stalin's Soldiers Fought*, 170.

the famous Sickle and Hammer (Serp i molot) factory in Moscow, police arrested a young engineer who refused to go to the army and urged his peers to join him in protest. Even more common than protest in the reports were instances of self-mutilation and suicide.[48] Among would-be "volunteers" in Komsomol-organized brigades, refusal also came with a cost. On State Committee for Defense (GKO) orders, youth organizers in Riazan province formed a Komsomol-Volunteer brigade of 1,203 paratroopers in November 1941, just weeks before the Germans arrived in the province. The local Komsomol head indicated that the large majority of the brigade volunteered. Nonetheless, at least eleven young men refused, including nine of ten recruited in the province's Dobrovskii district. These men faced expulsion from the league and likely further action by authorities, although reports on the brigade do not indicate what happened to them.[49]

Beyond police recordings of repression, arbitrary, presumably unrecorded executions are common features of veterans' memories of combat.[50] Such executions could even take place at the enlistment station. In an interview about his wartime experience, veteran Pinkhus Ostromogil'skii remembered being called up at age seventeen in 1942. He gathered with other young men at a recruiting center in Malgobek, Ingushetia, amid total disorganization. When several men tried to leave, authorities executed those whom they caught.[51] How widespread arbitrary executions were is unknowable. However, soldiers were probably aware that authorities were willing to use repression, official and unofficial, and this threat surely influenced their decision to enlist.

Civilian organizations put youth into arms throughout the war. For the year and a half from November 1941 to April 1943, Komsomol statisticians recorded approximately 520,000 young people as participants in the league's mobilization campaigns to Red Army and partisan units. Of those mobilized, 223,634 were women and 296,395 were men. Especially large numbers of young people joined partisan brigades, parachute units, ski brigades, and anti-air forces.[52] These figures did not include the ordinary mobilization of conscripts or units mobilized through the military's Vsevobuch program. Moreover, Komsomol groups were partially responsible for the incredible extramilitary mobilization in the first four months of the war. These early efforts undoubtedly produced more soldiers and partisans than the later mobilizations that the league registered. Establishing even

48. *Moskva voennaia*, 53, 55.

49. GARO f. P-3, op. 2, d. 67, ll. 1–2.

50. Reese, *Why Stalin's Soldiers Fought*, 170–71.

51. "Ostromogil'skii Pinkhus Ovseevich," *I Remember*, http://iremember.ru/minometchiki/ostromogilskiy-pinkhus-ovseevich/stranitsa-2.html.

52. RGASPI, f. 1m, op. 47, d. 102, l. 9.

an approximate estimate of the numerical impact of nonmilitary mobilization of youth is almost impossible. Without a doubt, though, the infusion of hundreds of thousands, if not more than a million, young people into the armed forces played a crucial role in tapping the Soviet Union's reserves of potential soldiers in the early part of the war.

Just as important and difficult as understanding the numerical impact of rapid mobilization is knowing why and how it occurred. Many experienced the war as an opportunity to realize aspects of themselves that did not fit into officially prescribed social norms in peacetime. It also provided material rewards and the possibility of advancement, much like the prewar Stalinist system. In other ways, too, Stalin's wartime regime represented an amplified version of the prewar USSR, magnifying existing support and the state's recourse to coercion. The most important aspect in the mobilization of Soviet youth was the conditioning they had undergone before the war. For a substantial number of young people, the war marked a continuation of Stalinist mobilization practices. It was a conscription campaign—a monumental one, to be sure. Yet the war was not unlike the campaigns they had known throughout the 1930s, a Stalinist form of acculturation that combined expressions of patriotism and the experience of repression. This system of paramilitary training and recruitment proved disastrously effective. In 1941, the fate of the regime hinged on the soldiers whose recruitment these mechanisms facilitated. The Soviet system of mobilization sent young people quickly and without preparation into a hideous struggle most could not hope to survive. It would allow the regime to emerge from the war, but much of this generation would not.

Labor and Order on the Home Front

The demands of war changed life for youth on the home front as well. As soldiers departed, those who remained were predominately women, adolescents, and the elderly. Political elites also departed in large numbers as they took responsibility for leadership in the expanded military or went into evacuation. Boris Chernousov, party secretary of Moscow province, claimed that the organization had decreased from a hundred thousand to thirty-five thousand. The departures from the Moscow area and elsewhere created a vacuum of labor and authority in the Soviet Union. Surveying the population that had remained, Chernousov said to a meeting of the province's Komsomol members, "We are placing our hopes on youth most of all as the force that will carry out our [the party's] work."[53]

---

53. RGASPI, f. 1m, op 5, d. 104, ll. 128, 130, 132.

Chernousov and other Soviet authorities would ask youth to fill the void by monitoring society and providing services the overstretched state could not during wartime.

One role politically active youth played was in policing the population. In the first days of the war in particular, chaos and lack of information led to the spread of rumors among Soviet people.[54] Police arrested those they believed were the sources of rumors, attempting to control information and opinions about the war.[55] An even greater fear was that the Germans were recruiting or sending spies to disrupt the Soviet home front.[56] As security forces became thin-spread, NKVD and Komsomol officials recruited youth to facilitate public order. On February 16, 1942, Nikolai Mikhailov reported to party secretaries that in villages along the front, "hundreds of suspect people," including "dozens of spies," were scouting the territory and spreading rumors. He claimed: "No one in any village asks for documents [of unknown people who arrive].... There are many incidents of so-called 'escapees from encirclement' living for weeks or for months in villages without coming upon a formation point or into the hands of authorities."[57]

Addressing this fear of devious wanderers, the Komsomol Central Committee on April 9, 1942, called for the formation of youth police brigades.[58] NKVD officials approved and gave instructions for the use of these brigades on April 18. The orders called for tight police supervision over the recruitment of the brigades and their activities.[59] Lower-level Komsomol groups were supposed to form units for protecting towns and various types of state and military property by April 25, 1942.

These brigades bore similarities to youth groups that had aided NKVD units in policing the railroads against hooligans and other vagrants in the mid-1930s but were formed on a larger scale and had magnified powers. According to the Ukrainian Komsomol's military department, the republic's youth league organized 201 brigades with 2,328 people. One of the more successful brigades uncovered a "counterrevolutionary group" that was alleged to be making a list of party and Komsomol members to give to the Germans on their arrival. Ukraine's youth leaders claimed that on average each brigade had stopped five or six

---

54. On limitations party leaders placed on military information in the Soviet press, see Berkhoff, *Motherland in Danger*, 30.

55. *Organy gosudarstvennoi bezopasnosti*, 2, no. 1:68–72.

56. Khaustov et al., *Lubianka*, 295, 309, 349–50, 350–51 (citing RGASPI, f. 17, op. 162, d. 36, ch. 2, ll. 42, 214; APRF, f. 3, op. 58, d. 256, ll. 67–68; APRF, f. 3, op. 57, d. 59, ll. 67, 68–70).

57. RGASPI, f. 1m, op. 47, d. 59, ll. 7–9.

58. Ibid., l. 27.

59. *Organy gosudarstvennoi bezopasnosti*, 3, no. 1:368–69.

"suspects, deserters, or other hostile elements," presumably sending these suspicious people to local authorities.[60] In a similar campaign in blockaded Leningrad, the Komsomol formed a regiment of four thousand people who worked with the police, clocking a million hours of patrols and detaining over thirteen thousand people as spies. Leningrad's Komsomol organizers also attempted to root out so-called *raketchiki*—people who marked points for German planes to bomb. Local activists organized groups of Pioneers to search for these collaborators and inform authorities. Besides these actions, by October 1942 the city's Komsomol had formed a regiment for firefighting and another for "defense of revolutionary order." According to a leader in Leningrad's Komsomol named Maksimov, in just one month these groups had stopped fourteen hundred "violators of revolutionary order [and] a large number of suspicious people."[61]

In Moscow, Komsomol members formed an underground in advance of the city's potential occupation in October 1941. On October 15, the GKO ordered the evacuation of state organizations in the city, driving people in the area into panic. Many Komsomol youth in the province burned their membership cards in advance of German occupation.[62] Youth in Moscow city formed the underground based on their disgust at what they saw as panic mongering and the real potential of German occupation of the city. When the danger to the capital passed, though, the underground continued to work as a secret organization to collect information on citizens.[63]

The underground's operations varied but primarily involved surveillance of Moscow enterprises and Muscovites themselves. Members seem to have been exclusively women, because young men had mostly left the city. One young woman—identified in the report as Comrade S.—checked Voikov factory, where the lack of security alarmed her. She had been on its premises for a half-hour without anyone checking her documents. During the summer of 1942, the underground began to record conversations members heard in public places. Underground members labeled the rumormongers as older women: "Lines were a hotbed of all sorts of false rumors and provocations of the notorious 'OWS' (one woman [*grazhdanka*] said) and 'OBS' (one *baba* [old woman] said) type." This label of OWS/OBS reflected stereotypes of women as the primary gossip spreaders, a youthful bias against older people, and the prevalence of older women in the city. When the underground took these rumors to party and Komsomol leaders,

---

60. RGASPI, f. 1m, op. 47, d. 25, ll. 80–84.

61. RGASPI, f. 1m, op. 5, d. 116a, l. 12.

62. OKhDOPIM, f. 641, op. 1, d. 20, ll. 5, 7, 8, 40, 49, 50; f. 652, op. 1, d. 2, l. 5.

63. OKhDOPIM, f. 635, op. 1, d. 320a, ll. 5–6.

some viewed them as dangerous, others dismissed them as unimportant, while a few took the rumors at face value, "going into a state of fright, of deep panic."[64]

Records of the group's activities are few, and whether party or policing authorities acted on its information is uncertain. The underground's anonymous chronicler provided cases of the group's failures that suggest its leaders took their work seriously. A Comrade K. received a safe ("conspiratorial") room and immediately invited her mother to live there. Against group operating procedure, the administration of the building learned that Comrade K. received the apartment as part of a secret assignment through the Komsomol. The chronicler wrote, "Her mother was aware of the entire conspiracy and . . . opposed her participation." When the police picked up Comrade B. on suspicion of prostitution during an operation, the underground member "unveiled the conspiracy" (*raskonspiriro-vala*), and the group threw her out soon after. Comrade S. lost her fake passport and "couldn't get another without our help." Her helplessness in the face of this crisis proved that she had "not one quality that would allow her the right to be in an illegal organization."[65]

In contrast to the initiative of the Moscow underground, summary information from the Komsomol Central Committee suggests that ordinary police were usually the organizers of these types of groups, giving the authorities extra eyes and ears. For example, in Tula province, under partial occupation in 1941–42, youth formed groups to monitor the region for deserters from the army. Yet an instructor from the central Komsomol's military department complained in the fall of 1942, "Brigades formed only in areas where there were soldiers of the NKVD's rear guard."[66] Although regular police may have played the main role in organizing irregular security from youth, the groups nonetheless expanded young people's authority. Through these brigades, political leaders hoped to supplement surveillance of the population that the war had made even more important but less practicable.

Youth not only played a role in filling gaps in security but in public services. In the darkest days of the blockade in Leningrad, the Komsomol enlisted members for elementary tasks of public health—including the removal of bodies. At a Komsomol Central Committee meeting in July 1942, Leningrad's youth secretary V. N. Ivanov offhandedly said, "I can't even begin to talk about the phenomenal work they [members] did removing corpses, shoveling snow, and so on."[67]

64. Ibid., ll. 17, 18.
65. Ibid., l. 19.
66. RGASPI, f. 1m, op. 47, d. 59, l. 66.
67. RGASPI, f. 1m, op. 5, d. 116a, l. 12.

In many cities of the home front, conditions in public spaces had deteriorated. Railroads were particularly hard hit as large numbers of soldiers, evacuees, and materiel flowed to and from the front. In Ivanovo, the province's Komsomol formed groups of five to seven members who would conduct spot checks of various enterprises and dormitories. At the city's train station, flies had taken over the buffet, where there was no hot water, plates, or mugs. The first waiting area at the station had 150 people, while the second had even more people, many of whom had been living there for up to two weeks. Although youth groups then cleaned up the station, the most disturbing aspect for organizers was that "individual district committees and Komsomol organizations" had "made peace with this disgrace."[68]

Among the law and order campaigns in which the regime expected youth to take a leading role, perhaps the closest to home for Komsomol organizers was containing child abandonment. Many children lost parents to the war, and the departure of parents either to the army or to distant workplaces left many others without authority figures. From 1943 to 1945 alone, police in receiving centers processed 842,144 children without parents or with absent parents.[69] Along with the police, Komsomol organizations were supposed to manage the massive numbers of abandoned children. The persistent inability of the regime to contend with these children demonstrated the limitations of young people and youth organizations as wartime instruments of state control.

The lack of state and parental control during the war allowed or forced many children to turn to crime. In the first three months of the war in Moscow, 10,186 minors received sentences for various infractions. According to NKVD Inspector of the Police Aleksandr Galkin, crimes by minors were generally not the work of orphans, but up to 90 percent were committed by children with absent parents. For the Soviet Union in 1941, Galkin counted 25,139 crimes by minors, including 20,816 thefts, 492 burglaries, and 161 murders.[70] While Komsomol leaders blamed the influence of antisocial elements for children's turn to crime, it was extreme vulnerability that seems to have created most juvenile delinquents. The paucity of official rations for nonworking children would have meant starvation without some form of supplementation.[71]

More alarming than child criminals were NKVD leaders' accusations that Germans were training children as spies on the front. A police report from December

---

68. RGASPI, f. 1m, op. 6, d. 19, ll. 62, 69.

69. Green, "'There Will Not Be Orphans,'" 36.

70. RGASPI, f. 1m, op. 7, d. 35, ll. 4–7, 9–10.

71. A study of the home-front economy claimed that for a twelve-year-old in Leningrad to rely on state rations alone would have meant "certain death." Barber and Harrison, *Soviet Home Front*, 79.

1941 detailed cases of children caught supposedly spying for the Germans. One of the detainees told his captors that the Germans had set up a small spy school in Bobruisk, Belorussia, where fifty orphans between eight and twelve learned how to conduct espionage.[72] At a July 1942 meeting of Komsomol leaders with NKVD authorities about the issue of abandoned children, Galkin claimed that though abandoned children and adolescents were not adults, they still could do significant damage in the hands of the enemy. Galkin asserted that "guys of that age went over to the Germans in occupied regions."[73] For police officials, the issue of security in wartime was more important than the well-being of children.

The problem of abandoned children created a wedge between police officials and Komsomol workers.[74] Youth workers in charge of children's issues criticized the police's overreliance on criminal prosecution. One Komsomol worker refuted Galkin by claiming that the typical case of child detention involved a police officer who would "arrest them [children], hold them for a few days, and then say: You, get out of my territory." Police were more concerned with ensuring that their statistics looked good than with dealing with the core of the issue.[75] Along these lines, in May 1943 the Komsomol's head of children's affairs, A. Sysoeva, investigated the status of children held in Sretenskii prison in Moscow. A representative case included a sixteen-year-old forced into life on the street after his mother was evacuated. Police arrested him when he stole a pound of bread from a factory, and to protest the disproportionality of his punishment, the teenager went on a hunger strike. Like the other children in the prison, he had violated the law. But Sysoeva argued that the drive for order had resulted in arbitrariness and excesses against the most vulnerable members of society.[76]

As a counterpart to administrative methods of controlling abandoned children, Komsomol committees were supposed to undertake measures to channel these children into factory schools and other institutions where they would contribute to the war effort. In many cases, though, youth organizers found themselves overwhelmed by these and other responsibilities. In September 1942, Galkin cited Sverdlovsk's Komsomol leader as saying of abandoned children, "We have more important tasks." This assertion was a political mistake, but it reflected a reality of the war: The state and its plenipotentiaries were overstretched, and children were a secondary priority.[77] Even gauging the numbers of abandoned

---

72. *Organy gosudarstvennoi bezopasnosti*, 2, no. 2:383–84.

73. RGASPI, f. 1m, op. 5, d. 118.

74. Green, "'There Will Not Be Orphans,'" 56–63; Livshiz, "Growing Up Soviet," 519–24.

75. RGASPI, f. 1m, op. 5, d. 118, l. 1.

76. RGASPI, f. 1m, op. 7, d. 70, ll. 71–74.

77. RGASPI, f. 1m, op. 7, d. 35, l. 20.

children posed difficulties. In Mytishchi district (Moscow province), the local inspector for patronage of children cited 389 arrests of children, most often for theft organized under the supervision of adults. At the same time, she claimed that lack of support from the Komsomol and other political authorities had made it impossible for her to assess the true scope of the problem of orphans and "half-orphans" in the region.[78]

Orphans continued to be a visible issue throughout the war. After conducting an investigation in Arkhangelsk province in May 1943, Sysoeva asserted that the problem was not only the suffering of children but the image of the Soviet Union these children presented to foreigners arriving with lend-lease goods. The children "molested the foreign sailors, asking things from them, stealing, and speculating." In one case, a foreigner threw candies on the ground and photographed the children. Poor conditions at orphanages and boarding houses for children only compounded the problem in the province, driving children out of these institutions and onto the street. The orphanage in Molotov city, for example, had no fuel for heating. Overall in Arkhangelsk province, 763 children ages twelve to sixteen were arrested, 676 for petty theft.[79]

For the state, the issue of abandoned children was not only one of protecting and controlling the smallest Soviets but also a question of productivity. With so many workers engaged in combat, the regime sought to expand the labor pool with adolescents or even children.[80] In May 1942, the Council of People's Commissars (SNK) issued a directive authorizing adolescents as young as fourteen to work in industry.[81] An internal Komsomol report from 1942 found that 3.89 million young people under eighteen were working in the agricultural economy alone.[82] In 1944, 2.46 million industrial workers were under eighteen, and of those, nearly a third were fourteen or fifteen years old.[83] Presumably some children under fourteen, driven by hunger or coercion, worked in the fields and the factory.[84]

The role of apprentice workers in industry was so important that it became the subject of one of the only youth films during the war, Lev Kuleshov and Aleksandra Khokhlova's *We Are from the Urals* (My s Urala). The film's main

---

78. OKhDOPIM, f. 652, op. 1, d. 2, ll. 69–70.

79. RGASPI, f. 1m, op. 7, d. 70, ll. 8–10.

80. Barber and Harrison describe this expansion tapping "disguised" unemployment. Adolescents are capable of working but in many modern states are unemployed so that they are free to receive education. Barber and Harrison, *Soviet Home Front*, 145. DeGraffenried, *Sacrificing Childhood*, focuses on the ways that wartime policy made self-sacrifice a key aspect of Soviet childhood.

81. *Direktivy KPSS*, 2:61–69. Cited in Livshiz, "Growing Up Soviet," 465.

82. RGASPI, f. 1m, op. 6, d. 20, l. 51.

83. Barber and Harrison, *Soviet Home Front*, 97.

84. Livshiz, "Growing Up Soviet," 449.

characters are Kuz'ma and Vania, students of a Factory Apprentice Education (FZO) school with good facilities and caring supervisors. After the two graduate, they receive assignments at a factory but want to follow Kuz'ma's sister, a nurse, to the front. Nonetheless, they commit themselves to production and become exemplary workers at their plant. Ultimately the film was never released. Nikolai Mikhailov denounced it to party leaders as "nonideological" and "antiartistic," particularly for its portrayal of youth's willingness to abandon their duty for the war. Moreover, he said that the scene where the young heroes dance in a Western style was "sickening." For these reasons, the Komsomol chief asserted that the film was guilty of a "lack of knowledge of the life of youth."[85]

The film, of course, did not reflect the reality of factory schools, but not for the reasons that Mikhailov cited. Conditions at real schools were not nearly as pleasant as in the movies. When youth ran away, it was most often for their home regions or more profitable work rather than for the army. Mikhailov's concern about children abandoning FZO schools was well placed, though. Youth who left the supervision of factory school authorities created a problem that merged the issue of abandoned children with the needs of the economy.

The reasons adolescent workers left Soviet institutions varied. At a meeting of factory school directors with Komsomol leaders in November 1941, one director, Beschastov, claimed that runaways recruited others to leave. Many children came from villages to work in factory schools. When they left the factory for their village, they wrote to friends who had stayed, urging them to leave and find work in the village economy.[86] Each factory school had its own concentration, and the more difficult specializations were more likely to drive away children. Students from outdoor construction schools ran away comparatively often, for instance.[87] Poor living conditions in FZO dormitories also pushed adolescents to run away. In at least one case, news about conditions drew the collective action of parents. A 1943 letter from the parents of children in the FZO program of the Ural Machine Factory implored the local Komsomol to intervene at the dormitory. Their children had reported thievery and a general indifference from school authorities. The parents wrote, "We can tell that they are unhappy with their conditions."[88]

FZO authorities often had no way to return adolescents to the schools, and they left with impunity. Although children were supposed to receive permission from a military official to leave the school, children obtained dismissal papers

85. Fomin, *Kino na voine*, 367–69 (citing RGASPI, f. 17, op. 125, d. 213, ll. 172–73). On the making of the film, see Bernstein, "Wartime Filmmaking on the Margins," 33–35.
86. RGASPI, f. 1m, op. 5, d. 100, ll. 5–7.
87. Ibid., l. 8.
88. RGASPI, f. 1m, op. 6, d. 81, l. 28.

whether they had a reason or not. At one school in Kuibyshev, students numbered 550 at the peak, but 340 had run away. Its director described the typical case where a student would come for dismissal papers under the pretense of going home to a nearby town to change dirty clothes for clean ones. "If you don't give them the papers," he said, "they'll run away all the same." Even Komsomol members ran away. Of the sixty-five members, twenty had fled. The director of another Kuibyshev FZO school had gone to the city police and asked officers to help by monitoring railways and docks, where children stowed away on transport or simply congregated. He even suggested that police could limit their surveillance to Saturdays, when students were most likely to run away. The police refused to help, though.[89]

Although some adolescents sought to avoid their wartime mobilization into the economy, others understood it as a replacement for school. Some youth were horrified that they would miss their education. For the precocious *intelligent* Georgii Efron, son of the poet Marina Tsvetaeva, the thought of working on a collective farm instead of studying was hard to bear. When he was not searching for food, he spent his time in evacuation in Tashkent devouring books in French and Russian to make up for what he perceived as a lack of culture.[90] Other youth welcomed their jump into the adult labor force. One Komsomol activist from Kolomna, speaking at a meeting of rural youth organizers in Moscow, worried that adolescents were becoming adults before they were ready. The common reaction among these young people was that school was no longer necessary: "Why should I go study when I am my own boss, earning as [much] as an adult?"[91]

Despite concerns about substituting work for education, the dominant opinion in Komsomol circles framed adolescent labor as a positive—an opportunity for maturation at the workplace. This framing drew on ideals from the 1920s that focused on labor as a force for imparting moral values to children, allowing them to contribute to the economy while learning skills.[92] Mikhailov hoped that by increasing the activity of adolescents in official youth culture, especially through the Komsomol, the positive features of labor could remain while social pressure would control the negative aspects. For this reason, he pushed for the league to lower its age minimum to fourteen to include the youngest workers. As Mikhailov explained to party Central Committee Secretary Andrei Zhdanov,

89. RGASPI, f. 1m, op. 5, d. 100, ll. 13, 23.
90. Efron, *Dnevniki*, 2:173.
91. RGASPI, f. 1m, op. 5, d. 117, l. 22.
92. Fitzpatrick, *Education and Social Mobility*, 144–55.

"In the conditions of war, the process of political upbringing for youth occurs quicker than in peacetime."[93]

Adolescents were not the only targets for league recruiting. Komsomol leaders viewed increasing membership as a general cure for the problems of chaos and mobilization on the home front. From January 1941 to January 1942, civilian Komsomol membership had decreased from 8.3 million to 3.5 million members.[94] A large number of those young people left for the army, entering its Komsomol organization, or joined the party. Statisticians also struck from the rolls youth who remained in occupied territories. Other young communists perished as civilians. The swift turnover in members did not allow anything close to an exact count of members. The apparent large decrease in membership alarmed central youth leaders, who associated raw membership numbers with their ability to mobilize young people and cultivate pro-Soviet attitudes among them.

In the fall of 1942, the Komsomol's Central Committee sent a closed letter to provincial organizations "On Admission to the Komsomol." The letter stressed that membership would increase young people's activity in the economy, by both decreasing complacency and mobilizing members into shock brigades. Additionally, the letter claimed that youth were "hungrily drawn" to politics and without guidance they might develop opinions about current events that were contrary to official narratives. There were young people who could or would join, but Komsomol leaders asserted that activists had merely taken youth who applied on their own initiative instead of actively recruiting potential members.[95] Attracting new members was easier to demand than to achieve. Even during peacetime, recruiting new members had required a mix of reward, coercion, and Soviet patriotism. During the war, nonmembers who volunteered or were coerced into military service had qualities and loyalties that made them probable candidates for membership. Correspondingly, it seems likely that the remaining nonaffiliated youth were more indifferent to the Soviet cause or were from marginalized groups unwelcome in Soviet political society.

For these youth, admission to the Komsomol had rewards and dangers during the war. Georgii Efron's mobilization orders in 1943 placed him in the labor army because of his connection to a Gulag prisoner, his father. Highly educated for a teenager, Efron demanded placement in an artillery school where his school peers received assignments. This attempt failed, and the local mobilization office informed him that if he had been a Komsomol member, he could have escaped

---

93. RGASPI, f. 1m, op. 6, d. 81, l. 40.
94. RGASPI, f. 1m, op. 6, d. 85, l. 1.
95. RGASPI, f. 1m, op. 6, d. 20, ll. 40–45.

the labor army. Of course, his father may have made it just as difficult to join the youth league as to enlist in artillery school. In the end, Efron deferred mobilization for another year, but at the time his scare had made him wish that he had been a Komsomol member.[96]

Membership also carried responsibilities and increased visibility. Keeping their distance from the youth league may have allowed young people to escape or defer mobilization, especially into militia and partisan units but also into factory shock brigades. Similar to the First Five-Year Plan, the war had made extraordinary mobilization the norm. Two months into the war, the youth press began a campaign to promote two-hundreders, youth who fulfilled two times their work norms.[97] By 1943, official figures claimed that 80 percent of industrial workers were involved in some kind of labor competition.[98] Youth groups were a focal point of organizing these competitions. In factories and on collective farms, youth leaders hoped to use groups to place extra burdens on workers to over-produce and conduct voluntary labor outside the workplace. How young people assessed the demands that came along with Komsomol membership is hard to know. Archival documents tend to record the extremes of patriotism and disdain for political regimes, but indifference fails to register on the historical record.[99] For some, the liabilities of membership probably outweighed the benefits.

Faced with demands to increase membership from above and indifference from below, local Komsomol groups still managed to enroll large numbers of youth in the league. What little qualitative evidence exists suggests that their methods built on the prewar tendency to encourage or even compel young people to join, sometimes enrolling them by list. At a Komsomol Central Committee meeting in 1944, the head of the army's youth league, I. Vidiukov, told a cautionary story of a Vsevobuch group in Rostov province. The local Komsomol secretary appeared at a training meeting and asked who would like to join the Komsomol. Those who joined went home. The others went marching for two hours. When they returned, the secretary repeated the question. Vidiukov quipped, "It turned out that more wanted to join."[100] The opaque minutes of district Komsomol committees are revealing about the process of admission when taken as a whole. Records show dozens or even more than a hundred young people joined at a single meeting, occurring weekly or biweekly, each with a small entry of their biographical data and the decision about their admission. No application was

96. Efron, *Dnevniki*, 2:144–45.
97. *Komsomol'skaia pravda*, September 24, 1941, 1.
98. Berkhoff, *Motherland in Danger*, 87.
99. Zahra, "Imagined Noncommunities."
100. RGASPI, f. 1m, op. 2, d. 227, l. 195.

refused. Given the large number of applicants, it seems unlikely that these com-mittees scrutinized them.[101]

In the army's Komsomol, membership practices were similar or even more lax. Nikolai Melnikov, by the end of 1941 the head of a youth group in a battalion, wrote that all the regimental secretaries understood membership policies: "No restrictions were put on joining. On the contrary, there was a directive that as many soldiers as possible should be induced to join." Instead of maximizing the production of wartime industry, the Komsomol's activity in the army consisted of maximizing wartime heroism. Before an advance—sometimes even while under fire—the Komsomol collective of a unit gathered as a means of creating solidarity.[102] In the army, too, membership was a double-edged sword. Melnikov asserted that Komsomol members received the most difficult orders but also were more likely to receive military decorations.[103]

The imperative to include more members also meant that disciplinary mea-sures decreased as the war progressed. In 1941 youth committees expelled a great deal of their members, 25,017, but by 1943 the number was 13,595, and in 1944 expulsions numbered 16,592—data for 1942 were lost or never gathered.[104] As calls to recruit new members grew, local organizers took a more forgiving tack. Even the issue of destroyed membership cards in advance of occupation became negotiable. In Voskresensk, a city in the southeast of Moscow province, the typical punishment for young people who had committed the "cowardly act" of burning their card was expulsion as late as March 1942. In April, though, several young women hit on an explanation that excused their misdeed: their parents had burned their cards. One even claimed, "It's possible the card fell into a book that my mother burned." By September, committees only reprimanded members for having burned their cards and apparently did not demand an excuse.[105] The main reason local youth organizers limited expulsions was the unspoken under-standing that harsh discipline was less important than retaining the ability to mobilize youth as Komsomol members.

Membership policies and wartime losses combined to create enormous turn-over in the Komsomol. At a meeting of organizers from the military's Komso-mol organizations in August 1942, one activist claimed that 73 percent of the members in his Forty-Third Army had joined in the past year.[106] Similarly, in the

---

101. For an example, see OKhDOPIM, f. 641, op. 1, d. 25.
102. RGASPI, f. 1m, op. 47, d. 109, l. 38.
103. Melnikov, "Road to Life," in *Soviet Youth*, ed. Novak-Deker, 228.
104. RGASPI, f. 1m, op. 33, d. 71, l. 36; d. 110, ll. 1–4; d. 130, ll. 15–18.
105. OKhDOPIM, f. 641, op. 1, d. 20, ll. 8, 21, 30, 40, 49, 94.
106. RGASPI, f. 1m, op. 5, d. 119, l. 15.

town of Mytishchi (Moscow province), the Komsomol organization fell from 12,000 members to 1,028 by the start of 1942, with 6,000 members enlisting and 5,120 going into evacuation. Over the course of 1942, it recruited 2,277 new members, making up 69 percent of its membership.[107] A report in the Komsomol Central Committee estimated that 30 percent of paid youth organizers had left their positions for some kind of army service at the very start of the war.[108] By July 1943, 79.3 percent of the secretaries of provincial youth committees had left their posts, while the turnover among district secretaries in the same period was nearly total—97.1 percent.[109]

Youth organizers presented the wartime turnover in cadres as an opportunity to develop new leaders, especially among women. In January 1941, women made up 43 percent of the Komsomol's members and an even smaller proportion of leadership positions.[110] By October 1942, the proportions had more than flipped. Women made up 63 percent of members and 68 percent of secretaries in local organizations in the civilian youth league.[111] Although women went into the armed forces during the war, young men went in larger numbers, leaving women to take their places in factories and on Komsomol committees. For youth leaders, the influx of women was a desirable necessity that they interpreted as the continuation of prewar recruiting practices.

In spite of the wishes of youth leaders, promotion of women often ran into obstacles. In Central Asia, Komsomol instructors who monitored local youth committees found that leaders discriminated against women routinely. One instructor reported that in Turkmenistan, local youth committees counted men as official Komsomol members and counted women separately as "little girls." Charshanginsk district's party secretary yelled at its youth leader for organizing the training of 105 young women as organizers: "Who allowed you to train women? Did you ask me? What do you want—for them to say abroad that our reserves [of soldiers] are finished?"[112] Reports about Central Asia drew on the long-standing notion that women there faced particular discrimination.[113] However, it seems that new women cadres were the objects of scrutiny elsewhere, too. In Molotov district, one female secretary proved "unclean in everyday life"—a likely euphemism for promiscuity or excessive drinking. Her replacement was no

107. OKhDOPIM, f. 652, op. 2, d. 7, l. 51.

108. RGASPI, f. 1m, op. 6, d. 86, ll. 10, 13, 14, 15.

109. RGASPI, f. 1m, op. 6, d. 86a, l. 30.

110. RGASPI, f. 1m, op. 23, d. 1395, ll. 17, 19; op. 126, d. 390, ll. 13, 14, 15.

111. RGASPI, f. 1m, op. 5, d. 12b, ll. 22–23; op. 6, d. 85, l. 1.

112. RGASPI, f. 1m, op. 6, d. 55, ll. 61, 84, 86.

113. Northrop, *Veiled Empire*.

better: "She organized drinking bouts and parties, and did not enjoy authority among youth in the district."[114]

Central Komsomol leaders hoped to solve cadre deficits by giving young women rapid administrative training. Recruitment for these schools, though, belied unrealistic standards for youth cadres during the war. When three training schools opened in 1942, the central instructor monitoring them noted with derision that its students were mere "rank-and-file [Komsomol] members." Their only qualifications were that they worked in white-collar professions.[115] Central leaders wanted to train experienced women cadres for leadership roles but none were available. When local organizers suggested that the war was partially to blame for turnover, youth leaders balked at this explanation, claiming that local groups had not worked hard enough to recruit or retain members.[116] Komsomol administrators acted as though an infinite number of youth were available to fill the league's ranks and become its activists if only lower-level organizers would pay more attention to cadres. This was not the case, of course. Politically active young people were in demand in all sectors of the wartime Soviet state. The best candidates had already enlisted in the army or used the war as an opportunity to advance to higher-level positions. The power of activism had stretched to its limit.

On the home front in general, regime leaders hoped that youth would take the place of the adult population as it departed for the front. The issue of governance during wartime intensified a long-term problem in the Soviet state: the need to rule a large country via a comparatively small governing class.[117] Before the invasion, the dearth of cadres had allowed young people swift upward mobility. In the extreme circumstances of the war, party and youth leaders continued to rely on young activists to compensate for shortages of labor and authority. Adolescent labor became an important part of the wartime economy, and Komsomol groups in places like blockaded Leningrad worked to recreate a semblance of public services in harsh conditions. In most cases, though, youth activism could not make up for the gaps in state control. In its place, chaos most often filled the void.

Restoring Order

The war turned decisively in the Soviet Union's favor at the beginning of 1943. At Stalingrad in January 1943, the Red Army destroyed Germany's Sixth Army

114. RGASPI, f. 1m, op. 6, d. 86a, l. 6.
115. RGASPI, f. 1m, op. 6, d. 12b, ll. 11–13.
116. RGASPI, f. 1m, op. 5, d. 127, l. 64.
117. On the general problem of cadres during war, see Stotland, "Ideologues and Pragmatists."

and took to the offensive. A half-year later, Soviet forces decisively beat back the German offensive at Kursk, placing the Wehrmacht on the defensive for the rest of the war. Although the Soviets had retaken limited occupied zones from the Germans earlier, the advances from 1943 onward meant the return of huge amounts of territory and people, some of which the country had annexed only in 1939 and 1940. The war would not be over for two more years, but Soviet leaders began to consider how they would manage the country's transition into peacetime, including the re-Sovietization of formerly occupied regions. The challenge in those areas was not just reestablishing authority, but reincorporating people whose survival under occupation made them the subject of suspicion. The problem of returning peace was not just the legacy of foreign occupation, though. As the end came closer, youth leaders worried about the impact of the war on youth. What would happen to a young generation that had experienced such violence and independence?

Soviet power was absent or weakened in many territories for as much as three years in the westernmost territories of the USSR. During the occupation, adolescents remained in their home regions both by choice and by chance. Although many tried to carry on with their lives, the war polarized occupied society, forcing Soviet people into accommodation with the occupiers or into resistance groups. As the tide turned in the war, resistance to the occupiers grew stronger as people under occupation sensed that they would have to account for their deeds to Soviet authorities. Antioccupation sentiment also increased because of German atrocities, including the abduction of millions of Soviets, very often adolescents, for forced labor in the west.[118]

After the initial retaking of occupied territories in 1943, authorities were most concerned with the practical issue of reestablishing Soviet institutions like the Komsomol in the regions that had been under occupation. Initially central youth leaders approached the question of cadres with raw quotas, ordering each home front provincial committee to send a precise number of activists to recaptured territories. Facing a shortage of qualified workers themselves, committees in the rear often sent people whom they considered expendable. Krasnoiarsk's youth committee sent cadres to Ukraine who had never been to the republic. Indeed, they had never held Komsomol positions. Among them, one was pregnant and refused to go.[119] A central Komsomol instructor claimed that thirteen of twenty-four workers sent from Omsk to Ukraine "deserted, scared by the first bombs."[120]

---

118. Dallin, *German Rule in Russia.*
119. RGASPI, f. 1m, op. 6, d. 165, l. 109.
120. RGASPI, f. 1m, op. 6, d. 92, ll. 43, 48, 51.

Hoping to avoid similar incidents, youth leaders sought workers who were both experienced and capable of contending with the violence of these territories. In spite of the Red Army's victories against the Wehrmacht, formerly occupied territories were still full of danger. Not only were some areas under the threat of German attack, but armed nationalist groups fought the regime. Anti-Soviet sentiment was especially strong in areas that the USSR had annexed only in 1939. Of the various groups, the Organization of Ukrainian Nationalists (OUN) presented the greatest challenge.[121] Its goal to found an independent Ukrainian state had complicated its relationship with the German occupiers, and members moved between resistance and collaboration at various times. The OUN's opposition to Soviet power was more consistent, though. Its continued struggle against Soviet authorities meant that well into the postwar period, authorities in the western borderlands faced civil war conditions.[122]

As the main forces of the Red Army moved westward, an important function of the Komsomol in reincorporated Soviet territories was as irregular police. Pro-Soviet youth became a key force opposing nationalists in communities.[123] Komsomol leaders, concerned with the need to defeat anti-Soviet partisans physically and ideologically, came to two conclusions. First, the best youth organizers would be young people from the region who had proven themselves in partisan groups as reliable, loyal cadres. Second, the next best youth organizers would be young people with connections to the western regions of the Soviet Union and "with a great deal of experience as Komsomol workers . . . physically fit and durable."[124]

In 1944, Komsomol leaders turned to national principles in recruiting cadres for reestablished committees in the west. In the spring of 1944, Komsomol leaders ordered lower-level committees to send thirty-two hundred ethnic Ukrainian organizers to Ukraine. The regions that had the largest quotas were often those where youth organizers had gone into evacuation. Kazakhstan's youth committee had to send 440 activists, for instance. Other provinces that received large quotas were places where there were simply many Ukrainians, such as the 112 organizers requested from Voronezh province.[125] The Ukrainian Komsomol also sent leaders to select cadres to come back to the newly liberated territories, prying them from resentful provincial leaderships in the east. One such Ukrainian youth worker accused local organizers in Bashkortostan's Komsomol and party of sabotaging

121. Dallin, *German Rule in Russia*, 114–22.
122. Rieber, "Civil Wars in the Soviet Union."
123. RGASPI, f. 1m, op. 6, d. 203, l. 115.
124. RGASPI, f. 1m, op. 6, d. 92, l. 51.
125. RGASPI, f. 1m, op. 6, d. 165, l. 1.

her mission, including denying her group access to the "comfort" train car—their due as party members.[126]

The problem of cadres only intensified over time. As the Red Army marched farther west, Komsomol organizers soon appeared in its wake. Those youth workers who initially arrived in liberated Ukraine were often the very same people who followed the army later. In the short period after the first Ukrainian territories were liberated, 889 new city and district youth secretaries had left their positions. Of those, a hundred were found incompetent. However, an even larger number, 250, had gone to western Ukraine as organizers.[127] The Red Army was a chain that pulled civilian workers along as authorities attempted to reestablish Soviet power. The most qualified—those who had proven themselves in dangerous areas—moved on to the new frontier.

The task of creating a bureaucratic infrastructure against a backdrop of violence belied the deeper challenge in the recaptured territories—the re-Sovietization of people. In part, this problem involved finding and punishing collaborators. This undertaking presented civilian authorities with new questions: What was the difference between collaboration and survival? Who could be forgiven and for what? And what could be done with those brutalized youth who emerged from the war?

In their initial attempts to deal with youth who had experienced occupation, Komsomol leaders urged a hard line against accused collaborators.[128] In recaptured areas of southern Russia, the Komsomol's Central Committee commanded brigades of instructors to reestablish youth organizations in those territories. In instructions to these brigades, Komsomol leaders demanded that the organizers root out former collaborators: "Purge the organization of German followers and people who comported themselves poorly during the occupation."[129]

As more territories returned to Soviet hands, youth leaders learned that various forms of reconciliation with occupying forces had been widespread. In May 1943, the Komsomol Central Committee hosted propaganda workers from regions still under German control. The central task for these activists was to consider how they would deal with young people who had been neutral during the war or had even collaborated with the Germans. An oft-repeated phrase was "it's no secret," followed by admissions of unpleasant realities that had occurred under occupation. A propaganda leader and former partisan from Smolensk province,

126. RGASPI, f. 1m, op. 6, d. 166, ll. 34–37.
127. RGASPI, f. 1m, op. 6, d. 166, l. 212.
128. Khaustov et al., *Lubianka*, 361–71 (citing APRF, f. 3, op. 58, d. 207, ll. 159–75).
129. RGASPI, f. 1m, op. 6, d. 86, l. 26.

A. Ia. Vinokurov, claimed, "It's no secret that some of our youth work for the police." The propagandist from Kiev province's youth committee, Karpenko, said, "It's no secret that many girls and women were herded into public houses [as prostitutes]."[130] It is difficult to know how many youth did collaborate, although Vinokurov's experience as a partisan lends credence to his assertions. Nonetheless, youth leaders accepted collaboration as a pervasive phenomenon.

The perception that a large number of young people had at least tolerated the occupiers caused youth leaders to call for leniency. While some had acted in unsavory ways, they concluded that young people were malleable enough to reform—or perhaps that there were too many of such youth to take a hard line against them. At a meeting of Komsomol propagandists from liberated territories in February 1944, Ol'ga Mishakova supported moderation toward youth who had lived under occupation. Some youth had been heroes in the war, but "not everyone can be a hero—a Zoia Kosmodem'ianskaia or those from Krasnodon [the Young Guard]."[131] Mishakova recast expectations for Soviet youth's wartime experience. Instead of demanding universal resistance to occupation, she maintained that it was better to accept that most youth had remained loyal to the USSR in their hearts, even if they had tolerated the occupiers to survive.[132]

Infiltration of young society by anti-Soviet ideas during occupation also concerned youth leaders. Rather than expelling young people, though, organizers' focus was on expunging these ideas. How to acculturate youth after occupation was a key issue at the Komsomol Central Committee's December 1944 plenum. A major concern was that Germans had allowed or encouraged religion.[133] The Soviet regime's own wartime alliance with the Orthodox Church complicated the actions that plenipotentiaries would take in formerly occupied regions. Attacking religion aggressively might awaken resentment among believers throughout the country. Thus Mishakova said that though the Komsomol was made up of atheists and needed to fight against religion ideologically, religious people had nonetheless "stood in defense of the motherland." Instead of direct attacks on faith, Mishakova and others recommended policies that would show youth the antiprogressive nature of religion. Above all, they stressed the use of "scientific propaganda" to expose the falsehoods of religion.[134]

---

130. RGASPI, f. 1m, op. 5, d. 152, ll. 22, 29, 30.
131. RGASPI, f. 1m, op. 5, d. 190, l. 92.
132. On Soviet propaganda about universal resistance, see Berkhoff, *Motherland in Danger*, 228–43. On legal attempts to deal with collaboration during the occupation, see Kudryashov and Voisin, "Early Stages of 'Legal Purges.'"
133. RGASPI, f. 1m, op. 2, d. 216, ll. 85, 109.
134. RGASPI, f. 1m, op. 5, d. 190, ll. 23, 91.

Religion was part of a broader program Germans had tried to spread among youth. In August 1943, Komsomol leaders commissioned reports about German organizations for local youth under occupation. These were primarily ethnic-based groups that formed in Ukraine, Belarus, and the Baltic states that attempted to attract youth to the German cause via local nationalism. One report euphemistically characterized the organizations as tools to turn young women into "slaves of German masters . . . to interest them in German victory." Komsomol Secretary for Military Affairs Aleksandr Shelepin, the future head of the league and a major figure in the party and KGB under Khrushchev and Brezhnev, received a similar report about the lasting effect of these groups in liberated territories. It concluded that the Germans had succeeded in spreading various social ills among youth: "among older schoolgirls, instances of prostitution; among boys, thievery, hooliganism, and many have been taken into petty trade and speculation."[135] Echoing the accusations of 1937–38 against "Trotskyist degenerates" in the Komsomol, in December 1944 Mishakova claimed that the Germans had tried to turn young people against Soviet power with alcohol, as well as "erotic books and films, pornographic poems and postcards." Moreover, foreign influences had not stopped with the Germans. As the war's end seemed to be nearing, Mishakova saw danger in the penetration of "bourgeois morals" via British and American media.[136]

Foreign occupation was not the only factor that had taken a troubling toll on youth. The war itself had made its imprint on young people who had fought. One group that particularly concerned regime leaders was partisans. In the partisan movement generally, party leaders worried that the freedom that the forest had presented had undermined Soviet behavioral norms and discipline.[137] Komsomol workers involved in the movement argued that the partisan experience had necessitated and encouraged brutality among young people. At a meeting of writers with partisans who had been behind enemy lines in 1943, one partisan spoke about a young man he called Vaniushka, an orphan and "previously a big hooligan who had been in prison." Now a partisan, it was "difficult to find a braver guy" than Vaniushka, a great fighter. Yet local peasants had also complained that Vaniushka drank himself into a stupor in their villages on stolen alcohol. The commander reconciled himself to working with Vaniushka and his kind but urged the writers to develop means of turning these brutal youth into cultured Soviet citizens.[138]

---

135. RGASPI, f. 1m, op. 53, d. 432, ll. 15, 51.
136. RGASPI, f. 1m, op. 2, d. 227, l. 107.
137. Slepyan, *Stalin's Guerillas*, 140–42.
138. RGASPI, f. 1m, op. 5, d. 151, l. 10.

Some youth who went through war were too far gone for rehabilitation, though. The secretary of Belorussia's Komsomol, Mikhail Zimianin, at a meeting of youth workers from liberated and occupied territories in May 1943, asserted that war itself was turning youth into irredeemable, ruthless fighters. He gave a gruesome example. After a partisan died in battle, his comrades decided to give his clothes to his mother. One of the partisans, though, "had become callous and brutal from war." He demanded the clothes from the mother, the only reminder she had of her son. When she refused, he beat her. The brigade's commander had him executed in front of all the men for "political banditism." Zimianin concluded that the executed partisan had not been bad but in the war "had become a beast and lost all human responsibility."[139] For Zimianin and other youth leaders, the cautionary tale of that partisan suggested a broader brutalization of youth who had experienced violence as part of their daily lives in occupied territories.

Cultural figures also believed that the violence of war had changed children's demands for entertainment. Workers at a May 1944 meeting of the artistic council of Soiuzdetfilm, the Komsomol-affiliated studio, considered what kind of films would be appropriate for the generation who had experienced the war. After the studio's most prominent director, Lev Kuleshov, a veteran of the avant-garde, proposed the studio shoot films about the outdoors, the chief screen-writing editor, Vladimir Shveitser, interrupted: how could the studio ignore the war as a factor and as a subject? "Of course, it is nice to be able to tie a tie and hunt woodcock," he said but continued, "We must orient ourselves toward the upbringing of a new generation after the shocks of the Patriotic War." Director Al'bert Gendel'shtein asserted that the war had fundamentally changed children: "A child from Leningrad . . . is an absolutely differently formed person with big thoughts." Films about the outdoors could not spark the interest of a generation who had experienced war.[140]

Although they viewed the negative effects of war as more pronounced in formerly occupied areas, Soiuzdetfilm's workers were also concerned about its effects on those young people who had spent the war at home. The poet and screenwriter Angiia Barto suggested that the same process that had matured children had also made them coldhearted. She complained that the studio's current plans included no "children's or youth films" but only films for adults that would not help children became cultured Soviet people. Nikolai Rozhkov, a screenwriter at the studio, countered that the children of the war could not be considered "youth" by peacetime standards but were effectively adults. Thirteen- or

139. RGASPI, f. 1m, op. 5, d. 152, ll. 3–4.
140. RGALI f. 2468, op. 2, d. 9, ll. 3, 7.

fourteen-year-olds had "joined the collective farm and even became its chair." The discussion hinged on whether a peaceful childhood could return or if the studio should make films that would appeal to youth's wartime experience. Nearly all the participants agreed, though, that films would have to address the experience of war somehow.[141]

In the Komsomol, too, youth leaders at the end of the war came to believe that the wartime experience on the home front had matured youth in complicated ways. During the early part of the war, Mikhailov had expressed the convenient opinion that participation in the economy contributed to adolescents' political development. At the first postwar meeting of the Komsomol Central Committee in November 1945, though, organizers addressed the unsavory effects of war. A worker at *Komsomol'skaia pravda*, Vasilii Koroteev, asserted that the war's influence on adolescents was mixed. On the positive side, adolescents had learned to work as adults. The negative side, though, was that the typical undersupervised adolescent boy during the war "drinks vodka and keeps company with girls." He maintained that in the countryside, largely bereft of young men, adolescents as young as fourteen were living with older women. This uncontrolled sexual activity Koroteev linked to a massive increase in venereal disease, five to ten times greater in some places. He concluded, "It's good that [young men] stopped being so soft and bad that [they] became so coarse."[142]

Anxieties about the behavior of young people reflected what would become the postwar concerns of the regime among youth. After the first part of the war had demanded total military and productive mobilization, re-Sovietization from 1943 onward placed political socialization back onto youth leaders' agenda. In formerly occupied territories, the perception that many young people had collaborated with the Germans was of particular concern. In contrast to Soviet popular culture, where all collaborators received their just due, many youth leaders believed that categorical exclusion was unreasonable and impractical. As in the aftermath of the Great Terror, youth whom security organs did not arrest—even those whose wartime records were not sterling—were redeemable. Youth leaders pushed local activists to verify, forgive, and remake those young people whose loyalty had not been absolute but who had not crossed the formal line into treason. This approach followed a general feeling in the regime that the war had changed young people throughout the country. It had robbed them of a peaceful childhood, making them into little adults.[143] As the war was ending, the

---

141. Ibid., ll. 8, 11.
142. RGASPI, f. 1m, op. 2, d. 234, l. 206.
143. DeGraffenried, *Sacrificing Childhood*.

regime's character builders strove for a return to a semblance of prewar normalcy but simultaneously asserted that the war generation was marked indelibly by its experience.

The war decimated the generation of youth who fought in it. Although Stalin stated that seven million Soviets died in the war, youth leaders must have known that the losses were much larger. The exact number of Soviet war dead is impossible to know, but a reasonable estimate put deaths at roughly twenty-seven million, including military and civilian casualties.[144] A report from October 1946 assessing the change in Komsomol membership during the war revealed the loss of an entire generation of the country's political class. At the start of the war, roughly ten million youth had been in the league and over the course of the conflict, another ten million joined. By the end of the war, only 7.6 million youth remained in the Komsomol. Of the missing twelve million, some young people outgrew the youth league, others joined the party, and more may have simply left the Komsomol. Without a doubt, though, the majority of them died in the war.[145] By one estimate, nearly half of the men who graduated from schools in 1941 died.[146] Another scholar asserts that 90 percent of the young men born in 1921 perished.[147]

In part because of these losses, the war became the defining achievement of Stalin's regime. It turned many people into Soviet patriots, convincing them that Stalinism was preferable to the National Socialist alternative. Some anticipated a postwar political relaxation that would never come.[148] For regime leaders, the war was no less momentous. Stalinist leaders believed that victory had demonstrated socialism's resilience and its inevitable worldwide triumph. Nonetheless, they considered the war itself an extraordinary period that had not reflected socialist normalcy, even though it had mobilized the power of the socialist state. This conception of the war as a period of extremes is only partially accurate. When the war placed enormous demands on state and society, the regime fell back on amplified versions of existing practices developed in the 1930s. The tremendous needs of the military and economy during war meant that youth culture focused almost exclusively on mobilization at the beginning of the conflict. At the war's end, though, Soviet character builders returned to the idea of disciplining youth for socialism.

---

144. Ellman and Maksudov, "Soviet Deaths in the Great Patriotic War."
145. RGASPI, f. 1m, op. 33, d. 232, ll. 27, 45, 47.
146. Somov, *Pervoe sovetskoe pokolenie*, 7.
147. Merridale, *Ivan's War*, 338.
148. Weiner, *Making Sense of War*, 367. Zubkova, *Russia after the War*, 35.

Conclusion

THE AFTERMATH OF WAR

Stalin's young communists believed they were living in socialism and working toward communism. Despite their faith in the USSR's historical mission,
the role youth would play under socialism was never set in stone. Contingency
often defined what the future of the great experiment would be. Most of all,
the threat of war shaped Stalinist youth culture. The impulse to stabilize society after the chaos of the First Five-Year Plan caused youth leaders to support
traditional gender roles, provide privileges for educated workers, and promote
cultured norms of behavior. The militarization of young society under Stalin
was explicit and pervasive. A consensus emerged that fitness and youth programs
were meant to prepare young people to fight. Beyond direct training for combat, youth activists sought to instill militarized discipline among future soldiers.
Whereas radical activists of the 1920s had wanted to overturn generational and
political hierarchies, the Komsomol of the 1930s trained youth to obey authority
figures in civilian life as one might obey an officer in war. Official youth culture
sought to extend these norms over an increasing number of citizens. In 1929, the
Komsomol was a relatively elite organization of activists that incorporated less
than 10 percent of the age-eligible population. By 1941, it had become a mass
organization incorporating 30 percent of youth.

The increased inclusiveness of Soviet youth culture came as Stalinist repression reached its apex. Even as Stalin's secret police worked ruthlessly to excise
a supposed fifth column from the population, youth leaders hoped that the
expansion of official culture would stop youth from taking the path from bad

behavior to becoming true enemies. It was rarely clear where the line between minor misdeeds ended and political crime began, except in cases where the NKVD arrested young people. When members transgressed without facing criminal charges, though, youth organizers often insisted they remain in the league precisely so that the Komsomol could watch and improve them as loyal citizens and future soldiers.

By the time Stalinist youth culture entered World War II, it had come to resemble the youth cultures of the country's enemies. Throughout the authoritarian world, the prospect of war caused youth organizations to expand their ranks, foster social and ideological discipline, and undertake extensive paramilitary training. Although the USSR would defeat its authoritarian enemies, the methods they shared for raising young people entered the postwar period through Soviet official youth culture.

The end of World War II both transformed and stultified the Soviet Union. The young people who emerged from the conflict were ready for change. The war had shown them extreme violence but also periods of freedom in the absence or weakness of political regimes. Millions had seen the world outside the USSR, albeit as soldiers in the Red Army or forced laborers in Nazi-occupied Europe.[1] On the home front, adolescents delayed or abandoned their educations for work in the wartime economy outside the supervision of adults. Their experience was a schooling of its own, teaching them about adult concerns. The war produced mature, worldly youth, but it also solidified Stalinism's hold over Soviet young people. For many Soviet citizens, the horrors of the German occupation had dispelled notions that capitalism (represented by the occupiers) presented an alternative to socialism. Moreover, youth who fought or toiled for the Soviet Union felt a new sense of ownership in the regime. For both regime leaders and for Komsomol youth, communist upbringing had proven its worth as a means of moral socialization.

The ultimate trial of the Soviet regime produced loyalty among the young generation but also the hope of a postwar relaxation in Stalinism.[2] As Soviet youth sought change, fissures in the regime's authority allowed subcultures to form among youth.[3] The apparent strength of Stalin's regime in Europe belied the internal weakness of the USSR, a country wrecked by war. The postwar occupation of Central and Eastern Europe, including the struggle with a nationalist insurgency in Ukraine, meant that Stalin's regime had restricted means to exert pressure within the USSR. In the immediate postwar period, it could not exercise

---

1. Edele, *Soviet Veterans*, 33–34.
2. Zubkova, *Russia after the War*, 101–16.
3. Edele, "Strange Young Men in Stalin's Moscow"; Furst, *Stalin's Last Generation*, 153–56.

authority over society to the extent that it had before the war, as limited and blunt as Soviet control had been then.

After the war, moreover, the motivations of terror in the 1930s had largely disappeared. The threat of war had created a sense of desperation among political elites that drove mass repression. With the war won, the overriding goals of Stalinist politics—to preserve and expand Soviet geopolitical power and Stalin's personal control—were virtually assured. Not only was the Soviet Union a military superpower, it had established a buffer zone in Eastern and Central Europe that would prevent a repeat of Germany's invasion. The victory also meant that Stalin's position in the country was unchallengeable. Despite the comparative moderation of repression, the regime remained capable of violence. One of the most infamous postwar incidents came in the so-called Leningrad Affair of 1949, when Stalin ordered the arrest of hundreds of Leningrad officials who had supposedly participated in a regional conspiracy against him.[4] Youth leaders, too, would become targets in the Leningrad arrests. Nonetheless, there would be no postwar purge on the scale of 1937–38.

Even though the urgency that motivated repression had diminished, social disorder among youth continued to be a source of anxiety in the USSR. The massive social dislocation of the war motivated new attempts to discipline society through policing and political culture. In the period of desperate shortages that followed the war, young people were among the most vulnerable Soviet citizens, contributing to a jump in "youth crimes" as orphaned and unsupervised children stole to survive. The reaction to these crimes was similar to the 1930s—a police campaign to curb juvenile delinquency.[5] Facing a new wave of supposed hooliganism, the Komsomol revived its efforts to keep youth within the grasp of the regime. In the postwar Communist Party, too, campaigns against degeneracy echoed the moral panic about the youth of the 1930s.[6] Indeed, it seems likely that many of the moralizing party members of the postwar period were from the cohort who had learned that "lifestyle cannot be separated from politics" in the Komsomol during the Great Terror.

After the war, the Komsomol continued to grow into an organization where adults monitored adolescents. Like their older siblings, postwar Komsomol members were predominately upwardly mobile school and university students rather than workers.[7] The dearth of cadres in the country, particularly

---

4. Khlevniuk and Gorlitzki, *Cold Peace*, 4–5, 79–89.
5. Furst, *Stalin's Last Generation*, 168–81.
6. Cohn, *High Title of a Communist*, 142–91.
7. Furst, *Stalin's Last Generation*, 48.

the absence of war-dead young adults, widened the existing divide between older, professional organizers and the younger rank and file. The number of provincial-level youth secretaries who listed their occupational background as "Komsomol worker" was just under 40 percent in June 1939 but by October 1945 included over 65 percent of these workers.[8] At the top of the league, the secretaries Nikolai Mikhailov and Ol'ga Mishakova both turned forty years old in 1946—five years older than Aleksandr Kosarev had been in 1938. Mishakova left the Komsomol that year but continued to be active in party work toward the moral socialization of youth, writing a dissertation titled "The Role of Upbringing in the Construction of a Communist Society." Mikhailov remained the league's chief until 1952, when the wartime Komsomol military secretary Aleksandr Shelepin replaced him. The former Komsomol head graduated into top posts in the party and Soviet government.

More than for any other reason, Mikhailov and his underlings remained faithful to communist upbringing because the war had proven it was part of the correct path from socialism to communism. An article from June 1945 referred to Stalin's meeting with Komsomol leaders in January 1935, where he had called for the league to become an organization of moral socialization. Ten years later, the article's author demanded a return to the "main task of the Komsomol—the communist upbringing of all youth."[9] Stalin and his followers did not see that their ideals for raising youth had evolved out of the anxious and violent conditions of the decade before World War II began. Instead, they saw a victorious system for creating a socialist society that, even in times of relative peace, would always need to cultivate youth ready to defend the country against external enemies. At a meeting of the Komsomol's Central Committee in 1944, a representative from the Red Army suggested the league might adopt policies from the Boy Scouts. V. N. Ivanov, the prominent blockade-era leader of Leningrad's youth organization, responded, "The party and Komsomol have twenty-five years of rich experience molding youth and cadres, [experience] that has absolutely proven itself."[10] Even as Soviet society evolved, key elements of interwar authoritarianism persisted in the basic contours of socialism.[11]

As the Soviet empire expanded into Eastern and Central Europe, Soviet advisers brought Stalinist youth culture with them. Mimicking the Komsomol, Eastern Bloc countries set up national youth leagues that claimed a monopoly on

---

8. RGASPI, f. 1m, op. 6, d. 355a.

9. N. Golyshev, "Velikaia bol'shevistskaia partiia vedet i vdokhnovliaet Komsomol," *Komsomol'skii rabotnik*, no. 11–12 (1945): 11–23.

10. RGASPI, f. 1m, op. 2, d. 212, ll. 121, 135.

11. Kotkin, "Modern Times," 161–64.

political socialization for the sake of communism.[12] In the developing Cold War, these organizations attempted to promote socialist culture as a defense against the decadent influence of capitalist popular culture. Much like the Soviet youth league, the Free German Youth organization, the equivalent of the Komsomol in East Germany, organized "order groups" to police youth whose interest in rock 'n' roll music leaders feared would lead to degeneracy.[13]

In the USSR, Stalinist aspiration to provide political socialization for all age-eligible young people ended with the inclusion of a majority of youth in the Komsomol by the 1960s.[14] For the ambitious in particular, league membership after Stalin was no longer desirable but mandatory for career advancement.[15] Soviet baby boomers from white-collar families joined because refusal would have closed admission to higher education.[16] Access to consumer goods and entertainment also motivated young people to participate in the Komsomol.[17] Entertainment and benefits became pillars of Soviet youth culture under Khrushchev and Brezhnev. The essence of official youth culture under late socialism emerged in the 1930s, though, when the Komsomol turned its focus to organizing activities meant to create discipline and cement a common identity among Soviet young people.

Soviet youth culture could still generate genuine enthusiasm among youth after the war. Echoing the mobilization of youth in the First Five-Year Plan and World War II, Khrushchev would appeal to youthful idealism in the 1960s in projects like the Virgin Lands campaign. Later, youth would enlist zealously to construct the Baikal-Amur Railway (BAM) under Brezhnev in the 1970s.[18] Only a minority of members would become serious activists, but political socialization in the Komsomol succeeded in creating a sense of socialism's permanence. Even as young people demonstrated cynicism about the materialism of Soviet society and became fans of capitalist popular culture, it remained difficult for them to imagine a non-socialist USSR.[19]

Communist upbringing was supposed to mold the society that would eventually create communism. Some fifty years after Stalin declared the victory of

---

12. For example, on Hungarian youth in the postwar period, see Kurti, *Youth and the State*, 140–79.

13. Fenemore, *Sex, Thugs and Rock 'n' Roll*, 23–24. See also Uta Poiger, *Jazz, Rock, and Rebels*; and Tsipursky, *Socialist Fun*, 54.

14. Kassoff, *Soviet Youth Program*.

15. Solnik, *Stealing the State*, 100.

16. Raleigh, *Soviet Baby Boomers*, 107.

17. Furst, *Stalin's Last Generation*, 3; Tsipursky, *Socialist Fun*, 189–220.

18. Ward, *Brezhnev's Folly*.

19. On belief in the permanence of the Soviet system, see Yurchak, *Everything Was Forever*, 207–37. For information on Soviet participation in capitalist popular culture, see Raleigh, *Soviet Baby Boomers*, 139–42; and Tsipursky, *Socialist Fun*, 54–73.

socialism, though, the Soviet state appeared hardly closer to this goal than it had been after the victory in World War II. Mikhail Gorbachev, himself the former secretary of the Komsomol at Moscow State University, was a true believer in the construction of communism. Toward this end, he championed reforms that effectively reversed the party's monopoly on the country's politics and economy. When perestroika challenged the ideological domination the party had enjoyed, however, it undermined the basis for Soviet rule as a whole. Komsomol membership ceased to be compulsory and stopped being a springboard to advancement, although some youth organizers, most famously the future oligarch Mikhail Khodorkovskii, successfully used their positions in the league to found businesses.[20] The drive to create communism no longer inspired the enthusiasm it had during the Stalin period or even during the postwar years, though. Mass membership in socialist youth associations soon melted away.[21] In some of these leagues, including the Soviet Komsomol, youth leaders attempted to repurpose their organizations as political forces independent of an umbrella political party.[22] Those that successfully transformed into political vehicles nonetheless lost their function in mass socialization. In Russia and other post-Soviet countries, the depoliticization of youth culture led to a vacuum filled by a proliferation of youth organizations affiliated with various regional, nationalist, and political movements.

The instability of post-Soviet societies and the resurgence of authoritarian nationalism in the 2000s created an interest in reviving Soviet-style mass organizations to mobilize youth for new political regimes. Groups like the pro-Putin organization Nashi (Ours) hoped to undercut the basis for what its leaders perceived as youth-supported revolts like Czechoslovakia's Velvet Revolution and Ukraine's Orange and Maidan revolutions.[23] At the same time, many older post-Soviet people viewed contemporary youth as lacking a moral foundation. Their anxiety over the deviance of young people also motivated attempts to revive a Komsomol-like organization.[24] The older generation yearned for a national program that would take charge of the moral socialization of youth, imposing behavioral discipline, national loyalty, and physical training—what Russians called patriotic upbringing. Although these demands were supposedly devoid of the political content of the Soviet era, they had their roots in the official youth culture of Stalinist socialism.

20. Hoffman, *The Oligarchs*, 100–126.

21. Solnick, *Stealing the State*, 104.

22. Pilkington, *Russia's Youth and Its Culture*, 169; Kurti, *Youth and the State*, 223.

23. For example, Aleksei Mukhin, a pro-Kremlin political author wrote of the role of youth in then-upcoming elections in 2007 and 2008, "Some threaten a 'color' [e.g., Orange] revolution, that is, an unconstitutional means of changing power." Mukhin, *Pokolenie 2008*, 5.

24. Blum, *National Identity and Globalization*, 134.

Appendix of Tables

TABLE 1. Komsomol membership (including military), 1923–45

YEAR	TOTAL	WOMEN		% AGES 15–24	TOTAL 15–24 (MIL.)
1923	284,544	52,072	18%	—	—
1924	406,660	63,846	16%	2%	29.1
1925	1,020,456	164,036	16%	4%	29.5
1926	1,640,107	323,811	20%	6%	30.8
1927	1,964,319	418,865	21%	7%	31.8
1928	1,936,977	433,396	22%	6%	32.7
1929	2,245,643	512,007	23%	7%	33.5
1930	2,466,127	606,846	25%	7%	34.0
1931	3,094,620	877,039	28%	9%	34.1
1932	5,358,630	1,624,570	30%	16%	33.8
1933	4,547,186	1,456,433	32%	14%	33.2
1934	3,750,975	1,206,318	32%	12%	31.4
1935	3,531,893	1,091,355	31%	12%	30.7
1936	3,623,010	1,101,395	30%	12%	30.1
1937	3,873,072	1,227,471	32%	13%	29.6
1938	4,375,604	1,421,258	32%	15%	29.4
1939	7,296,135	2,579,243	35%	25%	29.6
1940	10,223,148	3,373,177	33%	30%	33.9
1941	10,387,852	3,604,531	35%	30%	35.6
1942	3,494,536	1,859,109	53%	—	—
1943	2,618,574	1,718,181	66%	—	—
1944	6,727,955	—	—	—	—
1945	7,588,516	—	—	—	—

Source: Andreev et al., *Naselenie Sovetskogo Soiuza*, 121–26; RGASPI, f. 1m, op. 126, d. 393, ll. 5–6, 11, 20; op. 6, d. 85 l. 1; op. 33, d. 231, l. 1; d. 232, ll. 27, 45, 47.

Notes: Soviet censuses broke the population into age groups of five years, as do the post-Soviet Russian demographers Andreev, Darskii, and Khar'kova, who extrapolate their year-by-year estimates from these censuses. According to contemporary statistics from January 1939 and 1941 (not in the table), the percentage of Komsomol youth as part of the age-eligible population was 19.9 percent and 28.3 percent, respectively.

All data from January except 1942 and 1943, which include only civilian Komsomol. For comparison, on January 1, 1944, the Red Army's Komsomol groups included 2,230,116 members with 339,346 women. Figures for 1945 include only July.

TABLE 2. Komsomol members by class origin, 1923–36

YEAR	WORKERS		PEASANTS		OTHER		TOTAL
1923	80,241	28.2%	132,882	46.7%	71,421	25.1%	284,544
1924	165,104	40.6%	164,697	40.5%	76,859	18.9%	406,660
1925	437,187	42.8%	459,675	45.0%	123,594	12.1%	1,020,456
1926	716,711	43.7%	753,817	46.0%	169,579	10.3%	1,640,107
1927	836,760	42.6%	932,131	47.5%	195,428	9.9%	1,964,319
1928	841,512	43.4%	882,309	45.6%	213,156	11.0%	1,936,977
1929	1,046,504	46.6%	971,398	43.3%	227,741	10.1%	2,245,643
1930	1,188,400	48.2%	1,047,718	42.5%	234,549	9.5%	2,466,127
1931	1,509,823	48.8%	1,331,907	43.0%	242,414	7.8%	3,094,620
1932	2,498,945	46.6%	2,546,476	47.5%	—	—	5,358,630
1933	—	—	—	—	—	—	4,547,186
1934	—	—	—	—	—	—	3,750,975
1935	985,398	27.9%	2,285,135	64.7%	261,360	7.4%	3,531,893
1936	970,967	26.8%	2,391,187	66.0%	260,856	7.2%	3,623,010

Source: RGASPI f. 1m, op. 126, d. 336, ll. 18–23.

Notes: All data from January. Data from 1933 and 1934 contain no breakdown by class origin, likely because of the chaos that the large purge of those years caused. "Other" category for 1935 and 1936 contains both "white collar" (*sluzhashchie*) and "other" while previous years contained just the "other" category. For some years, totals from reports do not match the sum of the categories from the reports.

TABLE 3. Komsomol members by profession, 1929–41

YEAR	WORKERS	AG. WORKERS	KOLKHOZ	WHITE COLLAR	STUDENTS	OTHER	TOTAL
1929	683,589	326,144	862,731	279,544	149,412	108,444	2,409,864
	28.37%	13.53%	35.80%	11.60%	6.20%	4.50%	100.00%
1933	1,505,199	204,623	1,332,326	913,985	472,907	118,226	4,547,186
	33.10%	4.50%	29.30%	20.10%	10.40%	2.60%	100.00%
1934	1,146,693	168,305	1,189,103	735,336	442,446	69,092	3,750,975
	30.57%	4.49%	31.70%	19.60%	11.80%	1.84%	100.00%
1935	925,356	183,658	1,232,631	642,804	505,061	42,383	3,531,893
	26.20%	5.20%	34.90%	18.20%	14.30%	1.20%	100.00%
1936	931,113	173,904	1,202,839	663,011	597,797	54,346	3,623,010
	25.70%	4.80%	33.20%	18.30%	16.50%	1.50%	100.00%
1937	899,869	165,395	1,149,782	751,804	758,227	147,995	3,873,072
	23.20%	4.30%	29.70%	19.40%	19.60%	3.80%	100.00%
1938	1,075,190	117,409	1,266,671	914,437	1,006,391	112,915	4,375,604
	24.60%	2.70%	28.90%	20.90%	23.00%	2.60%	100.00%
1939	1,558,384	185,386	1,919,155	1,481,838	2,158,233	169,328	7,296,135
	21.40%	2.50%	26.30%	20.30%	29.60%	2.30%	100.00%
1940	1,679,491	196,356	1,922,377	2,041,702	2,833,033	200,599	8,677,202
	19.40%	2.30%	22.20%	23.50%	32.60%	2.30%	100.00%
1941	1,517,906	179,033	1,763,318	2,046,486	2,758,213	210,924	8,296,847
	18.30%	2.20%	21.30%	24.70%	33.20%	2.50%	100.00%

Source: RGASPI f. 1m, op. 126, d. 336, ll. 6, 18–23; d. 344, ll. 14, 15, 17; d. 358, 25–26; d. 372, ll. 40–41; d. 390, ll. 65–67.

Notes: All data from January except 1929, from October. Data from 1930 to 1932 are unavailable. The "white collar" category combines teachers, doctors, agronomists, and "other white-collar workers." "Students" combines grade school, technical school, and higher education students. The "other" category through 1936 includes independent farmers. For some years, totals from reports do not match the sum of the categories from the reports.

TABLE 4. Average age of civilian Komsomol membership, 1933–43

YEAR	TOTAL	ESTIMATE	OLD AVERAGE	YOUNG AVERAGE
1933	4,547,186	19.36	20.20	17.90
1934	3,750,975	20.00	20.80	18.50
1935	3,531,893	20.60	21.35	19.04
1936	3,623,010	21.29	21.99	19.55
1937	3,873,072	21.75	23.88	21.04
1938	4,375,604	21.71	24.07	20.98
1939	7,296,135	20.80	22.95	20.03
1940	8,677,202	20.38	22.24	19.62
1941	8,296,847	20.33	22.09	19.58
1942	3,494,536	20.27	19.45	20.90
1943	2,618,475	20.04	19.25	20.67

Source: RGASPI, f. 1m, op. 126, d. 336, ll. 6, 18–23; d. 344, ll. 16–17; d. 358, ll. 42–43; op. 6, d. 85, l. 6.

Notes: The youth organization gathered data about the age of its members based on groupings (e.g., seventeen and younger) making it difficult to estimate an average age for each group. This problem is particularly troublesome for the group "twenty-three and older" (1933–36) and "twenty-six and older," as a sizable group of members stayed in the organization well into their thirties. I compiled an estimate by averaging the age categories (e.g., 22–23 became 22.5) and making a reasonable guess about the average age for members over twenty-six (twenty-eight years old). The oldest and youngest averages use the oldest and youngest age, respectively, of each category. All data from January 1.

TABLE 5. Expulsions from Komsomol by age, 1936–40

	UNDER 17	18–19	20–21	22–23	24–25	26 AND OLDER
1936	585	2,742	4,713	4,972	3,666	3,506
	3%	14%	23%	25%	18%	17%
1937	2,407	8,700	13,813	16,358	14,350	17,112
	3%	12%	19%	22%	20%	24%
1938	2,595	8,193	11,929	11,767	12,477	16,908
	4%	13%	19%	18%	20%	26%
1939	2,171	6,546	8,665	7,070	9,613	9,908
	5%	15%	20%	16%	22%	23%
1940	4,059	11,403	10,468	6,372	7,747	5,864
	9%	25%	23%	14%	17%	13%

Source: RGASPI f. 1m, op. 126, d. 344, ll. 28–29, 32–33, 36–37, 40–41; d. 358, ll. 12–15, 36–37, 46–47; d. 372, ll. 11–12; d. 373, ll. 21, 24–25, 36–37; d. 373, ll. 29, 38–39; d. 390, ll. 16–18, 34–36, 52–54, 71–73.

Notes: 1936 data are for October through December. 1937 data does not include October through December.

TABLE 6. Expulsions from the Komsomol, 1936–40

	ENEMY ELEMENTS	BREAKERS OF KOMSOMOL DISCIPLINE	DEGENERATES	CAREERISTS	OTHER REASONS	TOTAL
Oct–Dec 1936	3,445	8,640	3,785	1,010	3,304	20,184
	17%	43%	19%	5%	16%	100%
Jan–Mar 1937	6,814	6,942	3,853	882	2,728	21,219
	32%	33%	18%	4%	13%	100%
Apr–Jun 1937	4,453	3,865	2,823	752	1,850	13,743
	32%	28%	21%	5%	13%	100%
Jul–Sep 1937	23,187	4,352	5,799	1,313	3,127	37,778
	61%	12%	15%	3%	8%	100%
Oct–Dec 1937	30,704	7,780	8,714	2,374	8,538	58,110
	53%	13%	15%	4%	15%	100%
Jan–Mar 1938	7,826	3,793	3,120	923	4,339	20,001
	39%	19%	16%	5%	22%	100%
Apr–Jun 1938	4,104	2,167	1,837	619	2,108	10,835
	38%	20%	17%	6%	19%	100%
Jul–Sep 1938	4,053	3,594	2,794	717	2,775	13,933
	29%	26%	20%	5%	20%	100%
Oct–Dec 1938	3,928	5,652	4,544	1,079	3,957	19,160
	21%	29%	24%	6%	21%	100%
Jan–Mar 1939	2,132	8,375	6,712	1,375	6,216	24,810
	9%	34%	27%	6%	25%	100%
Apr–Jun 1939	510	3,805	2,407	638	2,781	10,141
	5%	38%	24%	6%	27%	100%
Jul–Sep 1939	209	1,819	963	224	1,233	4,448
	5%	41%	22%	5%	28%	100%
Oct–Dec 1939	182	2,033	945	291	1,123	4,574
	4%	44%	21%	6%	25%	100%
Jan–Mar 1940	117	1,646	854	206	1,162	3,985
	3%	41%	21%	5%	29%	100%
Apr–Jun 1940	163	1,706	812	204	1,267	4,152
	4%	41%	20%	5%	31%	100%
Jul–Sep 1940	181	7,573	1,116	320	3,547	12,737
	1%	59%	9%	3%	28%	100%
Oct–Dec 1940	218	16,595	1,681	754	5,769	25,017
	1%	66%	7%	3%	23%	100%

Source: RGASPI f. 1m, op. 126, d. 344, ll. 28–29, 32–33, 36–37, 40–41; d. 358, ll. 12–15, 36–37, 46–47; d. 372, ll. 11–12; d. 373, ll. 21, 24–25, 36–37; d. 373, ll. 29, 38–39; d. 390, ll. 16–18, 34–36, 52–54, 71–73.

TABLE 7. Expulsions from Komsomol, 1933–36

	BREAKING PARTY LINE	BREAKING LABOR DISCIPLINE	UNFULFILLED KOMSOMOL DUTIES	CLASS ENEMY ELEMENT	BEHAVIORAL INFRACTION	CRIMINAL INFRACTION	RELIGION	TOTAL
1933 (Full)	20,570	50,622	55,206	61,026	18,461	24,124	2,266	232,275
	9%	22%	24%	26%	8%	10%	1%	100%
Jan–Mar 1934	1,383	6,536	9,144	6,473	3,709	3,802	377	31,424
	4%	21%	29%	21%	12%	12%	1%	100%
Apr–Jun 1934	1,842	10,909	13,673	8,049	5,915	7,225	873	48,486
	4%	22%	28%	17%	12%	15%	2%	100%
Jul–Sep 1934	921	4,477	5,977	3,492	2,763	3,556	236	21,422
	4%	21%	28%	16%	13%	17%	1%	100%
Oct–Dec 1934	1,326	5,786	8,318	5,967	3,707	4,611	422	30,137
	4%	19%	28%	20%	12%	15%	1%	100%
Jan–Mar 1935	6,489	2,445	4,562	8,750	4,633	4,951	546	32,376
	20%	8%	14%	27%	14%	15%	2%	100%
Apr–Jun 1935	1,129	3,312	7,679	6,112	4,264	5,395	420	28,311
	4%	12%	27%	22%	15%	19%	1%	100%
Jul–Sep 1935	757	2,138	5,635	6,280	3,163	4,076	223	22,272
	3%	10%	25%	28%	14%	18%	1%	100%
Oct–Dec 1935	1,269	3,312	9,444	10,466	4,722	5,603	423	35,239
	4%	9%	27%	30%	13%	16%	1%	100%
Jan–Mar 1936	1,005	2,313	8,138	6,655	4,256	4,190	379	26,936
	4%	9%	30%	25%	16%	16%	1%	100%
Apr–Jun 1936	538	1,476	4,997	1,933	2,876	2,645	180	14,645
	4%	10%	34%	13%	20%	18%	1%	100%
Jul–Sep 1936	2,703	1,519	4,840	3,357	2,615	2,473	159	17,666
	15%	9%	27%	19%	15%	14%	1%	100%

Source: RGASPI f. 1m, op. 126, d. 314, ll. 21, 22; d. 326, ll. 33–44; d. 336, ll. 25–40.

TABLE 8.   Komsomol admissions to the Communist Party, 1937–38

DATE	ADMITTED	RECOMMENDED	ADMIT/MONTH	REC/MONTH	ADMIT %
07/37–11/37	13,051	46,207	3,263	11,552	28%
11/37–2/38	15,672	53,082	5,224	17,694	30%
2/38–3/38	10,472	34,900	10,472	34,900	30%
3/38–9/38	92,744	175,112	15,457	29,185	53%

Source: RGASPI, f. 1m, op. 23, d. 1215, l. 84; d. 1285, ll. 73–75; d. 1192, ll. 7–13.

Note: All dates on first of the month.

Bibliography

ARCHIVES

Russian State Archive of Social-Political History (RGASPI)

f. 1m Central Committee of the Young Communist League (Komsomol)
    op. 2 Protocols and Stenographic Records of Plenums
    op. 3 Protocols of the Meetings of the Bureau
    op. 5 Stenographic Records of Meetings
    op. 23 Documents of the Departments of the Central Committee
    op. 33 Sector of Accounting and Statistics of the Department of Komsomol Organs
    op. 126 Department of Organizational Work, Sector of Accounting and Statistics
f. 6m Congresses of the Central Committee of the Young Communist League
f. 17 Central Committee of the All-Union Communist Party (Bolsheviks)
f. 73 Andrei Andreev
f. 74 Kliment Voroshilov
f. 82 Viacheslav Molotov
f. 558 Iosif Stalin

Russian State Military Archive (RGVA)

f. 9 Political Administration of the Red Army

State Archive of the Russian Federation (GARF)

f. 2306r People's Commissariat of Enlightenment
f. 7576 Committee for Physical Culture and Sport
f. 7952 State Publisher "History of Plants and Factories"
f. 8131 Procuracy of the USSR
f. 8355 Society of Assistance to Defense and Aviation-Chemical Construction (Osoaviakhim)

Russian State Archive of Literature and Art (RGALI)

f. 2468 Soiuzdetfilm

Central State Archive of Social Organizations of Ukraine (TsDAHO)

f. 7 Central Committee of the Young Communist League of Ukraine

State Archive of the Security Service of Ukraine (HDA SBU)

f. 16 Secretariat of the GPU-OGPU-NKVD-MGB-MVD-KGB

Department for the Preservation of Documents of the Social-Political History of Moscow (OKhDOPIM)

f. 644p Istrinskii District Committee of the Young Communist League
f. 648p Lopasne District Committee of the Young Communist League
f. 5358p Novo-Petrovskii District Committee of the Young Communist League

National Archive of the Republic of Karelia (NARK)
f. 779p Karelian Provincial Committee of the Young Communist League
f. 1229p Central Committee of Karelian Republican Young Communist League
f. 4070p Zaonezhskii District Committee of the Young Communist League

State Archive of Kyiv Province (DAKO)
f. 7p Kyiv Provincial Committee of the Young Communist League

State Archive of Riazan' Province (GARO)
f. 489p Riazan' District Committee of the Young Communist League

Smolensk Archive

PERIODICALS

Izvestiia TsK Komsomola
Komsomolets Karelii
Komsomol'skaia pravda
Komsomol'skii rabotnik
Molodaia gvardiia
Molodoi Bol'shevik
Pionerskaia pravda
Pravda
Vozhatyi

DOCUMENT COLLECTIONS

IX Vsesoiuznyi s"ezd VLKSM: Stenograficheskii otchet. Moscow: Molodaia gvardiia, 1931.
Artizov, A. N., et al. *Reabilitatsiia: Kak eto bylo.* Volume 1: *Mart 1953–fevral' 1956.*
    Moscow: Demokratiia, 2000. Volume 2: *Fevral' 1956–nachalo 80-kh godov.*
    Moscow: Demokratiia, 2003.
Bukov, K. I., M. M. Gorinov and A. N. Ponomarev, eds. *Moskva voennaia, 1941–1945:*
    Memuary i arkhivnye dokumenty. Moscow: Mosgorarkhiv, 1995.
Danilov, V. P., O. V. Khlevniuk, and A. Iu. Vatlin, eds. *Kak lomali NEP: Stenogrammy*
    plenumov TsK VKP(b), 1928–1929. 5 volumes. Moscow, 2000.
Danilov, V. P., S. A. Krasil'nikov, and L. Viola, eds. *Politbiuro i krest'ianstvo: Vysylka,*
    spetsposelenie 1930–1940. Moscow: Rosspen, 2006.
Danilov, V. P., R. Menning [Roberta Manning], and L. Viola, eds. *Tragediia sovetskoi*
    derevni: Kollektivizatsiia i raskulachivanie. Dokumenty i materialy. 5 volumes.
    Moscow: Rosspen, 1999–2006.
Desiaterik, V. I., et al. *Tovarishch Komsomol: Dokumenty s"ezdov, konferentsii i TsK*
    VLKSM 1918–1968. Moscow: Molodaia gvardiia, 1969.
Fomin, V. *Kino na voine: Dokumenty i svidetel'stva.* Moscow: Materik, 2005.
Ioffe, I. A., and N. K. Petrova, eds. *"Molodaia gvardiia" (g. Krasnodon)—*
    khudozhestvennyi obraz i istoristicheskaia real'nost': Sbornik dokumentov i
    materialov. Moscow: Veche, 2003.
Kariaeva, T. F., and N. I. Smorigo, eds. *Partiino-politicheskaia rabota v Krasnoi Armii:*
    Dokumenty. Moscow: Voennoe izdatel'stvo, 1985.
Khaustov, V. N., et al. *Lubianka: Stalin i NKVD-NKGB-GURK 'SMERSh'. 1939–mart*
    1946. Mezhdunarodnyi fond "Demokratiia," 2006.

Khlevniuk, O. V., et al. *Stalin i Kaganovich: Perepiska 1931–1936 gg.* Moscow: Rosspen, 2001.

Kniaz'kov, A. S., et al. *Voennyi sovet pri narodnom komissare oborony SSSR: Dekabr' 1934 g. Dokumenty i materialy.* Moscow: Rosspen, 2007.

Kodin, E. V. *Deti i molodezh' Smolenshchiny: 1920–1930-e gody. Sbornik dokumentov.* Smolensk: Madzhenta, 2006.

Malin, V. N., and A. V. Korobov, eds. *Direktivy KPSS i sovetskogo pravitel'stva po khoziaistvennym voprosam, 1917–1957 gg.: Sbornik dokumentov.* 2 volumes. Moscow, 1957.

On the Organization of Party Propaganda in Connection with the Publication of "The History of the C.P.S.U. (B.) Short Course." Moscow: Foreign Language Publishing House, 1939.

Pegov, A. M., et al. *Opolchenie na zashchite Moskvy: Dokumenty i materialy o formirovanii i boevykh deistviiakh Moskovskogo narodnogo opolcheniia v iiule 1941–ianvare 1942 g.* Moscow: Moskovskii rabochii, 1978.

Reshin, L. E., et al., eds. *1941 god: Sbornik dokumentov.* 2 volumes. Moscow: Demokratiia, 1998.

Stalin, I. V. *Sochineniia.* Moscow, 1949, 2007.

Stepashin, S. V., and V. P. Iampol'skii, eds. *Organy gosudarstvennoi bezopasnosti SSSR v Velikoi otechestvennoi voine: Sbornik dokumentov.* 5 volumes. Moscow, 1995–2007.

Tarkhova, N. S. *"Zimniaia voina": Rabota nad oshibkami, aprel'–mai 1940 g. Materialy komissii Glavnogo voennogo soveta Krasnoi Armii po obobshcheniiu opyta finskoi kampanii.* Moscow: Letnii sad, 2004.

Vilenskii S. S. et al., eds. *Deti GULAGa, 1918–1956.* Moscow: Mezhdunarodnyi fond "Demokratiia," 2002.

Viola, Lynne, et al. *The War against the Peasantry, 1927–1930: The Tragedy of the Soviet Countryside.* New Haven: Yale University Press, 2005.

Zolotarev, V. A., et al. *Russkii arkhiv: Velikaia Otechestvennaia.* Moscow: Terra, 1993–97.

DIARIES, INTERVIEWS, LITERATURE, AND MEMOIRS

Adzhubei, Aleksei. *Te desiat' let.* Moscow: Sovetskaia Rossiia, 1989.

Antonov-Ovseenko, Anton. *Vragi naroda.* Moscow: Intellekt, 1996.

Biriukov, Nikolai. *Chaika.* Moscow: Molodaia gvardiia, 1945.

Bronshtein, Valerii. *Preodolenie.* Moscow: Adamant", 2004.

Bulgakov, Mikhail. *Master and Margarita.* Richard Pevear, and Larissa Volokhonsky, trans. New York: Penguin, 1998.

Efron, Georgii. *Dnevniki.* 2 volumes. Moscow: Vagrius, 2004.

Garros, Veronique, Natalia Koronevskaya, and Thomas Lahusen, eds. *Intimacy and Terror: Soviet Diaries of the 1930s.* New York: The New Press, 1995.

Harvard Interview Project. 1950–53.

I Remember.

Iasnyi, V. K. *God rozhdeniia—deviat'sot semnadtsatyi.* Moscow: INTEK, 1997.

Kosterina, Nina. *Diaries.* http://www.prozhito.org.

Kravchenko, Victor. *I Chose Freedom: The Personal and Political Life of a Soviet Official.* New York: Scribner, 1946.

Leonhard, Wolfgang. *A Child of the Revolution.* New York: Collins, 1957.

Lotman, Iurii. "Ne-memuary." In *Lotmanovskii sbornik,* vol. 1. Moscow, 1995.

Mikhailova, E. M., ed. *Aleksandr Kosarev: Sbornik vospominanii.* Moscow: Molodaia gvardiia, 1962.

Novak-Decker, Nikolai, ed. *Soviet Youth: Twelve Komsomol Histories.* Munich: 1959.

Rotfort, Mikhail. *Kolyma—krugi ada: Vospominaniia*. Ekaterinburg: Ural'skii rabochii, 1991.

Tvardovskii, Ivan. *Rodina i chuzhbina: kniga zhizni*. Smolensk: Posokh, 1996.

FILMS

Bogdan Khmel'nitskii. Directed by Igor' Savchenko. Kyiv: Kievskaia kinostudiia, 1941.

Esli zavtra voina. Directed by Efim Dzigan. Moscow: Mosfil'm, 1938.

Frontovye podrugi. Directed by Viktor Eisymont. Leningrad: Lenfil'm, 1941.

My s Urala. Directed by Lev Kuleshov and Aleksandra Khokhlova. Stalinabad: Soiuzdetfil'm, 1943.

Strogii iunosha. Directed by Abram Room. Kyiv: Ukrainfil'm, 1936.

Vesennyi potok. Directed by Vladimir Iurenev. Moscow: Soiuzdetfil'm, 1940.

SECONDARY SOURCES

Alexopoulos, Golfo. "Portrait of a Con Artist as a Soviet Man." *Slavic Review* 57, no. 4 (1998): 774–90.

——. "Stalin and the Politics of Kinship: Practices of Collective Punishment, 1920s–1940s." *Comparative Studies in Society and History* 50, no. 1 (2008): 91–117.

——. *Stalin's Outcasts: Aliens, Citizens, and the Soviet State, 1926–1936*. Ithaca, NY: Cornell University Press, 2003.

Andreev, E. M., L. E. Darskii, and T. L. Khar'kova. *Naselenie Sovetskogo Soiuza, 1922–1991*. Moscow: Nauka, 1993.

Bailes, Kendall. *Technology and Society under Lenin and Stalin: Origins of the Soviet Technical Intelligentsia, 1917–1941*. Princeton, NJ: Princeton University Press, 1978.

Ball, Alan. *And Now My Soul Is Hardened: Abandoned Children in Soviet Russia, 1918–1930*. Berkeley: University of California Press, 1994.

——. *Russia's Last Capitalists: The Nepmen, 1921–1929*. Berkeley: University of California Press, 1987.

Barber, John, and Mark Harrison. *The Soviet Home Front: A Social and Economic History of the USSR in World War II*. London: Longman, 1991.

Barber, John, and Mark Harrison, eds. *The Soviet Defense-Industry Complex from Stalin to Khrushchev*. London: Routledge, 2000.

Barnes, Steven. *Death and Redemption: The Gulag and the Shaping of Soviet Society*. Princeton, NJ: Princeton University Press, 2011.

Belodubrovskaya, Maria. "Abram Room, *A Strict Young Man*, and the 1936 Campaign against Formalism in Soviet Cinema." *Slavic Review* 74, no. 2 (2015): 311–33.

Berghahn, Volker. *Militarism: The History of an International Debate, 1861–1979*. Cambridge: Cambridge University Press, 1981.

Berkhoff, Karel. *Motherland in Danger: Soviet Propaganda during World War II*. Cambridge, MA: Harvard University Press, 2012.

Bernstein, Frances Lee. *The Dictatorship of Sex: Lifestyle Advice for the Soviet Masses*. DeKalb: Northern Illinois University Press, 2007.

Bernstein, Seth. "Class Dismissed? New Elites and Old Enemies in the Soviet Komsomol, 1934–1941," *Russian Review* 74, no. 1 (2015): 97–116.

——. "Rural Russia on the Edges of Authority: Bezvlastie in Wartime Riazan, November–December 1941." *Slavic Review* 75, no. 3 (2016): 560–82.

——. "Valedictorians of the Soviet School: Professionalization and the Impact of War in Soviet Chess." *Kritika: Explorations in Russian and Eurasian History* 13, no. 2 (2012): 395–418.

——. "Wartime Filmmaking on the Margins: Soiuzdetfilm in Evacuation in Stalinabad, 1941–43." *Studies in Russian and Soviet Cinema* 9, no. 1 (2015): 24–39.

Binner, Rolf, and Marc Junge. *Kak terror stal bol'shim: Sekretnyi prikaz No. 00447 i tekhnologiia ego ispolneniia.* Moscow: Airo-XX, 2003.

Blum, Douglas. *National Identity and Globalization: Youth, State, and Society in Post-Soviet Eurasia.* Cambridge: Cambridge University Press, 2007.

Braithwaithe, Rodric. *Moscow 1941: A City and Its People at War.* London: Vintage, 2006.

Brandenberger, David. *National Bolshevism: Stalinist Mass Culture and the Formation of Modern Russian National Identity, 1931–1956.* Cambridge, MA: Harvard University Press, 2002.

Brooks, Jeffrey. *Thank You, Comrade Stalin! Soviet Public Culture from Revolution to Cold War.* Princeton, NJ: Princeton University Press, 2000.

Budnitskii, Oleg. "The Great Patriotic War and Soviet Society: Defeatism, 1941–1942," *Kritika: Explorations in Russian and Eurasian History* 15, no. 4 (2014): 767–99.

Carr, E. H. *The Bolshevik Revolution, 1917–1923.* 3 volumes. New York: W. W. Norton, 1985.

Carr, E. H., and R. W. Davies. *Foundations of a Planned Economy, 1926–1929.* London: Macmillan, 1969.

Chase, William. *Enemies within the Gates? The Comintern and the Stalinist Repression, 1934–1939.* New Haven: Yale University Press, 2001.

——. *Workers, Society, and the Soviet State: Labor and Life in Moscow, 1918–1929.* Urbana: University of Illinois Press, 1989.

Chubaryan, Alexander, and Harold Shukman, eds. *Stalin and the Soviet-Finnish War, 1939–40.* New Haven: Yale University Press, 2002.

Clark, Katerina. *Moscow, the Fourth Rome: Stalinism, Cosmopolitanism, and the Evolution of Soviet Culture, 1931–1941.* Cambridge, MA: Harvard University Press, 2011.

——. *Petersburg: Crucible of Cultural Revolution.* Cambridge, MA: Harvard University Press, 1995.

Cohen, Stanley. *Folk Devils and Moral Panics.* London: Routledge, 2011 [1972].

Cohen, Stephen. *Bukharin and the Bolshevik Revolution: A Political Biography, 1888–1938.* New York: Knopf, 1973.

Cohn, Edward. *The High Title of a Communist: Postwar Party Discipline and the Values of the Soviet Regime.* DeKalb: Northern Illinois University Press, 2015.

Corney, Frederick. *Telling October: Memory and the Making of the Bolshevik Revolution.* Ithaca, NY: Cornell University Press, 2004.

Dallin, Alexander. *German Rule in Russia, 1941–1945.* Boulder, CO: Westview, 1981.

Daniels, Robert. *The Conscience of the Revolution: Communist Opposition in Soviet Russia.* Cambridge, MA: Harvard University Press, 1960.

David-Fox, Michael. *Revolution of the Mind: Higher Learning among the Bolsheviks, 1918–1929.* Ithaca, NY: Cornell University Press, 1997.

——. *Showcasing the Great Experiment: Cultural Diplomacy and Western Visitors to the Soviet Union, 1921–1941.* New York: Oxford University Press, 2011.

——. "What Is Cultural Revolution?" *Russian Review* 58, no. 2 (1999): 181–201.

Davies, R. W. *Crisis and Progress in the Soviet Economy, 1931–1933.* London: Macmillan, 1996.

——. *The Socialist Offensive: The Collectivization of Soviet Agriculture, 1929–1930.* Cambridge, MA: Harvard University Press, 1980.

——. *The Soviet Economy in Turmoil, 1929–1930.* Basingstoke: Palgrave, 1989.

Davies, R. W., and Stephen Wheatcroft. *The Years of Hunger: Soviet Agriculture, 1931–1933*. London: Palgrave Macmillan, 2004.

Davies, Sarah. *Popular Opinion in Stalin's Russia: Terror, Propaganda, and Dissent, 1934–1941*. Cambridge: Cambridge University Press, 1997.

DeGraffenried, Julie. *Sacrificing Childhood: Children and the Soviet State in the Great Patriotic War*. Lawrence: University Press of Kansas, 2014.

Detskii karnaval: Letnyi prazdnik dlia detei srednego vozrasta. Moscow: Tsentral'nyi dom vospitaniia detei, 1939.

Dobrenko, Evgeny. "Socialism as Will and Representation, or What Legacy Are We Rejecting?" *Kritika: Explorations in Russian and Eurasian History* 5, no. 4 (2004): 675–708.

Druzhnikov, Iurii. *Informer 001: The Myth of Pavlik Morozov*. New Brunswick, NJ: Transaction Publishers, 1997.

Dunham, Vera. *In Stalin's Time: Middleclass Values in Soviet Fiction*. Durham, NC: Duke University Press, 1976.

Easter, Gerald. *Reconstructing the State: Personal Networks and Elite Identity in Soviet Russia*. Cambridge: Cambridge University Press, 2000.

Edele, Mark. *Soviet Veterans of the Second World War. A Popular Movement in an Authoritarian Society, 1941–1991*. Oxford: Oxford University Press, 2008.

———. "Strange Young Men in Stalin's Moscow: The Birth and Life of the Stiliagi, 1945–1953." *Jahrbücher für Geschichte Osteuropas* 50, no. 1 (2002): 37–61.

Edelman, Robert. *Serious Fun: A History of Spectator Sports in the USSR*. New York: Oxford University Press, 1993.

———. *Spartak Moscow: A History of the People's Team in the Worker's State*. Ithaca, NY: Cornell University Press, 2009.

Ellman, Michael, and S. Maksudov, "Soviet Deaths in the Great Patriotic War: A Note." *Europe-Asia Studies* 46, no. 4: 671–80.

Erickson, John. *The Soviet High Command: A Military-Political History, 1918–1941*. London: Macmillan, 1963.

Ermolov, Igor. *Russkoe gosudarstvo v nemetskom tylu: Istoriia Lokotskogo samoupravleniia, 1941–1943*. Moscow: Tsentrpoligraf, 2009.

Ewing, E. Thomas. *The Teachers of Stalinism: Policy, Practice, and Power in Soviet Schools of the 1930s*. New York: Peter Lang, 2002.

Fenemore, Mark. *Sex, Thugs, and Rock 'n' Roll: Teenage Rebels in Cold-War East Germany*. New York: Berghahn Books, 2007.

Figes, Orlando. *The Whisperers: Private Life in Stalin's Russia*. New York: Metropolitan Books, 2007.

Fisher, Ralph Talcott. *A Pattern for Soviet Youth: A Study of the Congresses of the Komsomol, 1918–1954*. New York: Columbia University Press, 1959.

Fitzpatrick, Sheila. "Ascribing Class: The Construction of Social Identity in Soviet Russia." *Journal of Modern History* 65, no. 4 (1993): 745–70.

———. *The Commissariat of Enlightenment: Soviet Organization of Education and the Arts under Lunacharsky, 1917–1931*. Cambridge: Cambridge University Press, 1970.

———. *The Cultural Front: Power and Culture in Revolutionary Russia*. Ithaca, NY: Cornell University Press, 1992.

———. *The Cultural Revolution in Russia, 1928–1931*. Bloomington: Indiana University Press, 1978.

———. "Cultural Revolution Revisited." *Russian Review* 58, no. 2 (1999): 202–9.

———. *Education and Social Mobility in the Soviet Union, 1921–1934*. New York: Cambridge University Press, 1979.

——. *Everyday Stalinism: Ordinary Life in Extraordinary Times. Soviet Russia in the 1930s.* New York: Oxford University Press, 1999.

——. "How the Mice Buried the Cat: Scenes from the Great Purges of 1937 in the Russian Provinces." *Russian Review* 52, no. 3 (1993): 299–320.

——. *The Russian Revolution.* 2nd ed. Oxford: Oxford University Press, 1994.

——. *Tear Off the Masks! Identity and Imposture in Twentieth-Century Russia.* Princeton, NJ: Princeton University Press, 2005.

Fitzpatrick, Sheila, Alexander Rabinowitch, and Richard Stites, eds. *Russia in the Era of NEP: Explorations in Soviet Society and Culture.* Bloomington: Indiana University Press, 1991.

Flynn, George. *Conscription and Democracy: The Draft in France, Great Britain, and the United States.* Westport, CT: Greenwood, 2002.

Fürst, Juliane. *Stalin's Last Generation: Soviet Post-War Youth and the Emergence of Mature Socialism.* Oxford: Oxford University Press, 2010.

Getty, J. Arch. *Origins of the Great Purges: The Soviet Communist Party Reconsidered, 1933–1938.* Cambridge: Cambridge University Press, 1985.

——. *Practicing Stalinism: Bolsheviks, Boyars, and the Persistence of Tradition.* New Haven: Yale University Press, 2013.

——. "State and Society under Stalin: Constitutions and Elections in the 1930s." *Slavic Review* 50, no. 1 (1991): 18–35.

Getty, J. Arch, and Roberta T. Manning, eds. *Stalinist Terror: New Perspectives.* Cambridge: Cambridge University Press, 1993.

Getty, J. Arch, and Oleg Naumov. *The Road to Terror: Stalin and the Self-Destruction of the Bolsheviks.* New Haven: Yale University Press, 1999.

Getty, J. Arch, Gábor T. Rittersporn, and Viktor Zemskov. "Victims of the Soviet Penal System in the Pre-War Years: A First Approach Based on Archival Evidence." *American Historical Review* 98, no. 4 (1993): 1017–49.

Geyer, Michael, and Sheila Fitzpatrick, eds. *Beyond Totalitarianism: Stalinism and Nazism Compared.* New York: Cambridge University Press, 2009.

Gill, Graeme. *The Origins of the Stalinist Political System.* New York: Cambridge University Press, 1990.

Gillis, John R., ed. *The Militarization of the Western World.* New Brunswick, NJ: Rutgers University Press, 1989.

——. *Youth and History: Tradition and Change in European Age Relations, 1770–Present.* New York: Academic Press, 1981.

Goldman, Wendy. "Industrial Politics: Peasant Rebellion and the Death of the Proletarian Women's Movement in the USSR." *Slavic Review* 55, no. 1 (1996): 46–77.

——. *Inventing the Enemy: Denunciation and Terror in Stalin's Russia.* Cambridge: Cambridge University Press, 2011.

——. *Terror and Democracy in the Age of Stalin: The Social Dynamics of Repression.* New York: Cambridge University Press, 2007.

——. *Women, the State, and Revolution: Soviet Family Policy and Social Life, 1917–1936.* Cambridge: Cambridge University Press, 1993.

Gooderham, Peter. "The Komsomol and Worker Youth: The Inculcation of 'Communist Values' in Leningrad during NEP." *Soviet Studies* 34, no. 4 (1982): 506–28.

Gorodetsky, Gabriel. *The Grand Delusion: Stalin and the German Invasion of the Soviet Union.* New Haven: Yale University Press, 1999.

Gorsuch, Anne E. *Youth in Revolutionary Russia: Enthusiasts, Bohemians, Delinquents.* Bloomington: Indiana University Press, 2000.

Grant, Susan. *Physical Culture and Sport in Soviet Society: Propaganda, Acculturation, and Transformation in the 1920s and 1930s.* New York: Routledge, 2012.

——. "The Politics of Physical Culture in the 1920s." *Slavonic and East European Review* 89, no. 3 (2011): 494–515.

Green, Rachel. "'There Will Not Be Orphans among Us': Soviet Orphanages, Foster Care, and Adoption, 1941–1956." PhD diss., University of Chicago, 2006.

Grekhov, V. N. "Rasprava s rukovodstvom Komsomola v 1937–1938 godakh." *Voprosy istorii*, no. 11 (1990): 136–51.

Guillory, Sean. "The Shattered Self of Komsomol Civil War Memoirs." *Slavic Review* 71, no. 3 (2012): 546–65.

——. "We Shall Refashion Life on Earth! The Political Culture of the Young Communist League, 1918–1928." PhD diss., University of California Los Angeles, 2009.

Hagenloh, Paul. "'Chekist in Essence, Chekist in Spirit': Regular and Political Police in the 1930s." *Cahiers du monde russe* 42, no. 2 (2001): 447–75.

——. *Stalin's Police: Public Order and Mass Repression in the USSR, 1926–1941.* Washington, DC: Woodrow Wilson Center Press, 2009.

Halfin, Igal. *From Darkness to Light: Class, Consciousness, and Salvation in Revolutionary Russia.* Pittsburgh: University of Pittsburgh Press, 2000.

——. *Stalinist Confessions: Messianism and Terror at the Leningrad Communist University.* Pittsburgh: University of Pittsburgh Press, 2009.

Harris, Adrienne. "The Lives and Deaths of a Soviet Saint in the Post-Soviet Period: The Case of Zoia Kosmodem'ianskaia." *Canadian Slavonic Papers* 53, nos. 2–4: 273–304.

Harris, James. "Encircled by Enemies: Stalin's Perceptions of the Capitalist World, 1918–1941." *Journal of Strategic Studies* 30, no. 3 (2007): 513–45.

Hellbeck, Jochen. *Revolution on My Mind: Writing a Diary under Stalin.* Cambridge, MA: Harvard University Press, 2006.

Hoffman, David. *The Oligarchs: Wealth and Power in the New Russia.* New York: Public Affairs, 2011.

Hoffmann, David L. *Cultivating the Masses: Modern State Practices and Soviet Socialism, 1914–1939.* Ithaca, NY: Cornell University Press, 2011.

——. "Mothers in the Motherland: Stalinist Pronatalism in Its Pan-European Context." *Journal of Social History* 34, no. 1 (2000): 35–54.

——. *Peasant Metropolis: Social Identities in Moscow, 1929–1941.* Ithaca, NY: Cornell University Press, 1994.

——. *Stalinist Values: The Cultural Norms of Soviet Modernity, 1917–1941.* Ithaca, NY: Cornell University Press, 2003.

Hoffmann, David, and Yanni Kotsonis, eds. *Russian Modernity: Politics, Knowledge, Practices.* Basingstoke: Palgrave, 2000.

Holmes, Larry E. *The Kremlin and the Schoolhouse: Reforming Education in Soviet Russia, 1917–1931.* Bloomington: Indiana University Press, 1991.

——. *Stalin's School: Moscow's Model School No. 25, 1931–1937.* Pittsburgh: University of Pittsburgh Press, 1999.

Holquist, Peter. *Making War, Forging Revolution: Russia's Continuum of Crisis, 1914–1921.* Cambridge, MA: Harvard University Press, 2002.

Hooper, Cynthia. "Terror from Within: Participation and Coercion in Soviet Power, 1924–1964." PhD diss., Princeton University, 2003.

——. "Terror of Intimacy: Family Politics in the 1930s Soviet Union." In *Everyday Life in Early Soviet Russia: Taking the Revolution Inside,* ed. Christina Kiaer and Eric Naiman. Bloomington: Indiana University Press, 2006, 61–91.

Hough, Jerry. *The Soviet Prefects: The Local Party Organs in Industrial Decision-making.* Cambridge, MA: Harvard University Press, 1969.

Husband, William. *"Godless Communists": Atheism and Society in Soviet Russia, 1917–1932.* DeKalb: Northern Illinois University Press, 2000.

Isaev, V. I. "Voenizatsiia molodzhi i molodezhyi ekstremizm v Sibiri (1920-e–nachalo 1930-kh gg.)." *Vestnik NGU* 1, no. 3 (2002): 63–70.

Jansen, Marc, and Nikita Petrov. *Stalin's Loyal Executioner: People's Commissar Nikolai Ezhov.* Stanford, CA: Hoover Institution Press, 2002.

Jones, David. "Forerunners of the Komsomol: Scouting in Imperial Russia." In *Reforming the Tsar's Army Military Innovation in Imperial Russia from Peter the Great to the Revolution,* ed. David Schimmelpenninck van der Oye and Bruce W. Menning. Cambridge: Cambridge University Press, 2004.

Kassof, Allen. *The Soviet Youth Program: Regimentation and Rebellion.* Cambridge, MA: Harvard University Press, 1965.

Kater, Michael H. *Hitler Youth.* Cambridge, MA: Harvard University Press, 2004.

Kelly, Catriona. *Children's World: Growing up in Russia, 1890–1991.* New Haven: Yale University Press, 2007.

——. *Comrade Pavlik: The Rise and Fall of a Soviet Boy Hero.* London: Granta, 2005.

——. "'A Laboratory for the Manufacture of Proletarian Writers': The Stengazeta (Wall Newspaper), Kul'turnost', and the Language of Politics in the Early Soviet Period." *Europe-Asia Studies* 54, no. 4 (2002): 573–602.

——. *Refining Russia: Advice Literature, Polite Culture, and Gender from Catherine to Yeltsin.* Oxford: Oxford University Press, 2001.

Kenez, Peter. *The Birth of the Propaganda State: Soviet Methods of Mass Mobilization, 1917–1929.* New York: Cambridge University Press, 1985.

Keys, Barbara. *Globalizing Sport: National Rivalry and International Community in the 1930s.* Cambridge, MA: Harvard University Press, 2006.

Kharkhordin, Oleg. *The Collective and the Individual in Russia: A Study of Practices.* Berkeley: University of California Press, 1999.

Khlevniuk, Oleg. *Master of the House: Stalin and His Inner Circle.* New Haven: Yale University Press, 2009.

——. *Politbiuro: Mekhanizmy politicheskoi vlasti v 30-e gody.* Moscow: Rosspen, 1996.

——. "The Reasons for the Great Terror: The Foreign-Political Aspect," in *Russia in the Age of Wars, 1914–1945,* ed. Silvio Pons and Andrea Romano. Rome: Annali, 2000, 159–73.

Khlevniuk, Oleg, and Yoram Gorlitzki. *Cold Peace: Stalin and the Soviet Ruling Circle, 1945–1953.* Oxford: Oxford University Press, 2004.

Kirschenbaum, Lisa. *Small Comrades: Revolutionizing Childhood in Soviet Russia, 1917–1932.* New York: Routledge, 2000.

Koenker, Diane. "Fathers against Sons/Sons against Fathers: The Problem of Generations in the Early Soviet Workplace." *Journal of Modern History* 73, no. 4 (2001): 781–810.

Konecny, Peter. *Builders and Deserters: Students, State, and Community in Leningrad, 1917–1941.* Montreal: McGill-Queen's University Press, 1999.

Koon, Tracy. *Believe, Obey, Fight: Political Socialization of Youth in Fascist Italy, 1922–1943.* Chapel Hill: University of North Carolina Press, 1985.

Kostyrchenko, Gennadii. *Tainaia politika Stalina: Vlast' i antisemitizm.* Moscow: Mezhdunarodnaia otnosheniia, 2001.

Kotkin, Stephen. *Magnetic Mountain: Stalinism as a Civilization.* Berkeley: University of California Press, 1995.

——. "Modern Times: The Soviet Union and the Interwar Conjuncture." *Kritika: Explorations in Russian and Eurasian History* 2, no. 1 (2001): 111–64.

Krylova, Anna. "Soviet Modernity in Life and Fiction: The 'New Soviet Person' in the 1930s." Ph.D. diss., Johns Hopkins University, 2000.

——. *Soviet Women in Combat: A History of Violence on the Eastern Front.* Cambridge: Cambridge University Press, 2010.

Kucherenko, Olga. *Little Soldiers: How Soviet Children Went to War, 1941–1945.* Oxford: Oxford University Press, 2011.

——. "Without a Family: Public Order, Social Welfare, and Street Children in the Wartime Soviet Union." *Australian Journal of Politics and History* 58, no. 3: 421–36.

Kudryashov, Sergey, and Vanessa Voisin. "The Early Stages of 'Legal Purges' in Soviet Russia (1941–1945)." *Cahier du monde russe* 49, nos. 2–3: 263–95.

Kuhr, Corinna. "Children of 'Enemies of the People' as Victims of the Great Purges." *Cahiers du monde russe* 39, nos. 1–2 (1998): 209–20.

Kuhr-Korolev, Corinna, Stefan Plaggenborg, and Monica Wellmann, eds. *Sowjetjugend 1917–1941: Generation zwischen Revolution und Resignation.* Essen: Klartext, 2001.

Kurti, Laszlo. *Youth and the State in Hungary.* London: Pluto, 2002.

Lapierre, Brian. *Hooligans in Khrushchev's Russia: Defining, Policing, and Producing Deviance during the Thaw.* Madison: University of Wisconsin Press, 2012.

Lewin, Moshe. *The Making of the Soviet System: Essays in the Social History of Interwar Russia.* New York: Pantheon, 1985.

——. *Russian Peasants and Soviet Power: A Study of Collectivization.* New York: W. W. Norton, 1968.

Livschiz, Ann. "Growing up Soviet: Childhood in the Soviet Union, 1918–1958." PhD diss., Stanford University, 2007.

Lovchenko, Liudmila. "Spetstrudposelentsy Severnogo kraia v tylu i na fronte, 1941–1945 gg." *Voprosy istorii*, no. 3 (2010): 140–43.

Lovell, Stephen, ed. *Generations in Twentieth Century Europe.* Basingstoke: Palgrave, 2007.

Mally, Lynn. *Revolutionary Acts: Amateur Theater and the Soviet State, 1917–1938.* Ithaca, NY: Cornell University Press, 2000.

Mannheim, Karl. "The Problem of Generations." In *Karl Mannheim: Essays*, ed. Paul Kecskemeti. London: Routledge, 1952.

Markwick, Roger, and Euridice Cardona. *Soviet Women on the Frontline in the Second World War.* London: Palgrave Macmillan, 2012.

McDonald, Tracy. *Face to the Village: The Riazan Countryside under Soviet Rule, 1921–1930.* Toronto: University of Toronto Press, 2011.

McLoughlin, Barry. "Vernichtung des Fremden: 'Der grosse Terror' in der UdSSR 1937/38." *Jahrbuch fur Historische Kommunismusforschung* (2001): 50–88.

McLoughlin, Barry, and Kevin McDermott, eds. *Stalin's Terror: High Politics and Mass Repression in the Soviet Union.* London: Palgrave Macmillan, 2003.

Merridale, Catherine. *Ivan's War: Life and Death in the Red Army, 1939–1945.* New York: Metropolitan Books, 2006.

Michalski, Milena. "Promises Broken, Promise Fulfilled: The Critical Failings and Creative Success of Abram Room's 'Strogii iunosha.'" *Slavonic and East European Review* 82, no. 4 (2004): 820–46.

Mukhin, Aleksei. *Pokolenie 2008: nashi i ne nashi.* Moscow: Algoritm, 2006.

Neuberger, Joan. *Hooliganism: Crime, Culture, and Power in St. Petersburg, 1900–1914.* Berkeley: University of California Press, 1993.

Neumann, Matthias. *The Communist Youth League and the Transformation of the Soviet Union, 1918–1932*. London: Routledge, 2011.

——. "Revolutionizing Mind and Soul? Soviet Youth and Cultural Campaigns during the New Economic Policy." *Social History* 33, no. 3 (2008): 243–67.

Nikonova, Ol'ga. *Vospitanie patriotov: Osoaviakhim i voennaia podgotovka naseleniia v Ural'skoi provintsii (1927–1941 gg.)*. Moscow: Novyi khronograf, 2010.

Northrop, Douglas. *Veiled Empire: Gender and Power in Stalinist Central Asia*. Ithaca, NY: Cornell University Press, 2004.

Novikova, Liudmila. *Provincial "Counterrevolution": The White Movement and the Civil War in Russia's North, 1917–1920*. Madison: University of Wisconsin Press, forthcoming.

Osokina, Elena. *Our Daily Bread: Socialist Distribution and the Art of Survival in Stalin's Russia, 1927–1941*. Armonk, NY: M. E. Sharpe, 2001.

Paperny, Vladimir. *Architecture in the Age of Stalin: Culture Two*. Cambridge: Cambridge University Press, 2002.

Parks, Jenifer. "Red Sport, Red Tape; The Olympic Games, the Soviet Sports Bureaucracy, and the Cold War, 1952–1980." PhD diss., University of North Carolina at Chapel Hill, 2009.

Payne, Matthew. *Stalin's Railroad: Turksib and the Building of Socialism*. Pittsburgh: University of Pittsburgh Press, 2001.

Petrone, Karen. *The Great War in Russian Memory*. Bloomington: Indiana University Press, 2011.

——. *Life Has Become More Joyous, Comrades! Celebrations in the Time of Stalin*. Bloomington: Indiana University Press, 2000.

Pilkington, Hilary. *Russia's Youth and Its Culture: A Nation's Constructors and Constructed*. New York: Routledge, 1994.

Pinnow, Kenneth. *Lost to the Collective: Suicide and the Promise of Soviet Socialism, 1921–1929*. Ithaca, NY: Cornell University Press, 2009.

Poiger, Uta. *Jazz, Rock, and Rebels: Cold War Politics and American Culture in a Divided Germany*. Berkeley: University of California Press, 2000.

Polian, Pavel. *Ne po svoei voli: Istoriia i geografiia prinuditel'nykh migratsii v SSSR*. Moscow: Memorial, 2001.

Priestland, David. *Stalinism and the Politics of Mobilization*. Oxford: Oxford University Press, 2007.

Raleigh, Donald J. *Soviet Baby Boomers: An Oral History of Russia's Cold War Generation*. Oxford: Oxford University Press, 2012.

Reese, Roger. *Stalin's Reluctant Soldiers: A Social History of the Red Army, 1925–1941*. Lawrence: University Press of Kansas, 1996.

——. *Why Stalin's Soldiers Fought: The Red Army's Military Effectiveness in World War II*. Lawrence: University Press of Kansas, 2011.

Rempel, Gerhard. *Hitler's Children: The Hitler Youth and the SS*. Chapel Hill: University of North Carolina Press, 1989.

Rieber, Alfred J. "Civil Wars in the Soviet Union," *Kritika: Explorations in Russian and Eurasian History* 4, no. 1 (2003): 129–62.

Rigby, T. H. *Communist Party Membership in the U.S.S.R., 1917–1967*. Princeton, NJ: Princeton University Press, 1968.

——. "Was Stalin a Disloyal Patron?" *Soviet Studies* 38, no. 3 (1986): 311–24.

Rimmel, Lesley. "A Microcosm of Terror, or Class Warfare in Leningrad: The March 1935 Exile of 'Alien Elements.'" *Jahrbücher für Geschichte Osteuropas* 48, no. 4 (2000): 528–51.

Rogovin, Vadim. *Stalin's Terror of 1937–1938: Political Genocide in the USSR*. New York: Mehring Books, 2009.

Rolf, Malte. *Soviet Mass Festivals, 1917–1991*. Pittsburgh: University of Pittsburgh Press, 2013.

Rossman, Jeffrey. *Worker Resistance under Stalin: Class and Revolution on the Shop Floor*. Cambridge, MA: Harvard University Press, 2005.

Sanborn, Joshua A. *Drafting the Russian Nation: Military Conscription, Total War, and Mass Politics, 1905–1925*. DeKalb: Northern Illinois University Press, 2002.

Semenov, Sergei. *Vozhaki Komsomola*. Moscow: Molodaia gvardiia, 1974.

Shearer, David R. "Elements Near and Alien: Passportization, Policing, and Identity in the Stalinist State, 1932–1952." *Journal of Modern History* 76, no. 4 (2004): 835–81.

——. *Industry, State, and Society in Stalin's Russia, 1926–1934*. Ithaca, NY: Cornell University Press, 1996.

——. "The Language and Politics of Socialist Rationalization: Productivity, Industrial Relations, and the Social Origins of Stalinism at the End of NEP." *Cahiers du monde russe et soviétique* 32, no. 4 (1991): 581–608.

——. *Policing Stalin's Socialism: Repression and Social Order in the Soviet Union, 1924–1953*. New Haven: Yale University Press, 2009.

Shtopper, Sebast'ian, and Andrei Kukatov. *Nelegal'nyi Briansk, 1941–1943*. Briansk: Klub liubitelei istorii rodnogo kraia, 2014.

Shulman, Elena. *Stalinism on the Frontier of Empire: Women and State Formation in the Soviet Far East*. Cambridge: Cambridge University Press, 2008.

Siegelbaum, Lewis. *Cars for Comrades: The Life of the Soviet Automobile*. Ithaca, NY: Cornell University Press, 2008.

Siegelbaum, Lewis, and Andrei Sokolov. *Stalinism as a Way of Life: A Narrative in Documents*. New Haven: Yale University Press, 2004.

Slepyan, Kenneth. *Stalin's Guerrillas: Soviet Partisans in World War II*. Lawrence: University of Kansas Press, 2006.

Slezkine, Yuri. "The USSR as a Communal Apartment, or How a Socialist State Promoted Ethnic Particularism." *Slavic Review* 53, no. 2 (1994): 414–52.

Smirnova, T. M. *Deti strany sovetov: Ot gosudarstvennoi politiki k realiiam povsednevnoi zhizni, 1917–1940 gg*. Moscow: Historia Russica, 2015.

——. "'V proiskhozhdenii svoem nikto ni povinen?' Problemy integratsii detei 'sotsial'no chuzhdikh elementov' v poslerevoliutsionnoe rossiiskoe obshchestvo (1917–1936)." *Otechestvennaia istoriia*, no. 4 (2003): 28–42.

Smith, Alison. *For the Common Good and Their Own Well-Being: Social Estates in Imperial Russia*. Oxford: Oxford University Press, 2014.

Solnick, Stephen. *Stealing the State: Control and Collapse in Soviet Institutions*. Cambridge, MA: Harvard University Press, 1998.

Solomon, Peter. "Local Political Power and Soviet Criminal Justice, 1922–1941." *Soviet Studies* 37, no. 3 (1985): 305–29.

——. *Soviet Criminal Justice under Stalin*. Cambridge: Cambridge University Press, 1996.

Somov, V. A. *Pervoe sovetskoe pokolenie: Ispytanie voinoi*. Moscow: Airo-XXI, 2015.

Stites, Richard. *Revolutionary Dreams: Utopian Vision and Experimental Life in the Russian Revolution*. Oxford: Oxford University Press, 1989.

Stone, David. *Hammer and Rifle: The Militarization of the Soviet Union, 1926–1933*. Lawrence: University of Kansas Press, 2000.

Stotland, Daniel. "Ideologues and Pragmatists: World War II, New Communists, and the Persistent Dilemmas of the Soviet Party-State, 1941–1953." PhD diss., University of Maryland, 2010.

Taubman, William. *Khrushchev: The Man and His Era*. New York: W. W. Norton, 2003.

Tepliakov, A. G. *Mashina terrora: OGPU-NKVD Sibiri v 1929–1941.* Moscow: Novyi khronograf, 2008.

Timasheff, Nicholas S. *The Great Retreat: The Growth and Decline of Communism in Russia.* New York: Dutton, 1946.

Tirado, Isabel A. "The Komsomol and Young Peasants: The Dilemma of Rural Expansion, 1921–1925." *Slavic Review* 53, no. 3 (1993): 460–76.

———. *Young Guard! The Communist Youth League, Petrograd, 1917–1920.* Westport, CT: Greenwood, 1988.

Trushchenko, Nikolai V. *Kosarev.* Moscow: Molodaia gvardiia, 1988.

Trushchenko, Nikolai V., et al., eds. *Pozyvnye istorii.* 8 volumes. Moscow, 1969–85.

Tsipursky, Gleb. *Socialist Fun: Youth, Consumption, and State-Sponsored Popular Culture in the Soviet Union, 1945–1970.* Pittsburgh: University of Pittsburgh Press, 2016.

Vaksburg, Arkady. *The Prosecutor and the Prey: Vyshinsky and the 1930s Moscow Show Trials.* London: Weidenfeld and Nicolson, 1990.

Vatlin, Aleksandr. *Agents of Terror: Ordinary Men and Extraordinary Violence in Stalin's Secret Police.* Madison: University of Wisconsin Press, 2016.

Velikanova, Olga. *Popular Perceptions of Soviet Politics in the 1920s: Disenchantment of the Dreamers.* Basingstoke: Palgrave Macmillan, 2013.

Viola, Lynne. "Bab'i bunty and Peasant Women's Protest during Collectivization." *Russian Review* 45, no. 1 (1986): 23–42.

———. *Best Sons of the Fatherland: Workers in the Vanguard of Soviet Collectivization.* Oxford: Oxford University Press, 1987.

———. *Peasant Rebels under Stalin: Collectivization and the Culture of Peasant Resistance.* Oxford: Oxford University Press, 1996.

———. *The Unknown Gulag: The Lost World of Stalin's Special Settlements.* Oxford: Oxford University Press, 2007.

Von Hagen, Mark. *Soldiers in the Proletarian Dictatorship: The Red Army and the Soviet Socialist State, 1917–1930.* Ithaca, NY: Cornell University Press, 1990.

Ward, Christopher J. *Brezhnev's Folly: The Building of BAM and Late Socialism.* Pittsburgh: University of Pittsburg Press, 2009.

Weinberg, Robert. "Demonizing Judaism in the Soviet Union during the 1920s." *Slavic Review* 77, no. 1 (2008): 120–53.

Weiner, Amir. *Making Sense of War: The Second World War and the Fate of the Bolshevik Revolution.* Princeton, NJ: Princeton University Press, 2001.

———. "Nature, Nurture, and Memory in a Socialist Utopia: Delineating the Socio-Ethnic Body in the Age of Socialism." *American Historical Review* 104, no. 4 (1999): 1114–55.

Wimberg, Ellen. "Socialism, Democratism, and Criticism: The Soviet Press and the National Discussion of the 1936 Draft Constitution." *Soviet Studies* 44, no. 2 (1992): 313–32.

Yurchak, Alexei. *Everything Was Forever, Until It Was No More: The Last Soviet Generation.* Princeton, NJ: Princeton University Press, 2005.

Zahra, Tara. "Imagined Noncommunities: National Indifference as a Category of Analysis." *Slavic Review* 69, no. 1: 93–119.

Zelenov, Mikhail, and David Brandenberger, eds. *"Kratkii kurs istorii VKP(b)": Tekst i ego istoriia.* Moscow: Rosspen, 2014.

Zubkova, Elena. *Russia after the War: Hopes, Illusions, and Disappointments, 1945–1957.* Armonk, NY: M. E. Sharpe, 1998.

Index

CPSIA information can be obtained
at www.ICGtesting.com
Printed in the USA
BVOW09*0108120817
491312BV00004B/5/P